SECRET
FLORENCE

Niccolò Rinaldi
Photos: Waris Grifi

Jonglez

Within each city is another hidden away. While the "visible" city may strike visitors and tourists alike as a labyrinth that no longer holds any secrets, there is beyond it another, more intimate, city of stratified layers. The earliest stones of the urban fabric, the neglected museums and deserted theatres – these, together with a thousand other enigmatic sites, make up this place. Not all the curiosities and signs that identify this other city date back to the Middle Ages and the Renaissance; some might well be much more recent. And yet, however often we have passed by them, we have failed – and continue to fail – to notice them.

This guidebook urges you to wander around the city, to look around you, because for those who are ready to read "between the stones" Florence becomes an open – or, at least, half-open – book. And how easy it is to fall into the habit of searching out the more surprising aspects of a city where the rhythm of life is the product of the activities of its residents and the very form of its urban fabric. Like Venice, Prague or Paris, Florence is full of hidden corners that preserve nuances of its history, its literature and the legends it has nurtured. Like them, Florence is a theatre of the unusual and the overlooked.

I too have learned a lot from compiling this inventory of curious details. As a native Florentine, I discovered a host of things that I did not know, or just suspected, becoming caught up in the task of deciphering traces which, at first sight, may appear to be of only minor significance. I know I will have missed a lot of these details, for by definition no such inventory can be exhaustive. In a task of this kind, discoveries lead on from one another – and, anyway, the very definition of what constitutes the "secret" Florence is a subjective one. Thus each reader is readily invited to complete the brief chapters with information they themselves glean from their own exploration of the city – and even more readily invited to share that information with us.

This guide is an encouragement to be sharp-eyed and attentive, for the cities in which we pass our time deserve to be approached as ancient yet living entities. Secret Florence aims to be an antidote, restoring that which has been forgotten. As a book that exists parallel to its subject matter, its goal is to stimulate our desire for adventure, to extend the boundaries of our knowledge of this marvellous city.

Note: It is for their often overlooked aspects that certain well-known locations (for example, the city walls) figure in this book. The text limits itself to the urban territory of Florence City Council, with the exception of certain neighbouring areas that are directly accessible from the city (for example, the Gualchiere). The confirmation of information with regard to access was, as always in Italy, complicated by the fact that arbitrary changes are sometimes made. Wherever possible, we would advise you to check on-site, thanking you in advance for any information on changes or errors. In rare cases, some of the places discussed were closed for temporary work as this guide went to press; however, they have been retained in the hope that they will soon reopen.

Here, I should also mention some excellent websites, maintained by teams of enthusiasts to whom the city owes a debt of gratitude (my own debt I readily recognise here): http://www.firenzesegreta.com/, http://firenzecuriosita.blogspot.com/, http://www.ioamofirenze.com and the UNESCO Florence site http://www.sitiunesco.it/.

My thanks to Cinzia Borsotti for her invaluable help, and to Thomas Jonglez, who has been fully committed to this project since our first conversations in Venice, when he expressed his faith in the ability of a member of the European Parliament to capture previously unseen aspects of the city as he wandered around his home city with eyes wide open. In effect, the rediscovery of our historic cities brings together exploration and reappropriation; it is, in the true sense of the term, a political act. But even more than that it is a pure joy.

Comments on this guidebook and its contents, as well as information on places we may not have mentioned, are more than welcome and will enrich future editions.

Don't hesitate to contact us:
• Éditions Jonglez, 17, boulevard du Roi
  78000 Versailles, France
• E-mail: info@jonglezpublishing.com

Niccolò Rinaldi (www.niccolorinaldi.it) was born in Florence in 1962. He has been head of the UN Afghanistan Information Office as well as assistant secretary general to the European Parliament. He is at

present a member of the European Parliament, elected within the constituency of Central Italy, which includes the Florence area. Within the European Parliament, he is head of the Italia dei Valori (IDV) party group as well as vice-chairman of the Alliance of Liberals and Democrats for Europe (ALDE). He is the author of travel books and reportage on Central Asia and Africa, as well as books on Florentine travellers.

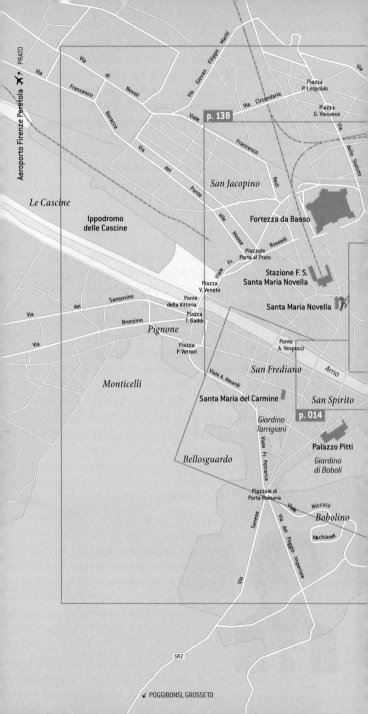

Aeroporto Firenze Peretola ✈ PRATO

Via

Via

Francesco

di

Baracca

Novoli

Via

del

Ponte

Via Filippo Marti

Via Giovan

Viale

p. 138

Via Circondaria

Francesco

Redi

Piazza
P. Leopoldo

Piazza
G. Viesseux

della Stazione

Via

San Jacopino

Le Cascine

Ippodromo
delle Cascine

Fortezza da Basso

alle

Mosse

Piazzale
Porta al Prato

Rosselli

Viale Fr.

**Stazione F. S.
Santa Maria Novella**

Santa Maria Novella

Via

dei

Sansovino

Bronzino

Via

Via

Pignone

Ponte
della Vittoria

Piazza
V. Veneto

Piazza
T. Gaddi

Piazza
P. Vettori

Ponte
A. Vespucci

Arno

Viale A. Aleardi

San Frediano

San Spirito

Monticelli

Santa Maria del Carmine

p. 014

*Giardino
Torrigiani*

Viale Fr. Petrarca

Palazzo Pitti

*Giardino
di Boboli*

Bellosguardo

Piazzale di
Porta Romana

Viale Senese

Via del Poggio Imperiale

Niccolò

Bobolino

Machiavelli

Via

SR2

↙ POGGIBONSI, GROSSETO

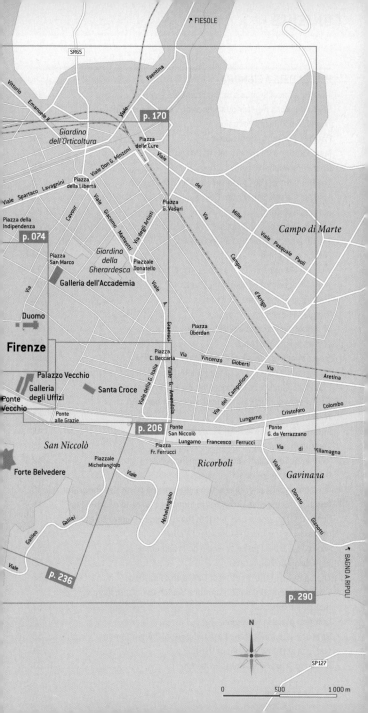

CONTENTS

DUOMO / SAN LORENZO

CONTENTS

SANTA MARIA NOVELLA

SS ANNUNZIATA

CONTENTS

CONTENTS

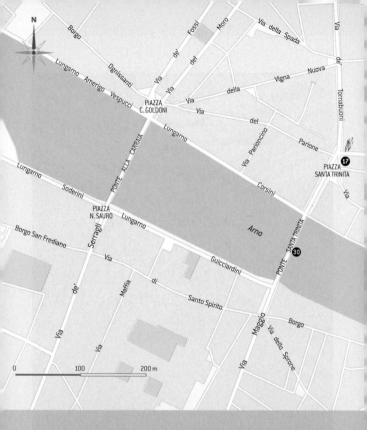

PIAZZA DELLA SIGNORIA

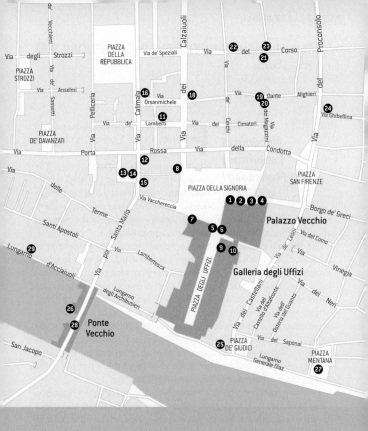

THE ALCHEMICAL SYMBOLS IN THE *STUDIOLO* ❶

Palazzo Vecchio

The Alchemical Laboratory of Francesco I de Medici

Francesco I de Medici (Florence, 25 March 1541 – Florence, 19 October 1587) commissioned a special *Studiolo* (study) within the Palazzo Vecchio. The decoration was in part the work of the most famous Mannerist painter of the day, Giorgio Vasari, who was commissioned to oversee the entire project (1570-1572), with the assistance of the humanist scholars Giovanni Battista Adriani and Vincenzo Borghini.

The *Studiolo* is actually divided into two parts: a study proper and an alchemical laboratory, the latter being a sort of *wunderkammer* in which Francesco I, who had little taste for politics, often took refuge. The prince would here engage in alchemical experiments or else delight in his collection of rare objects, all within a space that was decorated with a series of large-format paintings from his collection. The walls were, in fact, adorned with 34 paintings, mainly of religious or mythological themes. Other works included Mirabello Cavalori's *Wool Workshop* and Giovanni Battista Naldini's *Allegory of Dreams*, which undoubtedly reflects the interior of Francesco's nearby bedchamber. Pride of place went to a portrait of the duke's mother, Eleonora of Toledo, painted by Bronzino.

As already mentioned, the *Studiolo* became a place of refuge for Francesco, a man of complex and taciturn character. Soon after his death, his brother and heir, Ferdinando I, had the place dismantled (1590) – so completely that all trace of it disappeared. However, in the twentieth century it was "reassembled" after surviving traces of the ceiling frescoes made it possible for Giovanni Poggi (Superintendant of the Cultural Heritage in Tuscany) and Alfredo Lesni (Head of the Florence City Arts Department) to identify the original room in 1910. Miraculously, it was possible to restore the 34 paintings that had decorated the walls, together with eight sculptures in bronze.

Part of Francesco I's commission to Vasari for his *Studiolo* was for paintings of the four natural elements (Earth, Water, Fire and Air), upon which alchemists worked whilst pursing their explorations of Natural Philosophy within their laboratories; those laboratories themselves were, in fact, a symbol of the alchemical universe, a place of both Prayer and Work (*ora et labora*), a *laboratorium* and a laboratory. It is, however, unlikely that Francesco I actually performed alchemical experiments here; the place is much better suited to the reading of alchemical texts, with Francesco not venturing beyond the sphere of intellectual or theoretical alchemy (see following double page). However, the duke has left us a precious collection of paintings inspired by the theme of alchemical practice – in particular, the ceiling decoration of *Prometeo che riceve i gioielli della Nature* [Prometheus Receiving the Jewels of Nature]. Painted in 1570 by Francesco Poppi, this work shows Nature bestowing upon

Prometheus the "quintessence" necessary for the creation of the Philosopher's Stone. The image symbolises the creation of the Perfect Man, who is endowed with a Spirit enlightened by the Flame of Reason – the torch of which is associated with both Prometheus and Lucifer. Another work, this time by Vasari, depicts *Perseus and Andromeda*, the Greek myth which alchemists took to symbolise the hermetist disciple (embodied by Perseus) triumphing over the deficiencies of his lower nature (and over vanity in particular). As a result of this victory, the disciple is able to use the sword of true justice to free himself and hence reveal the higher, immortal nature of his soul (represented by Andromeda). The 1572 painting of *Atalanta and Hippomenes* by Sebastiano Marsili symbolises the disciple pursuing the primary material for the alchemical *Magnum Opus*, a theme which was the starting-point of a treatise on alchemy written in 1617 by the German alchemist Michael Maier (1568-1622) with the Latin title *Atalanta fugiens* (Atalanta in Flight). Hence, this association was a standard of Renaissance Hermetism.

Francesco I's reputation is such that it is difficult to argue that he possessed the virtues required of a true disciple of alchemical philosophy. On the contrary, he is remembered as a despot. Whilst Cosimo I (who was also interested in alchemy) had managed to preserve Florence's independence, Francesco behaved as a vassal of the Habsburg Holy Roman Emperor, imposing taxes upon his subjects in order to pay substantial sums into the imperial coffers. It is even said that his death was due to poisoning.

SEARCHING FOR A MYSTERIOUS FRESCO BY LEONARDO DA VINCI ❷

Salone dei Cinquecento
Palazzo Vecchio
Piazza della Signoria
• Open 9am to 7pm. Thursday and public holidays 9am to 2pm. Closed New Year's Day, Easter Sunday, 1 May, 15 August and 25 December

Lost or hidden?

The Hall of the Five Hundred (*Salone dei Cinquecento*) was the main chamber in the Palazzo Vecchio, and today it poses a real enigma. We know that the magistrates of the city commissioned Leonardo da Vinci to paint a fresco in this council chamber, and that the artist did produce a work depicting *The Battle of Anghiari*, but that fresco has now disappeared, leaving no trace. A real mystery: a fresco – and by Leonardo da Vinci to boot – that was once located in a specific place, right in the heart of Florentine government, and yet it seems to have vanished into thin air!

Experts have long been divided between two explanations. For the most part, art historians say that the fresco must have been done on plaster that dried too quickly, and this would explain why it deteriorated beyond repair. So, when Vasari was commissioned to redecorate the hall, he decided to paint over the previous fresco.

Another, smaller, group of experts indignantly reject the very notion that Leonardo did not know the basic techniques of fresco painting, also arguing that Vasari would not have dared lay hands upon the work of a master artist he admired above all others. Their hypothesis is that a second brick wall was

built just a few centimetres in front of the fresco, in order to preserve it; all one would have to do in order to admire Leonardo's work is demolish the wall with Vasari's fresco.

Given sophisticated new methods of restoration, one might think it would be possible to resolve this matter. Even without confirmation, the supporters of the second thesis are so confident of the survival of Leonardo's fresco that they argue there is a reference to it in Vasari's own work: if you look carefully at one of the standards that appear in the latter fresco you see it bears the words *Cerca, Trova* [Look, Find].

THE UFO OF PALAZZO VECCHIO

Palazzo Vecchio
Piazza della Signoria
• Open 9am to 7pm. Thursday and public holidays 9am to 2pm. Closed
New Year's Day, Easter Sunday, 1 May, 15 August and 25 December

Fifteenth-century Ufology

A room on the top floor of Palazzo Vecchio has long attracted particular interest from Ufologists and all those who argue for the existence of extraterrestrial life forms – or, indeed, from those who have simply heard about a Renaissance painting which is unique of its kind, apparently depicting a spaceship piloted by Martians.

The fifteenth-century painting is actually in a form reminiscent of a flying saucer, as it is a *tondo* measuring one metre in diameter. There were many paintings in this form at the time, but there is a peculiar detail in this work. The subject matter itself is the traditional depiction of *The Virgin and Child with St. John the Baptist*, but in the background the shepherd and his dog are not watching over their flocks but rather craning their necks to look up into the sky. And when you follow their line of sight, you see a strange circular object, painted in such a way that one has the impression it is rotating, or at least moving. To cap it all, the lower part of this curious grey-coloured "spaceship" seems to be surrounded by an aureole of spherical bodies, whilst the upper part bristles with projecting rods that remind one of antennas.

Looking at it nowadays, you would swear that this was a UFO – perhaps seen by the person commissioning the work, who then asked the artist (undoubtedly a pupil of Filippo Lippi) to "document" it. While all this may

seem highly improbable, it only took one architect to draw attention to this feature of the work (in 1978) for this painting to be raised to iconic status. It immediately underwent painstaking restoration and was subjected to sophisticated analysis both in Italy and the United States, in order to rule out the possibility of the "UFO" being a hoax created by later additions. However, the enigma has yet to be resolved.

Why are the shepherd and his dog looking at this strange object in the sky? And why was that object included here? Think what you will, there is no denying that the presence of this fifteenth-century spaceship has been a real boon for this undoubtedly minor painting.

PATROLLING THE CITY FROM ABOVE

• Reservations required, admission free; Tel: Monday–Sunday,
055 2768224 from 9.30am to 4.30pm,
or e-mail info.museoragazzi@comune.fi.it
• Visits should normally take place between 11.30am and 3pm, any day
of the week
• www.palazzovecchio-museoragazzi.it
• Warning: there are architectural barriers difficult for those of limited
mobility

> *An itinerary over 40 metres above ground level*

Palazzo Vecchio never ceases to amaze visitors, offering a wide range of visits and tours. After the launch of a tour designed for young people (Museo dei Ragazzi), another recent addition is the reopening of the patrol route used by guards as they did their rounds to watch over the city and protect the palace – the seat of government – from possible attack. Running around the entire palazzo – that is, offering a 360° view over the city – this route is located over 40 metres above street level, with a series of windows providing panoramic views over different parts of the city. There are other more conventional places where you can see Florence from above – the Parnassus Garden in Via Trento, Forte Belvedere, Fiesole, Villa Bardini, Piazzale Michelangelo, the Rose Garden – but the charm of this one is that, like the top of the church of Orsanmichele or the cupola of the Duomo, it offers a view of the city from within the urban fabric itself.

Apart from the stunning views, this patrol route is also fascinating from an architectural point of view: it is unique in Florence in that it has not been changed since the Middle Ages, remaining just as Arnolfo di Cambio designed it. While various other parts of the palazzo were being modified over the centuries, nobody turned their attention to this elevated route. Perhaps it was just too high up and too "military" in character – even for the extensive modifications carried out under Giorgio Vasari in the sixteenth century

MACHIOLATIONS FOR THE HOT OIL TREATMENT

At various points along the patrol route you see openings that were intended for pouring boiling oil over attackers. Now glazed over, these machiolations offer a view of Piazza della Signoria that will take your breath away.

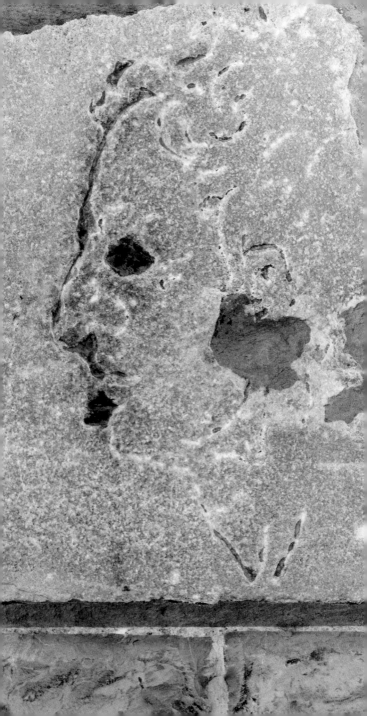

BOTHERING MICHELANGELO

Palazzo Vecchio
Piazza della Signor

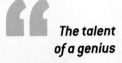

The talent of a genius

To the right of the main entrance to Palazzo Vecchio stands the statue of Hercules and Cacus; behind that sculpture – just above the bench now used by tourists – you can see the most famous work of antique "graffiti" in the whole of Florence. Look closely to make out the outline of a face – a sketch portrait that is attributed to Michelangelo himself. As might be expected, the story behind this original work carved "straight into the stone" is itself original. However, as is often the case with stories regarding works that have become part of popular tradition, there are two – contradictory – versions of that tale.

The first says that Michelangelo was constantly being pestered by someone who insisted on telling him rambling and irrelevant stories. One day, when the artist had his hammer and chisel handy, he carved this bore's portrait into the corner of the palazzo while pretending to listen, which would explain why the Florentines still refer to the figure in this carving as *L'Importuno*.

The second version has it that Michelangelo was here when he saw a convict brought for execution in front of the palazzo. Struck by the criminal's expression, he decided to try and capture it before the man was executed. As he had so little time – and didn't want to take his eyes off his "subject" – the only solution was to carve the image directly into the stone at shoulder height behind him. This would explain why the image is only sketched in, even if the artist has managed to capture the man's appearance; the very economy of means bears witness to Michelangelo's remarkable talent.

You decide which story you like best. What is beyond doubt is that this little masterpiece, carved into the wall of a busy public place, still gives rise to debate … and still attracts the attention of passers-by.

THE REMAINS OF THE CHURCH OF SAN PIER SCHERAGGIO

6

Via della Ninna

"Inside these walls the voice of Dante echoed within the people's councils"

San Pier Scheraggio takes less time to visit than any other church in Florence, though what you are visiting is not so much a church as the remains of a church. But these ruins are not tucked away somewhere or buried underground; they are there in plain sight. In Via della Ninna, almost opposite the main entrance to Palazzo Vecchio, you will find – against a wall of the Uffizi – two large arches surmounting elegant columns. The whole has been bricked in on the Uffizi side and is now disfigured by the presence of two windows. Furthermore, when you look down through some grates, you can also see the foundation of the church, whose presence here is commemorated by a discreet plaque. The inscription relates a very special detail about San Pier Scheraggio: *Tra le cui mura nei consigli di popolo sonò la voce di Dante* ["within whose walls, Dante's voice rang out in the people's councils"].

Built around the year 1000, the church stood near Dante's house, not far from Piazza della Signoria, and it is likely that the citizens of Florence gathered here in assembly during the more tumultuous periods in the city's history.

The place also possessed some fine works of art; Cimabue, for example, painted the frescoes in one of the naves.

Unfortunately, San Pier Scheraggio was very badly – that is, too well – located. In 1298, the Cimabue nave was demolished for building work on the Palazzo della Signoria or Palazzo dei Priori [Priors] as it was known as the time. When the Uffizi was built in the sixteenth century, the extant remains of the church were again in the way, so they had to be demolished. The one exception was part of a nave, which Vasari converted into a room that still makes up part of the ground floor of the Uffizi.

For a reason that is now unknown, these two arches, complete with their columns, were spared and incorporated within the wall. Nowadays giving the impression of a *trompe-l'oeil* architectural composition or "quotation", these few remnants are clear proof that this "city of many layers" still preserves some of its very earliest stones.

SELF-PORTRAIT BY BENVENUTO CELLINI ❼

Loggia dei Lanzi
Piazza della Signor

> **The grimacing creator of *Perseus***

Gazing ahead proudly as he holds out the bleeding severed head of Medusa, Benvenuto Cellini's *Perseus* is a powerful and dramatic figure. However, this is a "double" work of art, in the sense that the apparent image also contains another. To discover this, you have to go right into the Loggia dei Lanzi. (The name is derived from *lanzichenecchi*, the Italian version of the German term *landsknecht*, referring to the Lutheran mercenaries who camped out in this loggia prior to the Sack of Rome in 1527.) At the back of the statue, note how the carefully rendered musculature in the nape of the neck forms a human face. This is the self-portrait of Cellini himself, with a grimace that would definitely have been considered out of place on a monumental statue. Whether a joke at his own or his public's expense, this is a detail that your children (or friends) will be delighted to discover.

NEARBY

FARMACIA MOLTENI ❽
Via Calzaiuoli, 7 red • Tel: 055 215472

Dante himself was probably a customer here, given that this pharmacy was already registered with the Arte dei Medici e degli Speziali (Guild of Doctors and Apothecaries) at the end of the thirteenth century; its shop sign was distinguished by a diamond – indeed, this street junction used to be known as *Canto al Diamante* (Diamond Corner). The historic pharmacy would then have the grand dukes of Tuscany as its customers, and – much later – supply products to twentieth-century Italy's colonial armies engaged in Africa. Known as the Farmacia Molteni since 1892, the premises – both inside and outside – have suffered the ravages of time.

On the outside, traces of the medieval structure are still clearly visible in the large bolts for the old wooden shutters, while inside the vaulted ceiling gives some idea of just how old this pharmacy is.

The furnishings and interior decor date from the nineteenth century. The work of a Florentine celebrity of the day – the sculptor Giovanni Dupré – they are in flamboyant style. The cream colour scheme is enriched with ample use of gilded stucco-work – a glittering touch that was characteristic of the neoclassical revival, as are the flamboyant mirrors and the decorative motifs in the flooring. Despite these concessions to the ostentatious tastes of the time, the pharmacy still retains its character as a serious medical dispensary. In fact, at the end of the nineteenth century the sizeable laboratory installed in the back shop was the first in Italy to produce sterile medicine phials and other innovations.

CONTINI BONACOSSI COLLECTION

Via Lambertesca, 4
• www.uffizi.firenze.it
• Admission free, but only on request
• Tel: 055 2388809 or info.uffizi@polomuseale.firenze.it

Everyone hurries to the Uffizi; the excellence and abundance of its artistic wealth are enough to quench any thirst for culture. However, in the rooms adjacent to the great museum a small gem is tucked away, generally ignored even by the better-informed tourist. This is the Contini

Hidden store of masterpieces tucked away in the Uffizi

Bonacossi Bequest, which became part of the Uffizi in 1998: a miniature museum in itself, it comprises thirty-five paintings of excellent quality which were all chosen with great care and discernment by Count and Countess Contini Bonacossi, with expert advice from the art historian Roberto Longhi. Away from the hurly-burly of the main galleries, these rooms have an almost private feel to them. Here, you can enjoy a large number of terracotta and faience pieces by the Della Robbia Pottery, masterpieces by Sassetta and Bernini, a small selection of Spanish works (Goya, Velazquez, Zurbaran and El Greco) and works by various Venetian masters (Bellini, Veronese, Tintoretto, Jacopo da Bassano, Cima da Conegliano and Paolo Veneziano). There is also a fresco by Andrea del Castagno, an altarpiece by Cimabue and a Virgin by Bramantino.

In any other city, a gallery of this quality would be ranked as a prestigious museum in its own right. But in Florence – and within the immediate shadow of the Uffizi – it has to be content with the rank of unusual and little-known collection, a sort of back-up squad of masterpieces. However, this is no reason to ignore it – on the contrary.

THE LITTLE SECRETS OF THE VASARI CORRIDOR

• Visits by appointment, at the Uffizi Museum

This magnificent walkway was also a catwalk: in allowing the Grand Duke Cosimo I to get from Palazzo Vecchio (the ancient seat of power) to his apartments in the Pitti Palace without descending into the street, it provided not only safety and convenience, but also an expression of ducal prestige. The following are a few little known facts about what has become known as the Vasari Corridor:

By making use of structures that already existed – for example, the Ponte Vecchio – it was possible to design and complete this aerial walkway in less than five months. A true record!

Its construction required the removal of all the butcher's shops on Ponte Vecchio, which were in the habit of throwing their waste either into the Arno or nearby streets, thus creating a foul stench. The grand duke decided on a radical redevelopment of the bridge: the *beccai* [butchers] were moved to the Sant'Ambrogio area and their premises were taken over by the goldsmiths, who are still present today. It was around this time that the *renaioli* (see page 67) began sifting through the sand and silt below the bridge, in the hope of finding precious residues in the waste from the goldsmiths' shops. Sometimes the number of boats congregating around the bridge piers resulted in scuffles and arguments. It was thus decided that only one *renaiolo*, selected by the authorities, could enjoy the privilege of working under the goldsmiths' shops. The Corridor turns a corner as it passes from the Ponte Vecchio into the Oltrarno district. It would appear that the owners of the Torre Mannelli would not cede it for demolition. A local legend has it that these difficult owners died in mysterious circumstances. Just after the deviation around that Tower, there are two bricked-up doorways in the Corridor; they are due to the incorporation here of part of a private house. Unlike the Mannelli, various citizens were more than ready to accommodate Vasari's building work. The church of Santa Felicità is linked to the Corridor by a secret balcony, where a small window grating allowed the grand duke and his wife to attend mass without being seen themselves. During the Second World War, the Corridor suffered various vicissitudes. On a mere whim, Mussolini decided that, for Hitler's visit to Florence in 1939, panoramic windows should be created looking westward. They now offer a spectacular view at sunset. Spared by the retreating Wehrmacht (which did destroy all the other bridges in the city), the Corridor was used by the partisans to slip from one side of the river to the other. Incredible as it might seem, the Germans did not think of blocking access to it. The role this architectural feature played during the war inspired one of the episodes in Roberto Rossellini's *Paiscià*, a famous film which records so much of the destruction wrought at the time. Along with numerous portraits, in particular of the de Medici family (all the pictures of children make one feel one is inside a family photograph album), the Corridor contains the richest selection of self-portraits in the world. The "sitters" include Vasari, Leonardo da Vinci (perhaps), Velazquez, Rubens, Rembrandt, Canova, Ensor and Chagall. Certain artists – for example, Botero and Folon – have donated their self-portraits to the collection, but they are not yet on display.

FRESCO OF ST ANNE

Church of Orsanmichele
Via dell'Arte della Lana, 9
• Ground floor open Tuesday–Sunday from 10am to 5pm; closed Monday.
The sculpture museum (first floor) open Monday only from 10am to 5pm;
• Admission free

> **St Anne,
> Florence's
> forgotten
> patron saint**

Among its various treasures, the Church of Orsanmichele has a painting unique of its kind. On the curtain wall of the oratory, Mariotto di Nardo painted a fresco in the late fourteenth century that depicts St Anne in a rather curious posture: she is shown holding the city of Florence in her arms. Most saints are depicted at the moment of martyrdom or being venerated, but it is much rarer to see one clasping an entire city to her breast. The iconography denotes a very special relationship between saint and city. If you ask any Florentine, they will tell you without hesitation that the patron saint of the city is St John the Baptist, whose feast day (24 June) is celebrated with the famous "St John Fireworks". But everyone seems to have forgotten that Florence has another patron saint: St Anne, who is depicted here within a building that symbolises both the spiritual and physical well-being of the city (Orsanmichele served as a granary as well as a church). It was for this building that the city authorities commissioned a statue of St Anne from Francesco di Sangallo in 1522, to stand near the altar dedicated to her.

For centuries, St Anne's feast day (26 July) was celebrated in great pomp as an expression of the freedoms enjoyed by the Florentines. The saint was then adopted by the de' Medici as the patron of their dynasty. However, with the advent of the Counter-Reformation emphasis shifted onto Anne's role as the mother of the Virgin Mary, and it is only fairly recently that the city authorities have re-established the celebration of 26 July, which involves – among other events – a procession in front of Orsanmichele. These festivities are still quite a subdued affair compared with the fireworks that celebrate St John the Baptist – to whom various churches are dedicated (including Giovanni Michelucci's "motorway church") and a number of historic confraternities and guilds. Still, St Anne does have a unique privilege: she is the one shown embracing the city of Florence.

WHY WAS ST ANNE CHOSEN AS THE PATRON SAINT OF FLORENCE?
It was on 26 July 1343 – St Anne's feast day – that Florence threw off the "foreign" rule exercised by Walter VI, Count of Brienne and Duke of Athens. Hence, the association of the saint with the city's freedoms.

THE STRONGBOX IN THE NAPAPIJRI SHOP

Via Porta Rossa, 2 red, on the corner of Via Calimaruzza
• Ask the staff, they will accompany you

The Merchants' Strongbox

Napapijri, a sportswear shop in Via Porta Rossa, contains a largely-unknown treasure: a magnificent strongbox fitted within the dividing wall. According to experts, this masterpiece of craftsmanship dates from the 15th or 16th century – only in a city like Florence could such an antique crop up in such an unlikely place. In effect, the strongbox is a combination of marvels: within the stone wall a small niche was hollowed, within which was set a small nail-studded wooden door. However, this was only the first wall of defence in the strongbox, a veritable masterpiece of the locksmith's art (all the keys are original). Curiously, the receptacle in which one placed precious objects is not made of metal or wood; it is formed from sheets of sandstone fitted into the wall. Thus, at least three different materials – stone, metal and wood – were required to make this strongbox. In the same shop there are also several capitals

engraved with eagles clasping a bale of fabric (*torsello*) in their claws. They indicate that this was one of the halls of the *Arte di Calimala*, a rich guild involved in money-changing and the wool trade in medieval Florence. So the strongbox was likely created to hold precious documents or property of the guild or one of its members. Founded in 1182 by textile merchants, the *Arte di Calimala* played an important role in the history of the wool and textile trades. However, in 1770 it was closed by order of Grand Duke Piero Leopoldo I, when all the old guilds and corporations were replaced by a new Chamber of Commerce.

THE ORIGIN OF THE NAME *CALIMALA*

The etymology of this curious term is unclear. Some say it comes from the *Calle Maia* [Main Street] of Roman times, whilst others argue that it is derived from *callis malus* [street of ill-repute]. There are even some who argue it is derived from the Greek *kalos mallos* [fine wool]. Note that the street sign identifies this not as *Via di Calimala* but simply as *Calimala*.

PLAQUE TO GIUSEPPE LACHERI ⑬

Piazza del Mercato Nuovo, at the corner of the Capaccio (Loggia del Porcellino)

> *Celebrating a market trader*

Traces of Florence's history can be found in its streets and its language. Giuseppe Lacheri made his mark on both. Not far from the Loggia del Porcellino in Piazza del Mercato Nuovo a plaque commemorates this character who was for long a lively presence in one of the most typical street markets of nineteenth-century Florence.

Lacheri may not have been a man of wealth or great learning, but his reputation was such that it is still common to hear Florentines use the expression *Egli ha ragione, i'Lachera* (He's right, Il Lachera) to put an end to a dispute – in particular, to reject the unconvincing arguments of an adversary.

Lacheri was a simple market trader in San Lorenzo, and he acquired his reputation thanks to the no-nonsense readiness with which he replied to customers and fellow traders alike. Such frankness reflects a popular culture that is still very much part of Florence, a city that prizes itself on not "mincing its words".

The text on the plaque is significant: "It was in this old square that Giuseppe Lacheri (1811–1864), known as Il Lachera, became popular. A droll market trader, he was famous for the sort of authentic Florentine wit commemorated by Collodi."

Carlo Lorenzini – *alias* Collodi, creator of *Pinocchio* – wrote this brief yet affectionate portrait of the trader: "Lachera was the very embodiment of biting and wry wit, under the guise of a seller of baked pears or grape tarts, depending on the season."

Just like Collodi, the Florentines retain a fond memory of this popular market trader, of whom unfortunately no portrait survives. This plaque, raised in 2005, is a sign that within Florence – and the Loggia del Porcellino might be described as the very *heart* of Florence – popular wit survives to this day, making its mark both on the walls among which people live and on the language they use.

SCALES AT THE FARMACIA DEL CINGHIALE **14**

Piazza del Mercato Nuovo, 4 red
• Tel: 055 214221
• Open 9am to 1pm and 3.30pm to 8pm

Comfortable balance

The statue of the boar (*cinghiale*) gives its name not only to Loggia del Porcellino but also to another historic pharmacy within Florence, in Piazza del Mercato Nuovo. It was here that, in 1752, Girolamo Niccolò Branchi della Torre, an enlightened spirit of the day, would for a select audience of scholars and enthusiasts perform a series of chemical experiments that reflected the gradual shift from alchemy to the modern science of chemistry; indeed, the grand duke would call upon Branchi della Torre when setting up Tuscany's first rigorously scientific school of chemistry. The pharmacy, frequented by artists and men of letters, developed a sophisticated range of body products: creams, perfumes, oils and essences – all made with natural ingredients and all still available today.

Unfortunately, the premises of this historic pharmacy were badly damaged by the disastrous flood of 1966, although various precious furnishings did survive and are worth going out of your way to see. One of them is particularly interesting: an amazing pair of scales that lets you weigh yourself while seated comfortably in a specially designed chair. Based on the sort of scales the Romans used for weighing people, this is an apparatus that "indulges" the lazy and the overweight.

THE WHEEL OF *IL CARROCCIO*

Loggia del Porcellino
Piazza del Mercato Nuovo

> **Souvenir
> of the medieval
> Florentine *Carroccio***

Both good luck and misfortune are associated with the Loggia del Mercato Nuovo, one of the most bustling parts of the city. Let's start with the misfortune. At the centre of the Loggia del Porcellino take note of a curious detail, which may be missed among all the market stalls; to get a good look, it's better to get there before 11am or after 8pm, when the area is clear. On the floor is an engraving in marble of a six-spoked wheel, which commemorates the site where the Florentine *Carroccio* stood: this was a large four-wheeled chariot adorned with the city's coat of arms, around which medieval soldiers would gather when going into battle. The wheel was also used to punish insolvent debtors, guilty of a crime that was unpardonable in such a mercantile city as Florence. The punishment, repeated three times, involved the debtor being forced down abruptly, hitting his backside (*culo*) on the wheel. This practice was at the roots of various local expressions: *sculo* (bad luck) and *restare col culo per terra* ("to be broke"; literally, "be left with your backside on the ground").

Finally, note the small door in one of the corner columns. This leads to a narrow staircase that takes you up to a loft under the roof of the loggia. Unnoticeable from outside, this vast hall is used nowadays for occasional meetings or private dinner parties.

TRADITIONAL RITUAL INVOLVING THE FAMOUS *PORCELLINO*

Tourists seem to have taken the famous *Porcellino* to their hearts as much as the Florentines have. Tradition demands that once you get here you have to perform the following actions: 1) point out that the name of *porcellino* (piglet) is rather unsuitable as this is a full-grown boar; 2) rub the animal's snout, as have millions before you (judging by its high polish); 3) make a wish; 4) put a coin in the statue's mouth; 5) let it drop into the fountain; 6) note whether it catches on the grating or falls through; only the latter brings good luck, so in the former case start again.

This is an odd type of "sacrifice" to a statue which is less a celebration of the wild boar than of the artistic copy: the present statue is a copy of a work by the seventeenth-century sculptor Pietro Tacca, which is now in the Pitti Palace, and that original itself was inspired by a Greek statue in the Uffizi.

TRACES OF THE OLD INTERIOR OF THE 🔟 BUILDING THAT HOUSED THE ARTE DELLA LANA

- Cornliani – Calimala, 22 red
- Murphy & Nye – Calimala, 16 red
- Liu-Jo – Calimala, 14 red

The Calimala shopping mall occupies the ground floor of the building that once housed the Arte della Lana, one of the seven great craft guilds in Florence. Here, there are three clothes shops worth seeing – if only for the traces of their former interiors. While trying on formal wear (Corneliani) or more casual kit (Murphy & Nye), you can enjoy the sight of fourteenth-century frescoes, with arches, carved stone passageways, narrows staircases, capitals and high vaults.

> **14th-century frescoes, arches, carved stone passageways, narrow staircases, capitals and high vaults ...**

At Murphy & Nye there are even frescoes depicting various phases of wool (lana) production, which are all the more interesting as they are among the rare existing visual records of such processes. At Corneliani's, on the other hand, is a small chapel attributed to the Maestro del Bargello. As they are in listed buildings, these interiors have been tastefully restored, including the polychrome of the original frescoes, when possible. However, the modern shop fittings sometimes clash with the antique ones.

Still, what is most striking is the union of modernity and medieval architecture – an illustration that these large halls were originally intended as places of commerce. The bustle of customers and merchandise displays all seem to restore some of the original energy of these premises; paradoxically, the atmosphere of the original Arte della Lana hall survives better than it would have done if made into a museum.

As for the Liu-Jo shop, it occupies what used to be a long corridor running along the outside of a wing of the palazzo, but that was later incorporated within it. Inside, blocks of stone form a wall that has undergone numerous changes over the centuries. First an outer wall in the Middle Ages, then an interior wall, it is now part of a 21st-century shop.

PIAZZA DEL LIMBO: THE SQUARE THAT NO LONGER EXISTS

In April 2007, the International Theological Commission of the Roman Catholic Church ruled that limbo could no longer be considered as a "truth of faith". Limbo is notably mentioned in *The Divine Comedy* as a place of interlude that welcomes the souls of those who cannot reach Heaven because they died without having been baptised, as is the case for newborns.

However, Florence celebrates limbo in its own way with Piazza del Limbo, which was formerly the site of a cemetery for the stillborn and babies who died soon after birth.

THE "MESSAGES" IN PALAZZO BARTOLINI SALIMBENI

Palazzo Bartolini Salimbeni
Piazza Santa Trinità, 1

> "It is easier to criticise than to imitate"

Completed in 1532, this *palazzo* would give rise to controversy. In his designs, the architect Baccio d'Agnolo had shown a certain nonchalant daring; as is clear from the details of the façade, he had been more than happy to indulge the new taste for manifest echoes of the classical past. This building thus marked the advent within the city of the "Roman" style of Renaissance architecture, a style which may have been a hybrid but was not without its elegance. Vasari described Palazzo Bartolini Salimbeni as the "first in which one saw the windows adorned with pediments and the doorway accompanied by columns supporting an architrave, frieze and cornice." However, characteristic features of Florentine architecture were not totally omitted; look, for example, at the bench projecting from the bottom of the façade at street level. Still, that façade is noteworthy primarily for its unusual decorative columns and its triangular tympana. Overall, the design was taken as an attack upon the tastes prevailing in the Florence of the day – so much so that, just as happens nowadays, there was no lack of criticism and sarcasm. "This innovation," Vasari wrote, "would draw upon him [Baccio d'Agnolo] the censure of the Florentines, who overwhelmed him with mockery and satirical sonnets. He was scolded for having made a temple instead of a palazzo. This sarcasm so depressed Baccio that he almost lost his wits; however, he soon passed on to other things, thinking that the course he was following was the right one." If he did soon "pass on to other things", the criticism made such an impression upon the architect that he had the Latin inscription *Carpere promptus quam imitari* [Criticising is easier than imitating] engraved in plain view over the main doorway. And he would be proved right: his style was reassessed – and even imitated – with the advent of Mannerism.

WIDE AWAKE

The desire to communicate a message can be seen on other parts of this façade: another, more enigmatic inscription - *Per non dormire* [In order not to sleep] - appears over certain of the windows. Given that this motto comes from a family of wealthy merchants like the Bartolini Salimbeni, one might take this to be an exhortation to work – perhaps an allusion to the habit of getting to markets and auctions first in order to acquire the best merchandise.

The cornice is also decorated with three poppies, the family emblem. Given the somniferous properties of the opium associated with this flower, some have seen this as another allusion to sleep.

ANOTHER FLORENTINE INVENTION: ICE CREAM

Florence saw the invention not only of visual perspective (Leon Battista Alberti), Italian literature (Dante) and the telephone (Antonio Meucci), but also of ice cream. Such a delicious dessert could only be the brainchild of an artist, indeed, of a scholar-artist: Bernardo Buontalenti (1531–1608). In fact, this engineer, architect, decorator and inventor perfected previous attempts to create such a dish: before him, another Florentine by the name of Ruggeri had produced a sorbet for a cookery competition, which was described as "the most unusual dish that has ever existed". It was for the official visit of the Spanish to Florence that the Grand Duke ordered Buontalenti to come up with a dessert that would "leave these foreigners – in particular, these Spaniards – gawping". So the engineer invented ice cream – or, more exactly, a mix of milk and egg yolk blended together with honey as a sweetener, a drop of wine to heighten the taste and a pinch of salt to lower the freezing point. This was no longer sorbet, made by mixing snow and fruit, but rather real ice cream with a smooth, milky texture.

Of course, the history of ice cream did not stop there. Various improvements followed – for example, those introduced by Procope, a Sicilian chef working in Paris. However, the success of Florentine ice cream was such that Florence – and nowhere else – still produces the famous, smooth "Buontalenti" ice cream. In 1979, the ice-cream shop Badiani (Viale dei Mille, 20r) won the prize for the best "Buontalenti" in Florence – a very special flavour that is still protected by copyright. Other excellent ice-cream makers have also produced their own variety – including Baroncini

(an old dairy business that has since 1946 been located at Via Celso, 3r) and Da Roberto (Via Mariti, 3r).

The number of historic ice-cream shops in the city bears witness to the importance of this business in Florence over the centuries. These include the Gelateria Alpina (open since 1929 at Viale Strozzi, 12r) and Gelateria Veneta (open since 1925 at Piazza Beccaria, 7r). The Gelateria Vivoli (open since 1930 at Via Isola delle Stinche, 7r) is special because here one can not only enjoy the place's famous ice cream but also find a *buchetta* on the outside wall and, inside, a room decorated with a fresco of the Ponte Vecchio by Luigi Falai, a pupil of Piero Annigoni.

THE FRESCOES
IN *ANTICO RISRTORANTE PAOLI*

(18)

Via dei Tavolini, 12 red
• Tel: 055 216215

> *An old trattoria where Boccaccio meets Art Nouveau*

Boccaccio plays a leading role in the decor of the Antico Ristorante Paoli. Opened as a *trattoria-salumeria* by Pietro Paoli in 1824, this place with its typical marble tables is decorated with various works of art. Amongst them note the three lunettes frescoed with scenes from Boccaccio's *Decameron*. They were painted by Carlo Coppede, who in 1916 was commissioned to decorate the restaurant – thus perpetuating a tradition which had seen various artists work here at different periods in its history. The small *Saletta delle Rose* [Rose Room], for example, has splendid painted and ceramic decoration by one of the most important exponents of Italian Art Nouveau, Galileo Chini, who worked here just a few years later. The Villa Pecori Giraldi Museum in Borgo San Lorenzo is dedicated entirely to the work of this artist, one of whose descendants, Antonio Chini, decorated the Cantina Guidi.

The trattoria's collection contains other works, including a bust of the American president Woodrow Wilson, a painting by Annigoni (who also has his own museum in Florence; see p. 284), ceramics by Cantagalli dedicated to the various communes of Tuscany, and other valuable paintings.

15 GIUSEPPE GARIBALDI
Litografia del 1866, con firma autografa di Garibaldi, contornata di fiori e foglie essiccate

ITALIA E VITTORIO EMANUELE

IL DITTATORE DELL'ITALIA MERIDIONALE

AI VOLONTARI

PROCLAMA

Quando l'idea della Patria era in Italia la dote di pochi, si cospirava, e si moriva! Ora si combatte, e si vince. I patriotti sono abbastanza numerosi da formare degli eserciti, e dare ai nemici battaglie. Ma la vittoria nostra non fu intera. L'Italia non è ancora libera tutta, e noi siamo ben lungi dalle Alpi, meta nostra gloriosa. Il più prezioso frutto di questi primi successi è di potere armarci e procedere. Io vi trovai pronti a seguirmi, ed ora vi chiamo a voi tutti; affrettatevi alla generale rassegna di quell'esercito, ch'esser deve la Nazione armata, per far libera, ed una l'Italia; piaccia o no ai prepotenti della terra.

Raccoglietevi nelle piazze delle vostre città, ordinandovi con quel popolare istinto di guerra, che basta a farvi assalire quali il nemico.

I capi de' corpi, non formati, avvertiranno anticipatamente del loro arrivo in Napoli il Direttore del Ministero della Guerra, perché appagi l'occorrente. Per quei corpi, che più convenientemente potrebbero venir qui per via di mare, saranno date le opportune disposizioni.

Italiani, il momento è supremo. Già fratelli nostri combattono lo straniero nel cuore d'Italia. Andiamo ad incontrarli in Roma per marciare di là assieme sulle Venete terre. Tutto ciò ch'è dover nostro e diritto potremo fare, se forti. Armi adunque ed armati! Generoso cuore, ferro, e

"GIUSEPPE GARIBALDI" VETERANS' AND OLD SOLDIERS' MUSEUM

Torre della Castagna
Piazza San Martino, 1
• Tel: 055 2396104
• Open Thursday afternoon from 4pm to 6pm

Old Garibaldi Tower

This museum is not devoted solely to Garibaldi but to the "veterans and old soldiers" who played a part in the great epic of Garibaldi and his "Redshirts". Of course, all that took place 150 years ago and the veterans are long gone, so the existence of such a museum may seem an extravaganza due solely to a local association of enthusiasts. In fact, this association is spread nationwide in twenty-seven different branches, which bring together not only those with a passion for the period of the Risorgimento but also the old partisans of Garibaldi Division who fought in the former Yugoslavia. In Florence, the association owns a little gem, for its premises occupy the ground-floor, mezzanine and first floor of one of the finest medieval towers in the city, Torre della Castagna.

This tower, originally called Torre Baccadiferro, was renamed when the Florentine priors moved here in the thirteenth century. They had at first lived in the Bargello district but – as the passage from Dino Compagni's *Chronicles* cited on the nearby wall plaque records – they then took the decision "to shut themselves away within the Castagna Tower in order to put an end to threats from the powerful". This tower was indeed a small fortress, particularly robust because – unlike most of the other towers in Florence – it had not been modified or damaged, and it is now one of the few towers open to the public.

The credit for this is due to the Garibaldi Association, which readily opens its doors to all those who wish to consult its library of works relating not only to Garibaldi (obviously enough) but also the Renaissance. Once a week (on Thursday) you can also visit the curious museum that has been laid out within its small rooms: the collection comprises Garibaldi memorabilia, swords, other weapons, medals, portraits, busts … and the famous cushion used by the general. In short, not only an insight into a specific period of history but also the chance to see the inside of this superb tower.

ORIGIN OF THE TERM "BALLOT"

In Florence, the chestnuts (*castagne*) which the Florentine priors used when casting their votes are still called *ballotte*. Perhaps this is the origin of the verb "to ballot".

ALMS BOX IN THE CONGREGAZIONE DEI BUONOMINI DI SAN MARTINO ORATORY

Piazza San Martino
• Admission free
• Open all year round on working days from 10am to 12 noon and 2pm to 5pm; closed holidays and Friday afternoons

> **Age-old tact and discretion**

Although the small door of this oratory is always open and numerous groups of tourists visit it, the long history associated with its polychrome walls is far from over. Contrary to what you might think, the tradition of this very special institution continues.

It is often forgotten that there was a "political" origin to this Congregation, which was set up to provide assistance for the needy. When it was created by St Antonino, Prior of San Marco, in 1442, its purpose was to assist the "humiliated poor" – members of the affluent or even noble families ruined by their opposition to Cosimo de' Medici (who may have been an enlightened ruler but unhesitatingly destroyed those who didn't support his rule). These families, which due to their rank were ashamed to ask openly for assistance, could apply to the *procuratori buonomini* ("gentleman procurers") of the Congregation, knowing that they would remain anonymous.

The polychrome frescoes within the oratory illustrate the activities of these *procuratori*: paying for a funeral; providing a dowry for a young girl; assisting a woman in childbirth; settling an imprisoned man's debts; distributing clothing and food. These frescoes also illustrate certain rules which the *buonomini* followed: unlike all other confraternities, they did not wear easily recognisable uniforms and they provided assistance discreetly, keeping a record of the sums paid out in special notebooks.

The Congregation still performs its charitable work, and every four months selects certain families which have been "humiliated" by falling on hard times. While visiting the oratory you can also contribute to its work, making an offering in the old alms box in the form of a cross which is located to the side of the entrance. There is another box labelled *Per le istanze* (Requests); this is open day and night so that people can apply for charity anonymously.

ORIGIN OF THE EXPRESSION *RIDURSI AL LUMICINO* ("TO BE AT DEATH'S DOOR")

Relying on private donations and, by statute, not possessing any landed property, the Congregation used to put a small light (*lumicino*) on the altar when its funds had run out, thus appealing to the generosity of the faithful. This practice gave rise to the Florentine expression *ridursi al lumicino*.

LAMPREDOTTO: WHERE CAN YOU FIND THAT UNIQUELY FLORENTINE SPECIALITY MADE USING THE FOURTH STOMACH OF A COW?

At various places, including Piazza Cimatori, Piazza dell'Isolotto, Via Palazzolo, Piazza Sant'Ambrogio, Via Gioberti, etc.

Lampredotto is a mystery. All the regions and cities of Italy fervently – sometimes jealously – maintain their own culinary traditions, but only rarely do you find a dish specific to a single city. And in the case of *lampredotto*, that rarity concerns not only the recipe but also the basic ingredient, which outside Florence is definitely not a sought-after delicacy. The Florentines seem to be the only ones who appreciate this very special portion of a cow's innards: the fourth – that is, the last – of its stomachs. Just because it is the last, this organ is the cleanest – because the fodder that arrives here has already been filtered by its three predecessors – and its flavour when cooked is both strong and delicate, with the stomach consisting of a lean core and a more fatty covering. Nowhere else – not even in Tuscany – do people eat *lampredotto*, and this enigmatic exclusivity enjoyed by Florentines is complicated by where and how it is eaten. *Lampredotto* is not found on restaurant menus and only rarely on sale in butchers; in fact, the dish is sold by *lampredottai*, ambulant traders who sell the meat from carts either in a sort of sandwich or *in zimino* (with green vegetables). In the first case, the bread is unsalted, with the upper half soaked in the juice of the meat and the sliced *lampredotto* seasoned to taste with pepper. In the second case, the vegetables might include Swiss chard, for example.

Lampredottai are to be seen throughout the city, in the old centre or on the outskirts, with lovers of this local delicacy knowing where to find the best. The trade seems to be impervious to crises, even if recently threatened by EU regulations that banned the serving of the traditional glass of wine that accompanies the dish (though some prefer Coca-Cola, which is also sold by *lampredottai*) – happily the threat was resolved when the Italian authorities resisted. The little carts – local gathering-points to exchange the latest gossip – are particularly busy at lunchtime, perpetuating the tradition of what is one of the world's oldest examples of "fast food".

ANTICO VICOLO DEL PANICO OR VICOLO DELLO SCANDALO

From the Corso to Via Dante Alighieri

21

> *The alleyway that was opened up to separate the homes of two rival families*

Of all the old alleyways that cut through the heart of the old city centre there is one that does not appear on any map. This is the narrow Vicolo del Panico, whose name has nothing to do with "panic" – the accent is on the second syllable – but rather refers to a type of grain. To make things even more confusing, there is also another, official, Vicolo del Panico, which does appear on maps: it is a dead end leading off Via Pellicceria. To find the "unofficial" alleyway, you have to go to 49 red in the Corso, where an opening leads through to 8 Via Dante Alighieri (where, it would seem, the poet's house once stood).

Spanned at intervals by arches, this narrow twisting alleyway has a story that is even stranger than its name. It dates from the Middle Ages, when violent internal fighting was common in Florence. Following the victory of the Guelphs over the Ghibellines, the victors themselves were spilt by a schism between the Cerchi family and the more populist "White Guelphs" and the Domati family and the "Black Guelphs" who represented the more affluent classes.

Certain families within a specific district thus found themselves living near – or right next-door to – their new enemies. And it was very easy for someone to slip through a dividing wall in order to attack, rob or simply torment members of the opposing faction; some even feared that the dividing walls might be totally demolished to make way for a full-scale assault. This is why the city authorities decided that the dividing walls of such houses should be knocked down and replaced by a narrow alleyway separating "enemy" homes. One such alley was Vicolo del Panico, which was soon passing by the popular name of Vicolo dello Scandalo.

This alley remains one of the rare examples of such "peacekeeping" within the very fabric of the old city centre. The other Vicolo del Panico was named in the nineteenth century, when obviously the reasons behind the creation of the first no longer existed.

renrino nell Osteria del fico
accecato dall ira

Raccoglie sterco e quatto stimolato dal
di auolo

con un coltello
....

Lo Conducono in firenza

are di notte
Contenza

PICTURE OF THE DESECRATOR

Santa Maria de' Ricci church
Via del Corso, 25
• Open from 10.30am to 8pm
• The church is sometimes closed at lunchtime
• Curate's telephone: 333 3074339

> **Sixteenth-century cartoon strip depicting the punishment for desecration**

Almost opposite the entrance to Vicolo del Panico, the church of Santa Maria de' Ricci contains (at the far end of the last chapel on the left) a reproduction of a painting that is divided into nine framed scenes, rather like an early cartoon strip. These images recount how the church was built and dedicated to the Virgin as an act of reparation for the sacrilege that had been committed on 21 July 1501.

On the evening of that day, Antonio di Giovanni Rinaldeschi was passing by, having lost all his money at dice in the Albergo del Fico (Fig Inn). Happening to walk near a niche with an image of the Annunciation, he vented his anger by picking up a lump of horse dung and hurling it in the Virgin's face, an act of sacrilege that shocked all those present. Although partly due to excessive drinking, this outburst of anger cost Rinaldeschi his life: he was arrested, taken to the Bagello prison, given a summary trial and then hung from one of the building's windows.

The image of the Annunciation that was the object of this sacrilege is now in the choir of Santa Maria de' Ricci church, and the last chapel on the left has a reproduction of the cartoon strip telling the whole story. Better still, go to the Museo Stibbert, where you can see the sixteenth-century original, which has recently been restored.

For those interested to learn more, there is William J. Connell and Giles Constable's *Sacrilege and Redemption in Renaissance Florence: The Case of Antonio Rinaldeschi,* published in 2005. When an incident becomes a cartoon strip, it enjoys a certain popular success. Other narratives "crystallise" around it, revealing popular attitudes and beliefs.

THE PAINTING OF THE MEETING OF DANTE AND BEATRICE

Church of Santa Margherita dei Cerchi
Via Santa Margherita
• Open daily from 10.30am to 8pm

> *The true place of the meeting of Dante and Beatrice?*

Alongside the Corso, a road leads to the small church of Santa Margherita dei Cerchi (also known as Santa Margherita di Antiochia). For centuries maintained by the Cerchi family, it was adorned with a finely-coloured painting by Lorenzo de' Bicci. However, what attracts the attention of the rare visitors to this church is another painting in a very different style. The work of the English Pre-Raphaelite Marie Spartali Stillman, this painting depicts the meeting between Dante and Beatrice, which some say took place not in the nearby – and much larger – Badia Fiorentina but rather in this small intimate church. This is highly possible given that Dante's family lived just a short walk away, as did the family of Beatrice Portinari. This romantic encounter is so much the stuff of sentimental legend that there is even a tombstone claiming that Beatrice is buried in this church. The inscription has all the appearance of being a bluff since, having married a Bardi, it is logical that the real Beatrice would have been buried in her husband's family tomb within the Great Cloister of Santa Croce. It is only Beatrice's father, Folco Portinari, who was buried within these walls. Nevertheless, Santa Margherita does deserve its nickname of "Dante's Church".

ZABAIONE: INVENTED BY ST. PASQUALE BAYLON TO RESTORE FLAGGING MASCULINE FERVOUR

Santa Margherita is also where the Confraternity of Chefs used to gather. Their patron saint, St. Pasquale Baylon, deserves his position because he is said to have invented the recipe for *zabaione*: 1 egg yolk + 2 glasses of marsala+ 2 spoonfuls of sugar + 1 glass of water. He devised the recipe not in his spare time in the kitchen but as part of his pastoral activities. It was prescribed for those women who complained their husbands were no longer "up to the job".

QUIETEST PLACE IN FLORENCE

The Badia Fiorentina is where Dante is said to have first seen Beatrice and where Boccaccio later gave his course of *lecturae Dantis*, thus initiating the custom of public readings of *La divina commedia*. Today it is the sole church of the Italian community of the Monastic Fraternities of Jerusalem. They also have a hermitage up in the Mugello. The community practises total monastic silence right in the heart of the city, and their church – open from dawn to dusk – is a place of unnerving stillness – the quietest public space in Florence.

BEATRICE: A SYMBOL OF THE PATH OF SPIRITUAL ENLIGHTENMENT

Dante says he met Beatrice when he was 18 years old, even if he had first noticed her when he was nine and she eight. Some argue that he only saw her once and that he never even spoke to her. There is no biographical evidence to prove the matter one way or another.

Solely on the basis of the biographical information that Dante himself supplies in *La Vita Nuova*, we know that Beatrice (Bice) Portinari was born in 1265-66 and died on 8 June 1290. She has been identified as the daughter of the banker Folco Portinari from Portico di Romagna, who left her a substantial sum of money in his will dated 1287. We also know that Beatrice married the Florentine nobleman Simone de Bardi, by whom she had six daughters, and lived in a house next to Dante's in Florence. She founded the Ospedale di Santa Maria Nuova, today the hospital of central Florence.

Dante's dithyrambic praise of her Christian charity has immortalised her as *Beata Beatrice* [Blessed Beatrice]; it was under this name that Dante Gabriel Rossetti painted her in 1864, in a picture which shows the dove of the Holy Spirit appearing to her whilst carrying a rose in its beak.

The rose was the symbol of the *Fidelli d'Amore* (see p. 62) and also the flower of spiritual enlightenment and revelation. This is why the Litany of the Blessed Virgin Mary mentions a "mystic rose".

The courtly love of the twelfth and thirteenth century – for the first time since the Gnostics of the second and third century – glorified the spiritual dignity and religious virtue of women. Gnostic texts, for example, had exulted the Mother of God at the same time as the "mystical silence" of the Holy Spirit and the Wisdom of God.

If medieval devotions to the Virgin were an indirect veneration of women, Dante went one step further: he deified Beatrice, proclaiming her as superior to the angels and saints, as invulnerable to sin and almost comparable to the Virgin herself. Thus, when Beatrice is about to appear within the Earthly Paradise, a voice proclaims: "Come, O my spouse, from Lebanon" (*Purgatorio*, XXX, 11) – a famous line from the *Song of Songs* (IV, 8) which had been used by the Church in its veneration of the Mother of God.

In another passage (*Purgatorio*, XXXIII, 10), Beatrice applies to herself words that had first been used by Christ: "A little while, and ye shall not see me; and again, a little while, and ye shall see me." (John 16.16)

Beatrice represents Wisdom and thus the mystery of Salvation; Dante introduces her during the course of his three journeys of initiation into Hell, Purgatory and Heaven. She is presented as the idealisation of the Eternal Woman, the chosen means of communication that can lead to the metaphysical re-awakening and salvation of humankind.

This view of love and the veneration of womanhood as playing a part in the salvation of the human soul inspired the gnosis and esoteric initiations of the *Fidelli d'Amore* — as one can see in *La Vita Nuova* [New Life], which Dante dedicates to Beatrice. Written in 1292-93, this work describes initiation through spiritual love, with the figure of Woman being a symbol of *Intellectus illuminatio*, of the transcendent Spirit and Divine Wisdom that are destined to awaken the Christian world from the lethargy to which it has succumbed as a result of the spiritual ignobility of the popes. Thus, in the medieval writings of the *Fidelli d'Amore* one finds allusions to "a widow who is not such". This was the *Madonna Intelligenza*, who had become a "widow" because her spouse — the pope — was dead to the spiritual, having given himself over entirely to temporal affairs and corruption.

The veneration of the "Unique Woman" — and initiation into the mysteries of Love — were part of what made the *Fidelli d'Amore* into a sort of secret spiritual militia, employing an encoded language for truths that were to remain concealed from "the vulgar". This need for secrecy was urged by one of the most famous *Fidelli*, Francesco de Barberino (1264-1348), whilst another, Jacques de Baisieux, would say: "one must not reveal the counsels of love, but rather keep them carefully hidden". Scattered throughout Europe, the *Fidelli d'Amore* were linked with the troubadours and minstrels of the day, exalting the ideal of the Eternal Woman as associated with the supreme gift of the Holy Spirit (to which they referred as "Holy Love"). The veneration of Our Lady was their way of asserting the presence of the Paraclete (or "comforter") amongst the people with whom they settled. Royal courts were readily open to the *Fidelli*, themselves becoming "courts of love": this was famously true of the court of Alfonso X the Wise, king of Leon and Castille, and the court of Dinis I, the "troubadour" King of Portugal.

The *Fidelli* were not a heretical movement, but rather a group of free-thinking writers and artists who opposed the corruption of the Church and no longer recognised the popes as the spiritual head of Christendom. This opposition became keener after the bloody extermination of the Order of the Knights Templars by the king of France, Philip IV, and his "agent", Pope Clement V.

So, setting aside actual biographical details, the Beatrice of Dante's poem is, above all, a symbol of the Perfect Woman, of Divine Grace, and of the amorous soul that is a guarantee of spiritual immortality. Exemplifying the path of mystical purification, Beatrice represents that inner awakening which took place in Dante after his period of exile and his peregrinations in search of purification — peregrinations that finally came to an end when he re-discovered his immortal soul, symbolised by Beatrice.

THE FIRST CERTIFIED PORTRAIT OF DANTE

Palazzo dell'Arte dei Giudici e dei Notai
Via del Proconsolo, 16 red
• Open daily from 9am to 5pm
• For reservation telephone 055 240618 or e-mail museo@artenotai.org
• www.artenotai.org
• Admission: €8

A rare gem

T he premises of the old Guild of Judges and Notaries were restored in 2005, offering the opportunity not only for archaeological excavations in the basement but also for the creation of a restaurant on the ground floor and a museum on the first floor. It is the latter which contains a rare gem: the first certified portraits of Dante and Boccaccio. It was during the restoration of the frescoed walls of the first floor that various discoveries were made: the so-called Sant'Ivo lunette, a lunette of the *Arti del Trivio letterario* [depicting the figures of Grammar, Rhetoric and Dialectics] and a lunette with the portraits of the four writers who were considered to be the "founding fathers" of the Florentine Republic – at least, of the Republic as envisaged by Coluccio Salutati, the chancellor of Palazzo Vecchio. The portraits of two of these figures (Petrarch and Zanobi da Strada) have all but disappeared, with the exception of a few fragments. However, at either end of the composition one can clearly identify Dante and Boccaccio. Critics have no doubt about the authenticity of the Dante portrait, which shows a face which corresponds to the one depicted in the nearby Cappella della Maddalena frescoes in the Bargello (painted 1336-1337): the skin is slightly dark and the nose has its famous aquiline form, even if it is not hooked. Over the period of a century, famous artists painted other portraits here, with the *palazzo* becoming a veritable workshop for the city's homage to the literature in which it took such pride: Andrea del Castagno painted Leonardo Bruni, Ambrogio di Baldese painted Coluccio Salutati and the Latin poet Claudian (believed to be a native of Florence), and Pollaiolo painted Poggio Bracciolini.

FLORENCE, A NEW HEAVENLY JERUSALEM?

Designed by Jacopo di Cione – brother of Andrea Orcagna – the rose window on the ground floor is also a special feature of the building: it depicts the civil and political organisation of fourteenth-century Florence and the Cardinal Virtues.
The circular image of Florence shows the city as a new Celestial Jerusalem, protected by the Arnolfo-built ramparts and shown under the aegis of the lily, the cross and the Guelph eagle.
This provides part of the decor for the restaurant *Alle Murate*, which is renowned for its typically Tuscan cuisine. Do not forget to go down into the vaulted underground space of the restaurant as well, where there are Roman and medieval remains dating back to the first and ninth century.

DANTE, THE TEMPLARS AND *I FIDELLI D'AMORE*

The age of Dante Alighieri (1265-1321) was profoundly marked by the decline of the Order of the Knights Templars, and above all by the series of persecutions, imprisonments and condemnations to which the Order was subjected following its interdiction by the king of France, Philip IV, and Pope Clement V (clearly manipulated by the former). These events had a powerful impact upon Dante, who denounced this injustice before the political powers of the day. He went so far as to take part in an event in Florence that was a deliberate expression of support for Pope Boniface VIII, who in 1302 had been denounced as a heretic by the *États Généraux* summoned by Philip IV; in 1303, the king sent his troops to Florence to hold the pontiff prisoner in Palazzo d'Agnani for three days. The Templars, who were the pope's personal guard, were on this occasion supported by the local burghers, including Dante, and managed to free Pope Boniface VIII. However, he died just a month later in rather unclear circumstances; some even mentioned poison. Philip IV supported the immediate election of Clement V and set about persecuting the Templars, ultimately procuring their total destruction – in spite of the fact that a delegation (of which Dante was a part) had gone to Rome to argue their case before the pope in 1307. It is thought that Dante's initiation into the social and religious ideals underpinning the Templars came when he frequented their Florentine headquarters at San Jacopo, in Campo Corbolini. In this area, the Templars are credited with the original construction of the church of San Jacopo Sopr'Arno.

The Order aimed to promote, within the Christian faith and thence society as a whole, their ideal of spiritual perfection and temporal justice. To this end, they used poetry, song and the prose works of the Confraternity of Troubadours, advocates of a philosophy of "spiritual love" who were continually at loggerheads with the dominion exerted by Rome. Dante himself was one of these *Fidelli d'Amore* [The Faithful of Love].

The Confraternity of troubadours and minstrels had spread throughout the whole of Europe. The first traces of it are to be found in the poetry of the tenth and eleventh centuries, in courtly praise to the Mother of God and celebrations of the blessings of humanity. In a sense the descendants of the ancient *vates* (soothsayers) and bards, the troubadours wrote under the guidance of important spiritual masters, producing love songs and satirical lyrics that expressed esoteric truths. In short, they might be described as the "mouthpiece" of the different esoteric Orders that then existed in Europe, and there was a profound relation between their poetry and the kind of spirituality championed by the Templars.

Disgusted by the bloody destruction of the Order of the Knights Templars, Dante wanted to set the record straight for future generations, giving a masterly explication of its true aims in his literary masterpiece *La Divina Commedia*. It is interesting, for example, that in his *Paradiso*, from the third heaven inwards the poet is guided through the heavens towards his vision of God by St. Bernard of Clairvaux, who had been the spiritual father of the Templars. Similarly, when he reaches the highest of the heavens, the poet rediscovers Beatrice, his beloved and the expression of divine grace. There he has a vision of a white rose with a triangle at its centre; the latter symbolises love of the Holy Trinity, whilst the rose itself had been a symbol adopted by the *Fidelli d'Amore*.

The very decision to write the poem in the vernacular – the local dialect of *Toscan*, which is very close to modern-day Italian – was a gesture of revolt against Rome and its ecclesiastical Latin. It is also significant that in the eighth circle of hell called *Maleboge* (Fraud), Dante places two popes: Boniface VIII, condemned for simony (the sale of ecclesiastical honours) and Clement V, the corrupt pope who signed the condemnation of the Templars.

A "comedy" not because it is comic but because it ends well for all the characters who gain admission to Heaven, *La Divina Commedia* is made up of 100 *canti* and a total of 14,233 lines. Its three parts (*Paradiso, Purgatorio* and *Inferno*) are each made up of 33 *canti* of 40 to 50 tercets (verses of three lines). The *Inferno* also has an introductory *canto*, thus bringing the total of *canti* to 100; a symbol of absolute perfection ($100 = 10 \times 10 =$ the perfection of that which is perfect), this number is also to be found, for example, in the 100 names of the God of Islam. Each *canto* is made up of 130 to 140 lines of *terza rima* (that is, interlocking tercets). Thus, one continually finds multiples of the numbers 3, 7 and 10, all of which were heavily symbolic in the Middle Ages and might be taken to express the poet's devotion to the Holy Trinity, a special object of devotion for the Templars themselves.

Terza rima here involves hendecasyllabic lines (11 syllables) organised in rhymes that follow the schema ABA, BCB, CDC, EDE, and so on, with the central line of one tercet rhyming with the first and third of the following one. This structure is also known as "Dante's tercet", because he was the first to use it. Furthermore, the three books of the *Commedia* all end in a rhyme on the same word: *Stelle* (stars). It should be remembered that Mary, the mother of Christ, was often referred to as *Stella Maris* and again was an object of particular devotion for the Templars.

MERIDIAN IN FLORENCE'S ISTITUTO

1, Piazza Dei Giudici
- Tel.: 055 226 53 11
- info@imss.fi.it • www.imss.firenze.it
- Admission: €7.50, reduced: €4

Commemorating Florentine Science

The superb meridian that adorns the forecourt of the History of Science Museum was unveiled in 2008 and celebrates the combination of tradition (of which the museum is the custodian) and modernity.

The signs of the zodiac in glass are laid out in the ground along a calibrated copper standard that runs for fifteen meters from the Arno parapet (where the summer solstice is marked) to the museum entrance (where the winter solstice is marked). As well as functioning as a calendar, the instrument can also function as a solar clock, thanks to the calibrations in the metal. The gnomon, in fact, stands 6.19 metres high and consists of a double blade of bronze which rises from a water basin bordered with a wind rose.

Another traditional feature is the inclusion of a zoomorphic sub-meridian; the gnomon, in the form of a lizard's tail, indicates the exact moment when the sun is at its highest point. At night, the entire instrument is lit up, making it a feature of the city's urban landscape. The museum itself houses both a permanent collection and temporary exhibitions on specific themes. The former include some unique pieces: sundials, astrolabes, solar clocks, nocturnal clocks, compasses, armillary spheres, and several of Galileo's original instruments (including his famous first spyglass). The library and research centre underline this institution's importance as a custodian of Florence's past as a centre of scientific enquiry.

NEARBY

PONTE VECCHIO SUNDIAL

The sundial of Ponte Vecchio is an astonishing little meridian in the form of a shell. You hardly notice the meridian set on its column, hence it is often ignored. Besides, it is no longer in use.

There used to be a meridian at the Uffizi Gallery similar to the one at Santa Maria Novella, but it has disappeared.

WHO ARE THE *RENAIOLI*

Renaioli are "sand gatherers" (*rena* = sand) – or rather the descendants of those who for centuries used to collect the river sand that played such a part in the building of Florentine *palazzi*. These tough workers were not the only ones whose boats were to be seen on the Arno: right up to the Second World War, the river was home to barges carrying merchandise or providing floating stages for performances, and of course there were pleasure craft. However, the *renaioli* were undoubtedly the only ones who were still working the river at the time of the terrible flood in November 1966.

For centuries, these figures scrambled to sift through the sand immediately below the Ponte Vecchio, which might contain precious waste from the goldsmiths' shops above. Furthermore, during the Fascist period, this was one of the few jobs open to the regime's opponents, given that you did not need a party membership card to be a *renaiolo*. After the war it was *renaioli* who eventually (in 1961) recovered the head of the statue of *Spring*, which had still been missing when the Ponte de Santa Trinità was rebuilt after its destruction by the Germans.

AN EXCURSION ON THE ARNO WITH THE *RENAIOLI*

Arno embankment; access from Piazza Mentana
• From late May to late September
• Tel: 3477982356
• www.renaioli.it

> To see Florence from an unusual point of view

Having restored some of their boats, the *renaioli* are once more to be seen on the river Arno, powering their boats by means of the traditional *asta* – a pole similar to that used by the fishermen of African lagoons. One can book to go on excursions along the river which provide a very unusual view of Florence.

The fullest trip starts at the barrier that is located beneath Piazza Mentana, just before the historic premises of the *Canottieri Ponte Vecchio* [Ponte Vecchio Rowing Club], the perfect place to have an aperitif beforehand or – on the terrace of the club – enjoy dinner afterwards. The *renaioli* take you in front of the loggia of the Uffizi and then under the arches of Ponte Vecchio, offering you the chance to see the historic houses perched on the bridge from beneath. The trip continues in the direction of the Santa Trinità bridge – affording you a very unusual view of the piers of the central arch – and then as far as Ponte alla Carraia, without however venturing too close to the water barrage just before Ponte alla Vittoria. On the return trip, one passes close by the church "lapped by the Arno" – that is, San Jacopo, the apse of which rises up from the river itself.

PONTE VECCHIO GOLF CHALLENGE

Every December
• www.pontevecchiochallenge.it

> **New
> Florentine sport:
> golf on the river**

Every December since 1997, Florence has been home to the most spectacular – and bizarre – golf tournament in the world: the Ponte Vecchio Golf Challenge. The event was devised by Romano Boretti and is now held under his patronage, as owner of the internationally renowned "Conte of Florence" sportswear shop, which also produces a range of golfwear.

The Ponte Vecchio Challenge is played on a "course" that replaces the traditional, even banal, setting of some beautiful corner of the countryside with the river itself. The entire competition occupies the stretch of the Arno from the historic Ponte Vecchio to Ponte delle Grazie, the next bridge immediately upstream.

The result is a unique golf tournament, which allows for a limited number of strokes and no "strolling the greens" for the competitors. Still, the whole thing is highly spectacular for the public who follow it from bleachers on the Arno waterfront. The event is so unusual that a number of great champions have decided to take up the three-day challenge (even if the December weather is generally cold). The starting-point is between the arches on the eastern side of Ponte Vecchio, where scaffolding and green carpets are used to create teeing-off greens. From these special "balconies", the players drive towards the holes, which are located on four grass-turfed rafts in the middle of the river. And if your ball ends up in the water hazard … too bad!

This rather bizarre competition might make you think of those Japanese training grounds for golfers, where dozens of players occupy small carbon-copy playing terraces, happy to hit one ball after another onto an unlikely golf course located above the rooftops. However, the charm of the Arno has a rather different effect. The curious floating plots of green, the banks of spectators on the bleachers and the Ponte Vecchio transformed into a teeing-off green are all just one more metamorphosis of a river that decidedly takes many forms.

GIOVANNI UGOLINI WORKSHOP

Lungarno Acciaiuoli, 66–70r
• Tel: 055 2844969

A ll those who appreciated the charm of the collection at Florence's Opificio delle Pietre Dure (Workshop of Semiprecious Stones) can learn more about this unique art form at the Ugolini Workshop, which still practises the traditional craft of assembling semiprecious

Semiprecious stones in the twenty-first century

stones in compositions that highlight their colour and finished polish. The workshop does restoration work throughout the world although it continues to create settings of malachite, chalcedony, lapis lazuli, agate and jasper. The business, founded in 1868, has since widened its field of activity. While still practising a revitalised form of an ancient craft, it now also has a magnificent gallery of exhibits: still lifes and landscapes, inlaid boxes, tables and other furnishings adorned with semiprecious stones, and a number of decorative pieces that it would now be difficult to find elsewhere.

FORGOTTEN ORIGIN OF THE *LUCCHETTI D'AMORE* (LOVE PADLOCKS)

TRADITION *Terrace of the Lungarno dei Medici*

The tradition has now spread and Florence is not the only city to bear the brunt of it: as a seal of their bond with the city and with each other, loving couples fix a padlock to a historic monument and then throw away the key. In Florence, this ritual was long associated with the balustrade around the Benvenuto Cellini monument on Ponte Vecchio – a balustrade which the City Council has now taken measures to clear of all its padlocks. However, the determined padlockers have simply moved on a few metres, as can be seen from the railing covered with padlocks that runs along the river embankment opposite the Uffizi Loggia. The origin of this ritual of making a declaration of love (or some other vow) while closing the padlock and then throwing the key in the river is rather less well known. It is said that a student at the Army Medical Corps School attached the padlock from his barracks locker to a chain on Ponte Vecchio the day that he had to leave Florence. Little did he know that he was starting a custom that would enjoy greater and greater success – to the point of becoming a real nuisance.

CENTRAL ARCHES OF PONTE SANTA TRINITÀ

The rams guarding the Arno

Barely visible from the embankment – and almost impossible to see from the bridge itself – are two ram's heads which curve out over the Arno from the central arch of Ponte Santa Trinità.

These identical statues, located at either side of the bridge, are much more imposing than they appear from a distance. To fully appreciate them, you should either view them through binoculars from the embankment or, even better, take a boat out onto the Arno.

The ram is associated with war, and it is no coincidence that this animal motif appears on either side of the bridge. The ram looking up towards Ponte Vecchio protects Florence against the river spates which threaten from that direction (the waters flowing down from the Casentino mountains have often caused floods in the city); the ram looking towards Ponte all Carraia protects Florence against the foreign invaders whose ships often arrived upstream from the sea. Gossips will tell you that the worst of those enemies were the perfidious Pisans, although the truth is that when the bridge was built Pisa had long been part of the Grand Duchy of Tuscany; still, Florence continued to keep an eye on its old rival.

Destroyed by the retreating Wehrmacht on 4 August 1944, Ponte Santa Trintà was subsequently rebuilt *come'era e dov'era* ("as it was and where it was"). But not without difficulty: there were, for example, particular problems in reproducing the catenary curve of the arches, defined by the parabola of a heavy chain suspended from two points at either end. However, on 16 May 1958 the new bridge reopened, with the two rams present and ready for guard duty.

Of the four statues that grace the corners of the bridge, the one of "Spring" was restored without its head, of which no trace could be found. Then, three years later, one of the very last of the city's *renaioli* (see p. 66) happened to fish up the head, which could thus be set back in place – to the great joy of the Florentines, who celebrated the event.

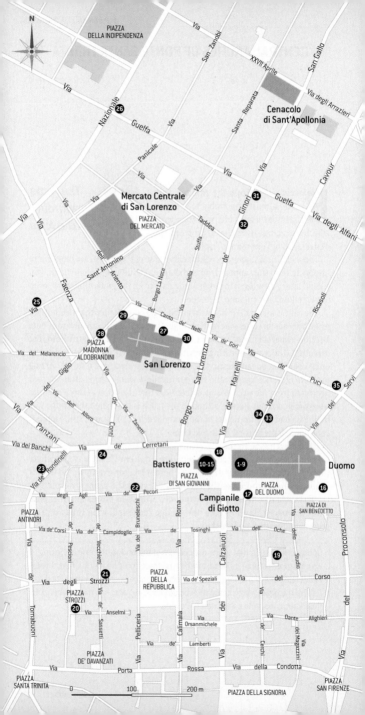

DUOMO / SAN LORENZO

OBSERVING THE SUN WITHIN THE CATHEDRAL

❶

Cathedral Santa Maria del Fiore
Piazza del Duomo
• Hours : Monday to Wednesday 10.00-17.00, Thursday 10.00-15.30,
Saturday 10.00-16.45, Sunday and holidays 13.30-16.45
• Admission free
• Solar observations with commentary by an astronomer in June; for
exact dates visit: www.operaduomo.firenze.it
• Entrance by the Porta dei Canonici (southern side of the Cathedral); tell
the custodians you want to see *"la meridiana"*

> **An exceptional astronomical phenomenon**

The astronomical activity of the cathedral of Florence cannot usually be witnessed: the chapel della Croce is normally reserved for the mass and the zodiacal inscriptions on the floor covered.

But, around four times a year, near the summer solstice (June 21), the cathedral provides an extraordinary spectacle that science buffs won't want to miss: one can observe the passage of the sun within the building itself. This feature was restored to full "working order" in 1996 and now the ecclesiastical authorities, working in conjunction with a committee dedicated to promoting public interest in astronomy, allow groups to observe the phenomenon; in theory, these groups should be limited to 150 people, but there were 250 on the day we visited. What one sees is the sudden apparition of a circle of light which then can be observed moving across the floor to come to rest exactly over a circle of marble whose position was calculated in 1475 by Paolo dal Pozzo Toscanelli (1397-1482). Apart from these special days, there is little visible trace of the astronomical activity associated with the church. During the Renaissance, astronomers were allowed to take advantage of the internal layout of the cathedral and the exceptional height of its cupola to carry out measurements that previously had been impossible. Toscanelli had assisted Brunelleschi in his calculations for the cathedral dome, and in 1475 he was allowed to install a bronze plaque (*la bronzina*) with an opening measuring about 5cm across. The light that passed through this opening fell to the floor of the building in the Cappella della Croce; the exact spot where it strikes at the time of the summer solstice is marked by a marble disk still visible today. In 1510, a wider circle whose diameter better corresponds to that of the ray of light was added (the original was kept out of respect for Toscanelli's work). This feature of the building was used in various types of astronomical work, including the reformation of the calendar. It has also served to study sun spots, the progression of eclipses, and the transit of Venus in front of the sun.

For more information on how such meridians work, see the following double-page spread.

XIMENES SUNDIAL

2

Santa Maria del Fiore cathedral
Piazza del Duomo

> **The highest sundial in the world**

Sundial meridians were often located in cathedrals, whose massive size increased the distance between the point of entry of the light and the point at which it struck the ground: the greater that distance, the more accurately scientists could calculate the angle of incidence. Another reason for the frequency of such scientific instruments within cathedrals was that the Church itself had an interest in them: they made it possible to calculate the exact date of Easter.

So, in 1754, almost 300 years after Toscanelli (see preceding double page), the Italian mathematician, engineer, astronomer and geographer Leonardo Ximenes (1716–1786) used such an opening to calculate the variations in the angle of inclination of the Earth's axis with respect to the plane of its elliptical orbit. His proposal to use the specific characteristics of the building (the height of the cupola made for unusually precise measurements) aroused the immediate interest of both civil and religious authorities.

In 1755 he obtained permission to have a marble meridian line inlaid on the floor of the Capella della Croce (this ran through the two previously installed marble disks). The angle of the solar image could be read directly from the calibrations on this line, with Ximenes' calculations finally concluding that the inclination of the Earth's axis changed by just over 30" (about one fiftieth of a degree) per century. Modern-day astronomers put the figure at around 47".

For Ximenes, it was essential that the observational readings be "absolute," so that they could be "transferable". This meant that he had to be able to give the precise size of all the instruments he used – for example, the height of the gnomonic opening above the floor of the cathedral. In fact, near the high altar (but not open to visitors) there is an elliptical paving stone that indicates the point that forms an exact perpendicular with the central axis of the opening. Within the stone are engraved standard measures of a *braccio fiorentino* (58.36 cm) and a *pied parisien* (32.48 cm). Ximenes had to overcome considerable difficulties in order to obtain the required precision in his measurements of the opening's height. For example, to measure the vertical distance from the opening to the floor (just under 90 m) he used a copper chain. When this was suspended down to the floor, however, the links stretched. And even that stretching varied according to the weight the individual link was actually supporting (i.e. its position in the chain). This meant that when the chain was returned to the horizontal, it was no longer the same length. Ximenes therefore decided to measure it when suspended, using the standard measurement he chose for the purpose: the *toise parisienne* (1.95 m). Another problem was the expansion of this metal standard due to increases in temperature. If this was not to invalidate his observations, he had to carry out all the different measurements on the same day and at the same time, allowing for the fact that the temperature within the cathedral varies depending on proximity to the lantern. The error in his final measurements was no more than 2 per 100,000 – a remarkable degree of precision for that period.

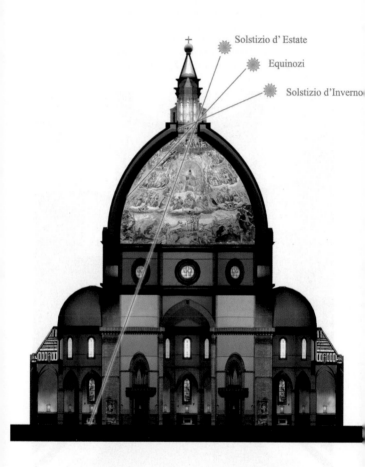

Solstizio d' Estate

Equinozi

Solstizio d'Inverno

HOW DOES A MERIDIAN WORK?

Instead of the using the shadow of a gnomon, these use a small hole placed at a certain height, through which the sun's light falls onto a meridian line (i.e. one aligned exactly north-south). The fact that the sun's rays perform the function of the shadow in a traditional sundial means that the opening is sometimes referred to as a "gnomonic opening." The higher the opening, the more efficient the meridian, hence the interest in using cathedrals (see the following section "Why are meridians installed in cathedrals?"); the circumference of the hole had to be no more than one thousandth of the height above the ground. Obviously, the opening had to be installed on the south side of the building in order to let in the rays of the sun, which lies to the south in the northern hemisphere.

The meridian line should run from the point which stands perpendicularly below the axis of the opening, not always easy to determine using the instruments available to scientists in the past (see "The Epic of Ximenes' Meridian"). The length of the line depends on the height of the opening; in some cases, where the building was not long enough to trace the entire meridian line across the floor (as was the case at Saint-Sulpice in Paris), an obelisk was added at its end, so that the movement of the sun's ray could then be measured up the vertical. In summer, when the sun is highest in the sky, the sun's ray falls onto the meridian line closer to the south wall (where that line begins) than it does in winter, when the sun is lower over the horizon and the rays tend to strike towards the far end of the meridian line.

The main principle behind the working of the meridian is that at noon, solar time, the sun is at its apex and, by definition, its rays fall straight along a line running exactly north-south. So, the exact moment when those rays strike the meridian line, which does run north-south, indicates the solar noon. Furthermore, the exact place on the meridian line where that ray falls makes it possible to determine the day of the year: the point right at the beginning of the line is reached solely on the day of the summer solstice, whilst the exact end of the line is reached on the day of the winter solstice. Experience and observation meant that the meridian line could be calibrated to identify different days of the year.

Once this was done, one could use the line to establish the date of various moveable feasts, such as Easter – one of the great scientific and religious uses of meridians. Similarly, one could establish the different periods corresponding with the signs of the Zodiac, which explains where one finds such signs indicated along the length of a number of meridian lines.

WHY WAS 4 OCTOBER FOLLOWED IMMEDIATELY BY 15 OCTOBER IN THE YEAR 1582?

THE MEASUREMENT OF TIME AND THE ORIGIN OF THE MERIDIANS

The entire problem of the measurement of time and the establishment of calendars arises from the fact that the Earth does not take an exact number of days to orbit the sun: one orbit in fact takes neither 365 nor 366 days but rather 365 days, 5 hours, 48 minutes and 45 seconds.

At the time of Julius Caesar, Sosigenes of Alexandria calculated this orbit as 365 days and 6 hours. In order to make up for this difference of an extra 6 hours, he came up with the idea of an extra day every four years: thus the Julian calendar – and the leap year – came into being.

In 325 AD, the Council of Nicaea established the temporal power of the Church (it had been called by Constantine, the first Roman emperor to embrace Christianity). The Church's liturgical year contained fixed feasts such as Christmas, but also moveable feasts such as Easter. This latter was of essential importance as it commemorated the death and resurrection of Christ, and so the Church decided that it should fall on the first Sunday following the full moon after the spring equinox. That year, the equinox fell on 21 March, which was thus established as its permanent date.

However, over the years, observation of the heavens showed that the equinox (which corresponds with a certain known position of the stars) no longer fell on 21 March...The 11 minutes and 15 seconds difference between the real and assumed time of the Earth's orbit around the Sun was resulting in an increasing gap between the actual equinox and 21 March. By the 16th century, that gap had increased to ten full days and so pope Gregory XIII decided to intervene. Quite simply, ten days would be removed from the calendar in 1582, and one would pass directly from 4 October to 15 October... It was also decided, on the basis of complex calculations (carried out most notably by the Calabrian astronomer Luigi Giglio), that the first year of each century (ending in 00) would not actually be a leap year, even though divisible by four. The exceptions would fall every four hundred years, which would mean that in 400 years there would be a total of just 97 (rather than 100) leap years. This came closest to making up the shortfall resulting from difference between the real and assumed time of orbit. Thus 1700, 1800 and 1900 would not be leap years, but 2000 would...

In order to establish the full credibility of this new calendar – and convince the various Protestant nations that continued to use the Julian calendar – Rome initiated the installation of large meridians within its churches. A wonderful scientific epic had begun...

The technical name for a leap year is a bissextile year. The term comes from the fact that the additional day was once placed between 24 and 25 February. In Latin, 24 February was the sixth (sextus) day before the calends of March, hence the name bis sextus, to indicate a supplementary sixth day. The calends were the first day of each month in the Roman calendar.

THE MERIDIAN OF SANTA MARIA DEL FIORE: THE HIGHEST MERIDIAN IN THE WORLD

From the 15th to the 18th century almost 70 meridians were installed in churches in France and Italy. Only ten, however, have a gnomonic opening that is more than 10 metres above floor level – that height being crucial to the accuracy of the instrument:

S. Maria del Fiore (Florence)	90.11 m
S. Petronio (Bologna)	27.07 m
St-Sulpice (Paris)	26.00 m
Monastery of San Nicolo l'Arena (Catania, Sicily)	23.92 m
Cathedral (Milan)	23.82 m
S. Maria degli Angeli (Rome)	20.34 m
Collège de l'Oratoire (Marseille)	17.00 m
S. Giorgio (Modica, Sicily)	14.18 m
Museo Nazionale (Naples)	14.00 m
Cathedral (Palermo)	11.78 m

WHY WERE MERIDIANS INSTALLED IN CATHEDRALS

To make their measurements more precise, astronomers required enclosed spaces where the point admitting light was as high as possible from the ground: the longer the beam of light, the more accurately they could establish that it was meeting the floor along an exactly perpendicular plane. Cathedrals were soon recognised as the ideal location for such scientific instruments as meridians. Furthermore, the Church had a vested interest as well, because meridians could be used to establish the exact date of Easter.

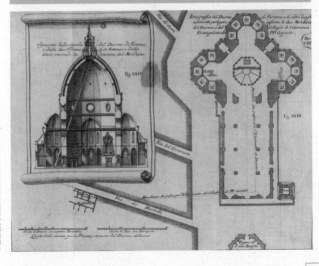

© Istituto e Museo di Storia della Scienza, Firenze

PAOLO UCCELLO'S CLOCK ❸

Santa Maria del Fiore cathedral
Piazza del Duomo
• Monday—Wednesday from 10am to 5pm; Thursday 10am to 3.30pm;
Saturday 10am to 4.45pm; Sundays and public holidays 1.30pm to
4.45pm
• Admission free

*Artist
employed in
the measurement
of time*

Even if their name is not immediately associated with the history of clockmaking, certain great Florentine artists did play an important role in the history of time measurement. After all, they lived in a city which was the birthplace of various master clockmakers, who would make Florence one of the centres of this nascent industry for centuries. For example, the architect Filippo Brunelleschi also invented timepieces; his clock in the Palazzo dei Vicari at Scarperia can still be seen today. Leonardo da Vinci may not have made clocks, but he did meticulously study their mechanisms. And it was Galileo himself who proved the isochronism of small oscillations. As for Paolo Uccello, his name is linked with the large clock that can be seen inside the cathedral over the main doorway. The original mechanism, subsequently modified a number of times over the centuries (the present one dates from 1761), was designed in 1443 by Angelo Niccolai degli Orologi, grandson of the Niccolò di Berardo who had built the clock at Palazzo Vecchio (since destroyed). Angelo's workshop was in a street that was subsequently renamed Via dell'Oriuolo (*oriuolo* being an old form of the word *orologio* – "clock").

Within the cathedral it was Paolo Uccello who painted the large circle with the twenty-four hours laid out in the sequence that was typical of the time – that is, what we would consider "anticlockwise" and starting from the bottom rather than the top. The first hour of the day was immediately after sunset, while the 24th corresponded to the hour of the evening *Ave Maria*. Thus, by beginning from the bottom, the hour at which the sun was at its zenith corresponded to the hour at the very summit of the clock face.

The Duomo clock measured out the rhythm of civic and religious life in Florence, although there were no chimes to strike individual hours. The face itself has only one clock hand – again the work of Paolo Uccello – even if the star-form design is so elaborate that you might be forgiven for thinking that there are actually three clock hands.

In 1750 the clock face was adapted to what was becoming the dominant 12-hour system, later imposed as the norm under Napoleonic rule. This new system had the great advantage of cutting the maximum number of chimes from 24 to 12 (thus reducing the possibility of error for those counting each chime to tell the time). In 1968 the clock underwent painstaking restoration of the original 24-hour format. The frescoes of the evangelists to the four sides of the clock face are also by Paolo Uccello.

OLD CONSTRUCTION HOIST AT THE DUOMO ❹

Santa Maria del Fiore cathedral
Piazza del Duomo
• Monday–Wednesday from 10am to 5pm; Thursday 10am to 3.30pm;
Saturday 10am to 4.45pm; Sundays and other public holidays 1.30pm to
4.45pm • Free entrance • Entrance to the cupola: Monday–Friday from
8.30am to 7pm; Saturday 8.30am to 5.40pm; first Saturday of the month
8.30am to 4pm; closed Sundays and public holidays • Admission: €6;
last tickets sold 40 minutes before closing time • Warning: there are 463
steps to climb!

> **Traces of building work on the cathedral**

The construction of a cathedral is a project that involves the whole city; acting as a catalyst on the life of the community, it can generate great tensions but also curious episodes of greater or lesser historical significance. And this is particularly true if – as was the case with Santa Maria del Fiore – building work continues over centuries. This explains why the very fabric of the cathedral and the surrounding area are rich in echoes of events that helped to establish the very identity of Florence.

The cupola over the choir of the cathedral was designed and built by Filippo Brunelleschi in the years 1420–1436. Given the huge dimensions of the project, a range of innovative techniques had to be used, both in the structural design of the cupola and in the handling of the thousands of tons of materials required to build it. For Brunelleschi, these technical problems offered another chance to demonstrate his genius, with the architect himself designing lifting equipment whose power of leverage was greatly increased by carefully designed gear systems. He even invented a system for installing tables high up on the structure, thus saving time by removing the need for the workmen to come down to ground level at mealtimes.

Brunelleschi's knowledge of machine design came from clockmaking, whose secrets he had learned while serving his apprenticeship with a clockmaker. And ten years after the construction of the cupola, his gear systems would again prove useful when they served to hoist into place the sphere atop the lantern – an operation in which the young Leonardo da Vinci was involved (see the collapse of the lantern in 1600).

The finished cupola rises 35.5 metres above the drum beneath – that is, 90 metres above ground level (107 metres including the lantern). It is estimated to weigh around 37,000 tons.

There is little surviving evidence of the building work itself. Most notable are two modest hoists fitted into wooden brackets under the central vaults of two of the so-called *tribune morte* (blank tribunes). These small structures around the outside of the drum beneath the oculi served to counteract the horizontal thrust exerted by the cupola.

Outside the cathedral – at the base of the drum, facing the premises of La Misericordia (that is, at the Via de' Calzaiuoli entrance to the building) – you can see the traces of another hoist in a niche.

BULL AT THE PORTA DELLA MANDORLA   **5**

Santa Maria del Fiore cathedral
Piazza del Duomo

"Cuckold"
door

I t is the Porta della Mandorla which leads to the summit of Brunelleschi's gigantic cupola, reached after 463 steep and sometimes narrow steps. Among the sculptural decoration of this doorway note the fine set of horns on the head of a bull which seems to be looking towards the house opposite him and to the left. It's said that this was the work of a waggish master mason, who placed the grim-looking bull there in order to mock a man whom all the world knew to be jealous of his young and beautiful wife.

NEARBY

LION NIGHTMARE   **6**

Another side doorway – this time on the left of the cathedral – is framed by two columns supported by a lion and lioness respectively. This is the Porta de Balla, or dei Cornacchini, and owes its name to a tragic episode.

In the fifteenth century Angelo, a neighbour of the Cornacchini family, had a terrible nightmare: he was being devoured by a lion identical to that supporting one of these two columns. The following day, to exorcise the fear caused by the nightmare, he came and put his hand within the large open mouth of the lion. Unfortunately, a large scorpion was nesting there and poor Anselmo died that very day from the sting he received on his thumb.

BLASPHEMOUS ANGEL OF THE DUOMO

Santa Maria del Fiore cathedral
Piazza del Duomo
First angel to the right of the doorway on the far right

Look carefully at the first angel to the right of the doorway on the far right of the Duomo's façade. All the doorways conceal a message, as was required of all entrances to a cathedral. In the arches over

Greeting from the Angel of the Sodomites

the openings are small sculptural groups that depict recognisable figures and recount a narrative. So far, so good. Nothing out of the ordinary; indeed, there is the usual multitude of angels and figures of greater or lesser significance.

In all Gothic cathedrals, what is striking are the masses of imaginary animals that crowd walls and roofs. However, among the angels of the Florence Duomo there is one whose gesture is, at the very least, disconcerting: there he is, clearly giving us the finger. Some – for example, David Leavitt – see this as a coded, but very clear message. This, they claim, is the Angel of the Sodomites.

The records of sodomy in Florence include, for example, Dante's depiction of his own teacher, Brunetto Latini, among the circle of sodomites in hell. And other literary sources provide extensive evidence that sodomy was widespread on the banks of the Arno. However, here it is architecture itself that refers even more blatantly to the practice, with an angel directing an insult at us by mimicking an erection from the very doorway of the Duomo. The gesture may pass unobserved amidst the numerous images that crowd the doorway, but it is a blasphemy of rare impertinence.

BACCIO D'AGNOLO'S ABANDONED PROJECT

"It looks like a cage for crickets," commented Michelangelo when looking up at the raised walkway that runs along only one of the eight sides of the cupola. And Baccio d'Agnolo, architect of the said walkway, was so discouraged that he did not complete the project. Unless the truth is that he himself had doubts about this "enclosure", which was intended to run as a sort of ring around the base of the cupola. The walkway would have been a spectacular construction, but it risked stunting the upward thrust of the cupola as a whole. And then there was the fact that Brunelleschi's calculations hadn't taken such an aerial construction into account, so the walkway might have compromised the statics of the whole structure. Whatever the reason, this complex project, on which work had begun ten years earlier, was abandoned in 1516, to the great satisfaction of Michelangelo and no real regrets from the city as a whole. The surviving stretch of Baccio d'Agnolo's walkway now stands as a solitary extravagance in mid-air. An odd sight, it is a reminder that the cathedral was for centuries the site of ongoing construction work, with this symbol of Florence being the object of discussions, proposals and debate.

CONCEALED SELF-PORTRAIT OF GIUSEPPE CASSIOLI ⑧

Right doorway to the Duomo
Santa Maria del Fiore cathedral
Piazza del Duomo

> **Strangled by a serpent for delivering work late**

Not all the anecdotes associated with the cathedral refer to the Renaissance. As was to be expected of such a major church, building work on Santa Maria del Fiore would, with dozens of interruptions, continue for a long time. Perhaps rather less expected is that it was not completed until the end of the nineteenth century: the façade was only officially inaugurated on 12 May 1887, that is six centuries after the laying of the first stone. And even then the doors were missing.

It was another decade before the doors for the left doorway, by Augusto Passaglia, were complete, and a further two years (1899) before the brothers Amos and Giuseppe Cassioli finished work on the right doorway. Having been severely criticised for this delay, Giuseppe Cassioli, with a certain irony, included a self-portrait in the bronze bas-reliefs decorating his door, showing himself being strangled by a snake. It is at about eye level on the right-hand side.

But even then work was unfinished. Not until 1903 were the central doors – again the work of Augusto Passaglia – inaugurated in a ceremony attended by King Victor Emmanuel III. Then – finally! – work on the façade came to an end.

NEARBY

THE BISCHERI INSCRIPTION ⑨

On the south side of the cathedral, near the bell tower, is an inscription just above eye level to the right of the visitors' doorway. Carved into marble, this announces the birth of a member of the Bischieri family. Due to the history of the Bischieri, the word has in Tuscan dialect become a synonym for "idiot." When planning to build the cathedral, the authorities of the Republic of Florence had to expropriate the homes of those who lived on the selected site. Each householder was offered a reasonable price; however, the Bischieri family refused point blank and would not budge. It is said that a mysterious fire then destroyed the houses that they owned, and thus they received only a derisory sum in compensation for their now-vacant plot. Another version has it that the Florentine authorities lost patience with them and exiled the entire family without compensation. Hence the use of their name to indicate someone who is stupid and pigheaded. Hence also the fact that the family preferred to change their name to Guadagni [Earnings]…

Where Via dell'Oriulo runs into Piazza del Duomo there is a plaque with the inscription *Canto dei Bischieri* [Bischieri Corner]; it indicates where the family used to live.

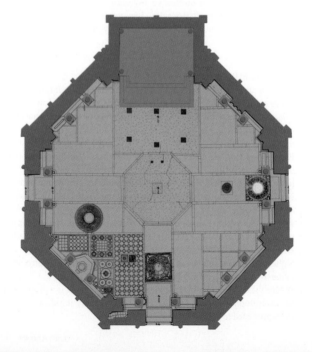

MARBLE SOLSTITIAL MARKER

Baptistery
Piazza San Giovanni
• Open from 12.15pm to 7pm; Sundays and holidays 8.30am to 2pm;
closed 1 January, Easter Sunday, 8 September and Christmas Day
• Admission: €3

*Traces
of the meridian
in the Baptistery*

Of all the various astronomical instruments installed within Florence's ancient buildings and monuments, the oldest is actually the least well known. It is to be found within the Baptistery and comprises a large circular floor plaque of marble between the north and east doorways. The plaque bears the twelve signs of the zodiac with a Sun engraved at the centre enclosed with the Latin palindrome (a phrase that reads the same forwards and backwards): *EN GIRO TORTE SOL CICLOS ET ROTOR IGNE* ("I am the Sun. I am that wheel turned by fire whose turning turns the spheres").

This is the last trace of the solar clock which was installed in the Baptistery some time before the year 1000. The building, dating from the fourth to fifth centuries, was a Christian place of worship in the seventh century, serving as a cathedral until, in 1128, it officially became the Baptistery.

Mentioned in the *Chronicles* of Flipppo Villani (1325–1407) as being on the lower edge of the lantern, a hole within a bronze plaque (no longer there) in the cupola allowed a ray of light to fall upon the signs of the zodiac that were laid out around the marble plaque. In the thirteenth century, the marble floor was replaced by one identical to the original, but without care being taken to place the plaque in its original position; hence, as Villani

explains, the solar clock no longer worked. However, the real reason for its demise was that the meridian had become obsolete due to the precession of the equinoxes.* So the hole was covered over and the solar clock was left to serve a merely decorative purpose.

However, the large marble solstitial plaque is no simple "defunct machine"; it is the oldest surviving trace of Florence's centuries-old interest in the stars.

Furthermore, the elegance of design and form make it a magnificent example of the arts applied to science.

*The precession of the equinoxes is due to the slow change in the inclination of the Earth's axis of rotation. This shift means that the axis of rotation itself actually defines a cone, completed about every 25,800 years.

THE CABBALA AND THE BAPTISTERY OF SAN GIOVANNI BATTISTA

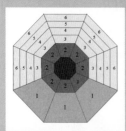

The Baptistery of San Giovanni Battista inherited the traditional forms of sacred geometry (see following double page) which had been used by the ancient Roman architects and artisans of the *collegiam fabrorum* and were the precursors of what one sees in Romanesque and Gothic architecture. Its floor-plan is an octagon measuring 25.6 metres in diameter, a form that is also often found in medieval baptismal founts, which frequently stood upon an octagonal base or rested upon a 'rotonda' of eight columns. St. Ambrose had argued that the octagon was a symbol of the Resurrection, thus here it symbolised the eternal life which the neophyte gained when baptised. In effect, the rite of Christian baptism comprised two highly symbolic phases: immersion in and emergence from water. The immersion, now reduced to sprinkling with water, corresponds to the disappearance of a sin-laden being within the waters of death, to purification and a return to the origins of life. The emergence from water symbolises the emergence of a purified being in a state of grace, reconciled with the divine source of a new life. The Baptistery's medieval baptismal founts stood at its centre and were decorated with geometrical motifs and the signs of the zodiac; it is said that their design had been inspired by Dante's *Divine Comedy*. Those founts were then transformed in 1576 by the craftsman Bernardo Buontaleni, working at the behest of Francesco I de Medici, and have survived to this day. The Baptistery's shape is intended to represent the eighth day (*octava dies*), that of Christ's Ascension. This is reinforced by an octagonal lamp, added in 1150.

The entire spiritual universe was the subject of the mosaics in the cupola, which were added from 1270 onwards. With gold backgrounds, they comprise eight sections (one for each side of the octagon) that were in turn divided into six parts, creating 48 compartments – a distribution that reflects the numerical logic of the Cabbala. Raban Maur (780/784?-856), abbot of Fulda in Germany, identifies this number of 48 (6x8) as the total of the biblical prophets who were admitted to divine ministry and received direct spiritual revelations. At the top of this decorative schema is a depiction of the hierarchy of angels surmounted by a *Last Judgement*, which itself is dominated by the large figure of Christ, at whose feet one sees the resurrection of the dead: to the right are the Just, received into heaven by the biblical patriarchs, to the left are the damned in a demon-filled hell.

A further symbolic reference to access to divine salvation is to be found in the three doors; the South Door, completed in 1336, was the work of Andrea Pisano, while the North and East Doors were the work of Lorenzo Ghiberti (the former completed in 1422, the latter begun in 1425). The number of these doors reflects the number of the Trinity, whilst their decoration is inspired by the Old and New Testaments, between whose ancient patriarchs and new apostles St. John the Baptist stood as a sort of link. The decoration of each door again was conceived on the basis of a numerical logic inspired by the Cabbala. For example, the south door has 28 rectangular panels depicting the acts and virtues of John the Baptist. They are laid out in seven vertical columns of four compartments each in horizontal alignment and enclosed within lozenges (of a lobate form known as *compasso gotico*). The first twenty panels depict episodes from the *Life of the Baptist*, beginning on the left (1-10) and continuing on the right (11-20). Then come the personifications of the Three Theological Virtues of *Faith, Hope* and *Charity* (21-23), to which are added *Humility* (24), and finally the four Cardinal Virtues of *Fortitude, Temperance, Justice* and *Prudence* (25-28). On the North Door, there are again 28 panels, this time depicting scenes from the New Testament, with the last two rows depicting eight saints: John, Matthew, Luke and Mark (the four Evangelists) and Ambrose, Jerome, Gregory and Augustine (the Doctors of the Church). Antonio Paolucci described this door as "the most important event in the history of Florentine art in the first quarter of the fifteenth century." The number 28 symbolises reflection within the Cabbala: just as the moon in its cycle of 28 days reflects the light of the sun, so it is the faithful who are to contemplate and reflect upon the images within these doors, absorbing their full meaning and thus gaining awareness of the virtues depicted therein – virtues that will lead them on the path towards the perfection of Heaven.

The East Door comprises ten panels depicting scenes from the Old Testament, here rendered in perspective depth; the technique of perspective was unknown before this period. Michelangelo called this door *la Porta del Paradiso*, the name by which it is still known.

The significance of the number 10 in the Cabbala arises from the Hebrew writings that claim God created the world by means of ten creative powers (Sephiroths). Ten was also associated with the realm that he first established, Paradise, where he set the first human couple. When Man fell into original sin (the sin of sexual corruption), God gave him the Ten Commandments, so that by following them through the course of his life he might regain the Eden of the original Paradise. Ten is the number of the whole; it summarises God's creation.

The three doors of the Baptistery one sees today are actually copies of the originals. Removed in 1990 because they were being damaged by pollution, the originals are now in the Museo dell'Opera del Duomo, preserved within nitrogen-filled containers.

TOMB OF THE ANTIPOPE JOHN XXIII

Baptistery
Piazza San Giovanni
• www.operaduomo.firenze.it
• Open from 12.15pm to 7pm; Sundays and holidays from 8.30am to 2pm;
closed 1 January, Easter Sunday, 8 September and Christmas Day
• Admission: €4

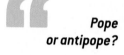

*Pope
or antipope?*

Baldassare Cossa was elected Pope John XXIII by the Council of Pisa in 1410 – a council he had helped to organise and, above all, finance. He died in 1419 at Florence, a city which had been his ally.

He was however an "antipope" only until 1415, the year in which he was deposed and recognised as Pope Martin V in Rome. Having maintained his rank as bishop, he would be buried in the Florence Baptistery – certainly not a place for the tomb of a heretic. Indeed, he was long considered as one of the legitimate leaders of the Church – as can be seen from the papal *Annuaries* published up to 1947 and from the mosaics in the Papal Basilica of St Paul in Rome, which include his portrait as pontiff.

However, Pope Angelo Roncalli was not of this opinion, deciding to

disavow the apostolic succession of Baldassare Cossa by himself taking the name of John XXIII (a decision that raised doubts among historians). Curiously enough, Cossa's predecessor – another "antipope", Alexander V – was to see the legitimacy of his apostolic succession recognised, with the next pope to take the name Alexander being known as Alexander VI. The antipope John XXIII did not enjoy the same fate. Still, his imposing tomb remains in the Baptistery as some sort of compensation.

ANTIPOPES: A QUESTION OF LEGITIMACY

The election of antipopes was one of the most striking symptoms of the deep conflicts with the Church; it also demonstrates the role that politics played in the choice of a pontiff. The antipopes were elected by "dissident" conclaves and were not recognised by the guardians of Roman Catholic orthodoxy, even if their situation was not always clear-cut: for example, the antipope John XXIII was buried with the full honours of his rank in one of the most prestigious places of Catholic worship – which would not have happened if he had been a heretic. The first antipope, Hippolytus, reigned from 217 to 235, in opposition to Pope Pontian, with whom he would later be reconciled. He subsequently died a martyr of the Church. Numerous antipopes reigned for only a short time, elected as the result of temporary disagreements. However, from 1378 onwards, the antipopes of Avignon formed a consolidated system of alternatives to the head of the Church in Rome. Indeed, in 1437, the antipope Benedict XIV would, according to a suggestion repeated in two historical novels (Jean Raspail's *L'Anneau du pêcheur* and Gérard Bavoux's *Le Porteur de lumière*), appoint various cardinals to secretly nominate other antipopes in order to prolong the "Avignon line". This "line" ended with Benedict XVI (1470–1499), but in the meantime yet another claimant to the throne of St Peter had been elected: Felix V (1439–1449). So, at one time, there were three putative popes. The election of antipopes came to an end after 1499, but the practice probably contributed to the calls for ecclesiastical renewal that inspired the Protestant Reformation.

GHIBERTI'S CONCEALED SELF-PORTRAIT

Porta del Paradiso
Baptistery

> **Signature of the creator of the *Porta del Paradiso***

There are various portrait busts concealed within the doors of the Baptistery, whose very weight has become legendary: Galileo himself commented that even if they were pushed shut very gently, the whole building would tremble the moment they struck the threshold.

This masterpiece by Lorenzo Ghiberti, which Michelangelo dubbed the *Porta del Paradiso* ("Gates of Paradise"), contains a self-portrait of the artist himself. Bald and with a wry expression, he is to be seen in the frame of the left-hand door at the fifth level (the levels are read left to right and from the bottom upwards). At the same level, on the right-hand door, is a portrait of Bartoluccio Ghiberti, his presence here a tribute from his adoptive son and pupil Lorenzo.

RECYCLED STONES

Just like other cathedrals – for example, that in Pisa – the Florence Baptistery (originally a cathedral) was built using masonry, sometimes dressed stones, taken from elsewhere. This would explain the incongruous presence – near ground level, to the left of the north doors – of a sculptured frieze decorated with a naval scene and some figures. It probably came from a Roman sarcophagus.

Another recycled stone is to be seen to the upper right of the east doors, facing the Duomo. Here, a curious inscription that has nothing to do with the cathedral is set into the wall.

THE ELM TREE AND THE SAN ZENOBIO COLUMN

Piazza del Duomo
Opposite the left doorway of Santa Maria del Fiore cathedral

*Commemorating
the passage
of a miracle-
working corpse*

It is to be hoped that now Piazza del Duomo is rid of the traffic that was choking it, San Zenobio's column will be restored to its rightful place within the city centre. To date this granite monument surmounted by an iron cross has made no more impression than a street lamp – particularly as there is nothing particularly ostentatious about it. However, the height of the column and its position – between the Baptistery and the Duomo – are clear indications that it once had very precise meaning and importance.

St Zenobio (337–417) was Florence's first bishop. He was credited with a wide range of miracles, including the resurrection of the son of a French pilgrim (a miracle that is commemorated by a plaque on the façade of Palazzo Valori e Altoviti). Some years after his death, when his body was being transferred from San Lorenzo to Santa Reparata (which stood on the site of the present cathedral), the bier happened to brush against a dead elm tree whose branches suddenly began to put forth shoots. Immediately this was claimed as a posthumous miracle. Tradition has it that all this occurred on 26 January 429, although we have no date for the raising of the column to commemorate the miracle. Still, we do know that the original column was swept away by the floods of 1333 and then rebuilt soon afterwards.

Though there is an inscription on the column – plus a carving of an elm tree – the name of Zenobio means nothing to modern-day Florentines, and even less to tourists. They all pass by this simple yet fairly obvious monument without realising that it bears witness to a story that is an integral part of the very identity of Florence.

WHAT BECAME OF THE WOOD OF THE MIRACULOUSLY REVIVED ELM?

The wood itself became a precious relic, used to make the crucifix in the church of San Giovannino e dei Cavalieri (in Via San Gallo) and to provide the panel for a painting of the Miracle of San Zenobio by an artist known as Il Maestro del Bigallo. Zenobio was so popular that, together with St Antoninino Pierozzi, he became the patron saint of the diocese of Florence.

TRACES OF ANCIENT UNITS OF MEASUREMENT IN THE BAPTISTERY

⑭

Piazza del Duomo

It's a foot!

Before the advent of the metre, the arms and feet of sovereigns were often the bases for standard units of measurement. To make these units known to merchants and citizens, these lengths were reproduced on stone slabs and plaques that were then placed on public display. Some of these can still be seen: curious rectangles engraved in stone on the two columns that flank the south doors of the Baptistery.

The column on the left has two rectangles, one within the other, whose function is yet to be explained. However, on the column on the right, the simple, larger, rectangle represents a "Lombard foot". Introduced by King Liutprand (690?–744), this new unit of 38 cm by 51.5 cm was part of the arsenal of regulations intended to unify the Italian peninsula under the often resented rule of the Lombards. For example, these rulers often clashed with the papacy. Tradition has it that Liutprand himself was 1.73 metres tall – an exceptional height for the time – and that his right foot measured 25.4 cm and his left 26.1 cm; hence the measure of 51.5 cm, the sum of the two. However, these precise figures were disproved when Liutprand's actual remains were discovered in his tomb within San Pietro in Ciel d'Oro, a church in Pavia, his capital, and the king was shown to have been of average height. Still, a thousand years after his rule, Liutprand's foot continued to be used as a unit of measurement in some Italian cities.

WHAT PRECEDED THE METRIC SYSTEM?

On 28 July 1861 Italy officially adopted the metric system. Before that, each province – or even city – had its own units of measurement, sometimes based upon the size of a monarch's foot or arm or hand. This confusion explains why such standards were often displayed in public places, primarily markets, where vendors and customers could consult them. Some of these old units of measurement can still be seen in Volterra and Barga.

In Florence, the most commonly used units were the *braccio fiorentino* (58.4 cm) and the *canna agrimensoria* (2.92 m). The Florentine foot (*piede fiorentino*) was the same length as the *pied parisien* (32.48 cm). This latter had become something of a standard measure throughout Europe thanks to the renown enjoyed by the architects of France's Gothic cathedrals.

BROKEN PISAN COLUMNS

**A gift
of Pisa**
The broken porphyry columns on either side of the Baptistery doorway seem to have been left there by mistake, but they were gifts presented to Florence by the city of Pisa in gratitude for its help against Lucca in 1117. Although damaged in transit, they were nevertheless set in place to avoid wounding Pisan sensibilities, as relations between Florence and Pisa were not as cordial as they might have been.

NEARBY

WHERE THE CATHEDRAL LANTERN CRASHED TO THE GROUND

In the middle of the grey paving slabs behind the cathedral there is a round plaque in white marble. This unidentified marker in itself identifies the place where the lantern atop the cathedral crashed to the ground on 17 February 1600. This was no ordinary incident of structural damage, for the lightning on this occasion had brought down two tons of building materials, with the gilded bronze ball and cross alone weighing some eighteen quintals. Fortunately nobody was injured, but the noise echoed throughout the city, with pieces of the lantern subsequently being found as far away as Via dei Servi. The lantern, the work of Andrea del Verrocchio, had been raised to the top of the cathedral in 1468, using special machinery designed for the occasion by Leonardo da Vinci. And after the collapse, Grand Duke Ferdinand I hurriedly took measures to have the damage repaired and the lantern restored. Just two years later, it – together with ball and cross – was back in place. However, the grand duke did more than just trust the skill of his engineers. In agreement with the archbishop, he sought divine protection for the restored lantern by having two small lead containers set within the arms of the cross, each containing precious holy relics and Latin inscriptions that invoked protection against lightning. To prevent any future such accidents, the lantern is nowadays protected by a lightning conductor.

MUSEO DELLA MISERICORDIA DI FIRENZE

Piazza del Duomo, 19–20
• Open Monday from 9am to 12 noon and 3pm to 5pm • To visit the
museum on another day, e-mail info@misericordia.firenze.it or call, a
few days in advance (indicating the number of people), 055 239393,
Monday–Friday from 8am to 1.30pm or 2.30pm to 5.30pm
• Admission free

> **Treasures
> of a powerful
> archconfraternity**

The collection of the Misericordia is important for two reasons, historic and artistic. Historically, because for more than seven centuries this confraternity has been supplying services to the sick and needy; with constantly updated equipment and a fleet of ambulances, the organisation has branches throughout the region. Artistically, because the collection in the historic premises of the Oratory contains such masterpieces as a statue by Benedetto da Maiano, a sculptural group by Luca della Robbia (over the altar) and Ghiberti's famous *Virgin Mary*. The premises themselves are located just opposite the Campanile di Giotto (Giotto's bell tower), in front of which there are always a couple of ambulances parked and ready for duty.

Since 2005 some of the rooms in the Oratory have been given over to the creation of a small museum which is open one day a week. The objects on display give some idea of the customs and duties of the confraternity. For example, there are the traditional black uniforms, the urns used when the confraternity voted, books and documents, religious furnishings and various items of silverware. There are also works linked with the high altar of the Misericordia – including Santi di Tito's *St Sebastian* – and a collection of drawings and watercolours relating to the sixteenth-century building that houses the confraternity.

The whole collection is laid out in a hushed and private space where it is rare to encounter other visitors; indeed, the atmosphere here is more that of a place of worship than an organisation dedicated to assisting the sick and needy and providing emergency care.

On the same floor as the museum you can also see the historic chamber where members of the Council of the Misericordia used to meet. In all the rooms open to the public, the keen-eyed visitor will note not only traces of the history of the confraternity but also some of the practical and vocational spirit behind this "church of the artists" – an institution which has played a role in Florentine life for over seven centuries.

ROSICRUCIANS: AN ORDER OF ESOTERIC AND MYSTICAL CHRISTIANITY

The name of this esoteric Order comes from that of a German elder who lived around 1460 and was known as Christian Rosenkreutz (Christian Rose-Cross). Together with twelve disciples deeply versed in Christian mysticism, he set up an Order dedicated to the study of the religious and scientific learning of the day. Having established themselves in the south of Europe, these scholar-mystics came into contact with the spiritual and cultural learning of the Islamic world – in particular, with Sufism. These contacts remained close for a long time, thus creating a spiritual link between East and West. Tradition has it that the Rosicrucians had superhuman powers thanks to their profound knowledge of hermetism and alchemy; that they knew how to create the philosopher's stone; that they spoke directly to God, Christ, the saints and the angels; and that through these contacts they learned divine wisdom and the secrets of immortality. Their reputation for supernatural miracle-working powers continues to this day, without it being clear where reality ends and fantasy begins. The Rosicrucians very quickly faded into anonymity from the fifteenth century onwards, becoming a secret society. Indeed, no new member was accepted before the death of an existing member – thus keeping the numbers equal to 1+12, on the model of Christ and his twelve Apostles. In 1614 a work written in German (with the Latin title *Fama Fraternitatis*) was attributed to Christian Rosenkreutz, though its actual author was the theologian Johannes Valentinus Andreae (1586–1654), who was supposedly the spokesman of the Order of Rosicrucians and signed himself as its "Grand Master". He describes the origins, history and mission of the Rosicrucians, who were striving to restore primordial Christianity and rid the Church of the secular vices to which it had fallen prey.

When Freemasonry evolved in the eighteenth century, it embraced Rosicrucianism, establishing in 1761 the 18th degree of *Prince of the Rose Cross* or *Knight of the Pelican* – a strictly Christian division (the bird being a Christian symbol of charity, abnegation and sacrifice).

Several scholars – such as the English physician and philosopher Robert Fludd in his 1629 *Summum Bonum* – distinguish between the Rose Cross and Rosicrucianism, with a further distinction later being made between Rose-Cross Masons and former Freemasons. The bases for this distinction are as follows:

Rose Cross refers to he who has achieved spiritual illumination, the Master who knows and applies divine mysteries because he is spiritually and inwardly in the image of Christ, the Supreme Being. Here, the emblem of the Rose Cross represents complete Enlightenment, the spirit (Rose) which enlightens and guides matter (Cross).

Rosicrucian: the disciple who has chosen to adopt the discipline that leads to the higher level of Rose Cross. The symbol of the Rose Cross here symbolises the love (Rose) and the perfection (Cross) that are to be achieved.

Rose-Cross Mason: this is the symbolic initiate who has achieved the 18th degree of Freemasonry. In this case, the Rose Cross placed at the centre of a set-square and pair of compasses represents the perfection and justice of Christ's message.

WROUGHT-IRON ROSICRUCIAN ARMS

Restaurant *Buca San Giovanni*
Piazza San Giovanni, 8
Tel: 055 287612

> **Secret meeting-place of the Rosicrucians**

This is a typical Florentine *buca* – literally meaning "hole" – the term used in the city for basement restaurants. The rooms here were once part of the sacristy of the Baptistery, which gives you some idea of their historic importance; the restaurant's premises are in fact listed. Certain furnishings date from the Middle Ages and the Renaissance – for example, the altar which has been converted into the restaurant bar, various decorations and coats of arms on the walls and a fresco (in the main room) which is attributed to the Giotto school.

Rich in a sense of history, the whole underground space has a mysterious atmosphere. It is no great surprise that the followers of Rosicrucianism, in the first half of the twentieth century, should have chosen this as their secret meeting-place. The fact that the rites of this confraternity were celebrated here is confirmed by a detail which may not be apparent to the layman but is immediately clear to the initiated: a wrought-iron grille featuring the symbol of the Rosicrucians.

TORRE DELLA PAGLIAZZA

Hotel Brunelleschi
Piazza Elisabetta, 3
• Tel: 055 27370
• Free admission on prior booking with the hotel at the following address: info@hotelbrunelleschi.it

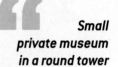

> *Small private museum in a round tower*

Numerous tower residences survive within the city, most still inhabited or incorporated within other buildings; indeed, you could follow an itinerary from one tower to another that would take you across the city as across a chessboard. However, only one of these towers is round, and it stands in a small square just a short walk from the Duomo. This exceptional shape may be because the original construction was Byzantine, being built by Greek solders while they were defending the city against the Goths; built on the site of the *piscina* – or water basin – of Roman thermal baths, the tower was supposedly intended as an addition to the city's fortifications. However, some claim that the structure dates from a few decades later and was built by the Lombards.

Whereas the puzzle of its origin may perhaps be insoluble, we do know something of the vicissitudes the tower has passed through. For a time it was used as a female prison; the *pagliazza* ("straw") refers to the material used as bedding in the cells. Then it was converted into the bell tower for the church of San Michele alle Trombe, before almost totally disappearing when it was incorporated into a building used as housing and warehouses. More recently, the tower has been converted into a hotel. But far from involving some cheerless "updating", this superb restoration/conversion by Italo Gamberini has stripped away the building that once blocked the view of the tower and highlighted its circular form, as well as its place within the context of the piazza (itself now enjoying new life thanks to full street lighting).

The restoration work revealed that the tower's foundations date back to the Romans and the end result elegantly highlights the medieval style of the structure. Inside, a remarkable little museum has been installed, which is not restricted to hotel guests and gives access to the underground area where you can admire the vaults and undressed stone walls.

As well as the remnants of the Roman baths, the museum has a fine collection of pottery and fragments dating from the Roman era (first century AD), together with objects manufactured in later periods; there are even some seventeenth-century ceramics from Montelupo. All these archaeological pieces were found during the on-site excavation and restoration work. Quite apart from the artistic value of its artefacts, this unique museum is a fine example of the historic stratifications to be found within – and under – a Florentine building.

SALA MARAINI

Gabinetto Scientifico Letterario G.P. Vieusseux
Piazza Strozzi, 1
• Tel: 055 288342
• Visits on request Monday, Wednesday and Friday from 9am to 1.30pm;
Thursday 9am to 6pm

The
Far East
in Piazza Strozzi

While the Sala Mariana may only be a room in a library, it has a very special atmosphere. This collection of material relating to the Orient was put together by the Florence-born traveller, ethnologist and Orientalist Fosco Maraini (1912–2004) and comprises a collection of 70,000 photographs and more than 8,000 books (most of the publications so rare that they are only found here). The library also has a constantly updated collection of magazines and journals on Japanese culture, some of which are complete as far back as the 1930s. The photographs on the walls depict some of the key moments in the life of Maraini, who was also a Himalayan mountain-climber. Not only are there pictures of the historic expeditions by the great Orientalist Giuseppe Tucci (in 1937 and 1948) and of expeditions by the Italian Alpine Club to Karakorum and the Hindu Kush region, but images of a range of countries in the Far East and South-East Asia: from Japan to Pakistan, Nepal to Tibet, Korea to Cambodia. Such a series of fascinating journeys and adventures reflects the boundless curiosity that inspired Fosco Maraini throughout his life.

If the writer wished to bequeath his precious library and photographic archive to the Gabinetto Vieusseux, he was in part inspired by a desire to re-establish the connection between the continent he loved and the city of his birth, for up to the 1930s there had been close scientific links between Florence and Asia.

What is striking is the breadth and homogeneity of this collection dedicated to Asia, the multiple aspects of the continent being illustrated by both texts and images. The photographic archive by itself is remarkable and would be the pride of even the most selective of universities.

There are other fascinating rooms in the Gabinetto Vieusseux, but the Sala Maraini is unique in Florence. The staff are welcoming and the director himself is very helpful. Wandering amidst these books and images, you can – within the very heart of Palazzo Strozzi – engage in a voyage of rediscovery that takes you back over the highlights of a long-running "love affair" between a Florentine and the Far East.

SCULPTURE OF A LITTLE DEVIL
Corner of Via degli Strozzi and Via de' Vecchietti

*A devil
on a horse*

On the corner of Palazzo Vecchietti at the junction of Via degli Strozzi and Via de' Vecchietti is a bronze statue of an insolent, jeering little devil. The work of Giambologna (or Jean de Boulogne, Douai, 1529 – Florence, 1608), it was commissioned by Bernardo Vecchietti to commemorate a mysterious incident in Florence's history.

In 1425 a Dominican friar, Pietro da Verona (see below), a sort of precursor of Savonarola, was preaching against heresy in Piazza del Mercato Vecchio (now Piazza della Repubblica) when a startled black horse ran into the square. The monk, immediately realising that this was a ruse of the Devil to distract his listeners, raised his hand to make a large sign of the cross over the satanic beast. The possessed beast withdrew and disappeared around the corner of Palazzo Vecchietti, leaving nothing but a plume of smoke and a strong smell of sulphur…

PIETRO DA VERONA

Pietro da Verona, or St. Peter Martyr, was born in Verona in 1205 to a Cathar family. Having become a Dominican, he gained a reputation for his visceral opposition to heretical ideas and was appointed head inquisitor for Lombardy, where he became known for the number of victims he condemned to burn at the stake. When he later moved to Florence, he established a sort of Christian militia to fight against the *Patarini*, a movement of clergy and populace rebelling against the excesses of certain prelates and their way of life. It is said that he feared his life would come to violent end due to the hatred he aroused. And that is what happened on 6 April 1252, when a certain Pietro da Balsamo split his head open with a billhook; the murderer later repented his crime and himself became a Dominican. In the numerous paintings of this murder, one sees the saint almost impervious to the cleaver buried in his skull. Only two years after his death, he was canonised as St. Peter Martyr by Pope Innocent IV, who thus exalted the role he had played in fighting heresy. Two violent clashes are said to have occurred in 1244. Historians now have cast doubts on such stories, even if there are two columns in Florence that were raised to commemorate these events: one, la Colonna della Croce al Trebbio, stands at the corner of Via del Moro, Via delle Belle Donne and Via del Trebbio, the other, la colonna Santa Felicità, stands in the square of the same name.

PRIVATE MUSEUM OF THE *CASA DEL TESSUTO* ㉒

Via dei Pecori, 20–24r
• Tel: 055 15961

An unknown museum

Two brothers with the delightful names of Romolo and Romano Romoli – direct descendants of the Egisto Romoli who founded the *Casa del Tessuto* ("Home of Textiles") in 1929 – have transformed this city-centre shop into a space where there is always something going on. This is not only somewhere to find the very best textiles, but twice a week it also offers lessons for young couturiers and pupils from all over the world. There are also courses and talks on the history of the city. As for the customers, you might well find some famous figures – not only actors and writers, but also the emperor of Japan and the queens of Denmark and Holland, all delighted by a rich array of cottons, silks and linens in a range of colours and designs.

The business also owns a real gem: a small museum illustrating the history of textiles. The collection includes a precious sixteenth-century weaving loom, various ancient scissors and pins, scales and numerous other instruments, plus a vast assortment of thread and bobbins. There is more than enough to offer a fascinating insight into the history of fabric-making, plus such wonderful curiosities as peacock-feather fabric.

NEARBY

PALAZZO RICHARD-GINORI   ㉓
Via Rondinelli, 17r • Tel: 055 210041

Palazzo Ginori is one of the rare places in the city that commemorates Carlo Lorenzini, better known as Carlo Collodi. The history of the Lorenzini family was linked with that of the Ginori, founders of a porcelain factory now renowned worldwide. Carlo's mother worked as a maid for the Ginori and his father was their cook; his brother then worked as an administrator in the porcelain factory which the Ginori had founded in 1735 (the business was renamed Richard-Ginori after having been bought out by the Richard Company in 1896). Today, the palazzo houses a magnificent exhibition room complete with exposed vaulting, faience-framed leaded windows and rich furnishings. Here, in a building that has a charming little courtyard, you can see an exhibition of Richard-Ginori porcelain as well as ceramics and porcelain from other major manufacturers. There are also some works of art. A plaque on the façade records that Collodi frequently stayed in the palazzo, even as an adult. In fact he was the guest of his brother, and it was within these walls that he wrote a large part of *Pinocchio*, while still pursing his interests in Freemasonry and esoteric symbolism (see following double page).

PINOCCHIO: THE FIRST MASONIC PUPPET

Though not officially recognised, Carlo Collodi's membership in the Freemasons is widely believed to be confirmed by a range of evidence: he started a satirical newspaper entitled *Il Lampione* (The Lamp Post) in 1848, with the express aim of "illuminating all those held in thrall by the shadows"; his participation in the campaigns of Giuseppe Garibaldi, a famous *carbonaro* advocating liberal ideas and undoubtedly a Mason; his close relationship with Mazzini, who was a well-known Mason and of whom Collodi declared himself to be a "passionate disciple". Furthermore, the guiding principles of the Freemasons – *Liberty*, *Equality* and *Fraternity* – are embodied in *The Adventures of Pinocchio*: Liberty, because Pinocchio is a free being, who loves liberty; Equality, because Pinocchio's sole aspiration is to be equal to everyone else, accepting that all are born equal to each other; Fraternity, because this is the feeling that seems to motivate the characters at various points in the story. *Pinocchio* was also immortalised in a film by the American Walt Disney, himself a high-ranking Mason, and embodies the three founding principles of universal freemasonry: freedom of thought and will; psychological and social equality; fraternity between individuals, who can thus achieve universal understanding. More than a simple children's story, *Pinocchio* is an initiatory tale, as is Goethe's *Faust* and Mozart's *The Magic Flute*. It can be read at various levels as a Masonic parable, with the multiple meanings reflecting themes and formulas associated with the stages of initiation. Indeed, it is due to these veiled allusions to an initiatory path that Pinocchio owes its extraordinary success (its sales in twentieth-century Italy were second only to those of *La divina commedia*), for the various stages in the plot offer subliminal echoes of cognitive archetypes. A formidable didactic instrument, *Pinocchio* takes its place alongside the official educational literature of its day. A moral tale deeply imbued with the message of political emancipation, it is one of Tuscan culture's greatest contributions to Freemasonry. Pinocchio is subject to a long course of development. Initially nothing more than a "rough" piece of wood (just like the "rough" stone that all the uninitiated have to cut and shape), he must become "polished" (a term which in the Masonic vocabulary means "enlightened"]. The very name of Pinocchio derives from *pinolo*, the Italian word for "pine nut", thus there is a connection with pine trees, traditionally associated with Christmas – and Christmas itself is a symbol of the spiritual rebirth that the neophyte will experience when he receives the light of initiation.

Furthermore, it is no coincidence that the central character of the tale, Geppetto, is a carpenter, as was Joseph, the father who raised Jesus Christ. As a carpenter, Geppetto is also a demiurge ("creator", "artisan") in the Platonic and Gnostic sense of the term. A little later in the tale, the Blue Fairy descends from heaven to teach Pinocchio free will, and when he asks if he has finally become a real boy she significantly answers: "No, Pinocchio. The vow of your father Geppetto will not fully come true until you deserve it. Set yourself to the test, with courage, sincerity and passion, and one day you will become a real little boy." This is precisely what is said during Masonic initiation, with regard to apprenticeship and the bearing of responsibility. The voice of the Cricket is definitely that of conscience, urging the puppet to go "to school" – another Masonic symbol for conscience and awareness. The initiation of Pinocchio also comprises a series of trials that involve all four elements: air (the presence of numerous birds in the story, and the puppet's flight on the wings of a dove); earth (the coins buried in the ditch); fire (which burns his feet) and water (with various episodes, right up to the final chapter, involving swimming and drowning). Pinocchio is also prey to "sleep", another Masonic metaphor for the non-activity of the uninitiated; and it is precisely when he is asleep that the Blue Fairy gives him a kiss (a kiss also being part of the Masonic rite of the Templars). When hanged, Pinocchio dies, but he is resuscitated through a purge/purification – that is, by elevating himself to a higher level of initiation. Among the other references to Freemasonry there is the island of industrious bees, which recalls Hiram's Temple of Solomon, with its four hundred pomegranates. That is also the exact number of the small bread buns which the Blue Fairy prepares together with cups of coffee and milk (the colour contrast of black and white is another feature of the Temple and a symbol of the contrast between good and evil). The Cat, the Fox and the Firefly all embody the temptations of an easy and profane life, with limping and lameness being other allusions to Masonic symbols. The puppeteer Stromboli and the Land of Toys again represent the vanities of this world, and Pinocchio's transformation into a donkey reveals he has fallen to the level of beasts. To save himself, he must return to the path of enlightenment. The puppet must find his father/demiurge, but he can only do so after passing through a biblical trial: being swallowed by a whale like Jonah, the central figure in a myth that is fundamental in all the great monotheistic religions and all schools of esotericism. Being reunited with Geppetto, who bears him on his shoulders as he swims through the primary element of water, Pinocchio finally becomes a "real little boy", one of the truly "enlightened".

FACE ON SANTA MARIA MAGGIORE CHURCH ㉔

Church of Santa Maria Maggiore
Via de' Cerretani

> *A priest's petrified head?*

I t's still there, looking out of a window that is not a window, watching who knows what from the upper side wall of Santa Maria Maggiore church in Via de' Cerretani. It isn't trying to hide, yet to see this stone head you have to look upwards. Depicting a woman, it was undoubtedly carved around 1327, the year when the astrologist Francesco Stabili – better known as Cecco D'Ascoli – was condemned to be burned at the stake. Just before the execution, a priest claimed to know the details of the pact the astrologist was said to have made with the devil. Satan, according to the cleric, had assured Francesco that he would escape all danger if he took a sip of water. "Above all, don't give him anything to drink," he urged, thus imposing a further torture on the wretched man condemned to die in the flames.

In response, Stabili is said to have told the priest: "And you … you'll never move your head from there!" Immediately the cleric's head turned to stone, becoming set within the wall where you can still see it.

Inevitably, this image of a head perched so high up on the walls of a church has over the centuries generated the most unlikely urban legends. One tells of a market gardener who brought into town a bell she could use to warn all those who didn't live within the city that the gates were about to close. Another version says that the bell was rung so that the gates could be re-opened for those who were late. Whatever the truth, the Florentines are said to have commemorated this donor by having her face carved on the church wall.

Another story goes that this is the head of a woman who turned to stone when cursed by the condemned man she was mocking as he was being led to his execution.

You can make up any story you wish, with this face ultimately proving only one thing: the stones of Florence are so soulful that legends are bound to arise around them.

WHERE LEONARDO DA VINCI'S *MONA LISA* WAS HIDDEN AND THEN RECOVERED

It is no accident that the hotel at No. 2 Via Panzani is called "La Gioconda", because it was here – under the bed in Room 20 – that police discovered Leonardo's famous *Mona Lisa*, which had been stolen from the Louvre by an Italian nationalist who wanted the world's most famous painting to be returned to his fatherland (on payment to himself, that is). Once recovered, the painting was returned to the French State, which is undoubtedly the rightful owner of the work – not something that can necessarily be said of the pieces appropriated during the Napoleonic campaigns. The only trace of the painting in Florence is the name of this hotel, previously the Hotel Tripoli.

"POSTERS" AT PALAZZO VIVIANI

Via Sant'Antonio, 11

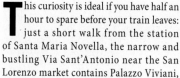

Baroque dazibaos in honour of Galileo

This curiosity is ideal if you have half an hour to spare before your train leaves: just a short walk from the station of Santa Maria Novella, the narrow and bustling Via Sant'Antonio near the San Lorenzo market contains Palazzo Viviani, which is known as *Palazzo dei Cartelloni* because of its rather strange façade. Viviani was a famous seventeenth-century mathematician and he had the front of the building covered with three inscribed "posters" (*cartelloni*): one to either side and a smaller one in the middle. The Latin texts are by Viviani himself and describe and celebrate the astronomical discoveries and inventions of Galileo: the telescope, the "Medici planets" (actually moons of Jupiter), Sun spots, the resistance of solids, projectile trajectory, a proposed solution to the problem of calculating longitude at sea. These are all depicted in the bas-reliefs that surmount the main doorway, together with a bust of the great astronomer by the sculptor Giovan Battista Foggini.

But Viviani did not use the *cartelloni* simply to praise Galileo's scientific achievements; he was also concerned to stress his faith and moral probity. Hence, these inscriptions have something of the air of a political manifesto. Having died while still suspected of heresy, Galileo had not even had the right to a proper funerary monument, and two centuries later he was still susceptible to contemptuous attacks by the Church.

Another curiosity is that this palazzo seems to have been built on the site of the home of the Del Giocondo family, who commissioned Leonardo da Vinci's *Mona Lisa*, also known as *La Gioconda* after the sitter's family name.

NEARBY

HOUSE OF SCALES

Via Nazionale, 160r • Tel: 055 496305

Although the shop window is not particularly inviting, the *Casa della Bilancia* (House of Scales) is undoubtedly unique. It only stocks scales and meat slicers, providing a full range of customer services: sales, technical advice, spare parts, maintenance, repairs and restoration of old machines. The shop has changed little since it first opened in 1870 and it is still run by the same family, with five generations extending between the founder, Cornelio Carretti, and the present owner, Vittorio Carretti.

CEILING OF THE OLD SACRISTY

Church of San Lorenzo
Piazza San Lorenzo
• Tel: 055 214042 (Opera Medicea Laurenziana)
• Open Monday—Friday from 10am to 5pm
• Admission €2.50; free for children under 6 years
• Accessible to those of restricted mobility

> **Painted stars immortalising a specific date**

The star-studded fresco on the cupola of the old sacristy at San Lorenzo captures the appearance of the night sky on a specific date. Exactly the same arrangement of heavenly bodies is to be seen within the cupola of the Pazzi Chapel in Santa Croce church (see p. 213), which is all the more extraordinary as the works were commissioned for two different places by two different families (the Medici and the Pazzi respectively). The relation between these two night skies long remained a mystery, but recent restoration work and detailed study of the position of the planets and stars, of the ecliptic and its angle, have made it possible to identify the specific night depicted. The gilding and rich turquoise colour of this fine nocturnal view celebrate 4 July 1442, the day of the arrival in Florence of René of Anjou, the man who – it was hoped – would lead a new crusade against the Infidel. Among his various titles (King of Sicily, King of Hungary, Duke of Bar, King of Anjou and Lorraine, Count of Guise and so on), René – who was the son of the Queen of Spain and brother-in-law to the King of France – possessed a title that was even richer in evocative power: King of Jerusalem. Furthermore, in 1442, René was 33 years old, the same age as Christ when he died on the Cross. However, the hoped-for crusade was not all a question of religion: the Holy Land at the time attracted the interest of various great Florentine families, who were bankers to the papacy, Guelf in allegiance (like René himself) and well-versed in overseas trade. This "fixed" night sky was not created solely with a celebratory function but was also rich in hermetic significance (see following double page). In effect, it was intended to draw on the celestial energy of Jerusalem and "crystallise" it within the vault of the sacristy. The maintenance of this energy would thus support Florence's claim to the heritage of ancient Jerusalem and at the same time justify its temporal ambitions. The fresco has been attributed to Giuliano d'Arrigo – known as *Il Pesello* – who was famous for his paintings of animals. However, such a prodigious scheme also required the services of a highly skilled astronomer: Paolo dal Pozzo Toscanelli (1397–1482), who was an eminent Florentine scientist as well as being "astrologist" to Cosimo de' Medici and a friend of Filippo Brunelleschi (architect of both cupolas). These relations between scientists and artists give an insight into the fervent religious life of 15th-century Florence, and partly explain the interest of these two astronomical frescoes. They are not just expressions of artistic skill but an assertion of the divinatory role of astronomy: the stars indicate "the way", while the architectural form – in particular, the curved vault of a cupola – is seen as creating a chamber of meditation that can enclose the cosmic forces capable of exerting an influence on earthly events.

HERMETISM AND THE TOMB OF LORENZO DE MEDICI

Medici Chapel
Church of San Lorenzo

A hidden message

In the Medici Chapel within the Church of San Lorenzo stands the monumental tomb of Lorenzo de Medici, Duke of Urbino (1492-1519). Few of those who visit it realise that this is the burial place of the grandson of the greatest patron of occult learning in Renaissance Florence, Lorenzo il Magnifico. Nor is it widely known that there is concealed significance to the artwork of the tomb itself, designed by Michelangelo. The artist began work in 1519, dedicating himself to the task right up to his departure for Rome in 1534, before the completion of the initial project. During his younger years, Michelangelo is known to have studied alchemy and alchemical symbolism figures in the tombs, with the male and female statues – of *Dawn* and *Dusk* or *Day* and *Night* – embodying the beginning and end of the hermetist *Magnum opus*, the return to a primordial androgynous state, a perfect synthesis of man and woman.

Interestingly, the three figures on the tomb – Lorenzo himself and the figure of the Man and Woman – form a perfect triangle and thus express the perfection of the Body Present (Lorenzo), the Absent Soul (Dusk) and the Free Spirit (Dawn). One thus has the two universal periods of activity and repose which underlie all life, regulating the cycles of existence – that which the Hindus refer to as *manvantara* (action) and *pralaya* (inertia) and which are here represented by Day and Night.

In the traditional symbolism of Day as derived from Jewish thought, Creation lasted six days, whilst the seventh day symbolises eternal life. In the second *Book of Esdras*, also known as the *Ascension of Isaiah*, the soul is freed from the body and undertakes a journey that corresponds to the six days of the Creation of the World and the seventh day that corresponds to God's day of rest. Thus, the soul must pass through seven heavens. Each day, it experiences the creation of Self through the different creations of God, so Day symbolises a "stage in the ascension of the spirit".

Another rabbinical exegesis of *Genesis* sees the seventh day not as that of the Lord's Rest after his work of Creation – God cannot be tired – but rather as an instant when God deliberately ceased to intervene in the world, an instant when he surrendered command of and responsibility for the Universe to Man, so that humankind could make itself worthy to one day receive the Creator, who would come to live together with his Creation. Thus, the seventh day symbolises a time of action, of a Humanity left to its own devices; it is the time of responsibility and culture, seen in opposition to Nature, which was created in six days and then handed over to mankind for them to develop their own activity. It is also seen in opposition to the eighth day, which will be the day of Renovation, when Creator and Created will be reunited in a Universe of perfect harmony.

The traditional symbolism of Night sees it as a period of gestation, of the development of the potential which will then emerge into day as a manifestation of life. To enter night is to return to the phase of the indeterminate, the indefinite – to pre-existence. Like all symbols, there is a dual aspect to night: that of a period of shadows and darkness, within which ferments all future life, and that of the period of preparation for the day, when the light of life will break forth.

In mystical theology, night also symbolises the disappearance of all distinct knowledge, of that which can be analysed and expressed; it is a time when the senses are denied access to the physical bases for knowledge. In other words, as a time of obscurity, or subjectivity, night is a time for the purification of the spirit, with its emptiness and deprivation corresponding to the purification and revitalisation of the memory. The aridness and dryness are themselves a reference to the purification of desires and affections based upon the senses – and even of the highest aspirations; sleep purifies all of these and brings with it renewed vigour.

Night is the time when things cannot be seen; Day is when they are made manifest. Above them, the genius of the spirit (embodied in Lorenzo de Medici) meditates the secret thoughts of the elevated soul.

MONUMENT TO ANNA DE' MEDICI

Via del Canto de' Nelli

> *Last descendant of the Medici family*

Behind the basilica of San Lorenzo is a monument that is rather different to all the others and yet still passes almost unnoticed. The regal and confident woman seated here in an almost flirtatious pose is however commemorated every 18 February (the anniversary of her death in 1743) by a procession that ends at this monument. Thus the city pays its respects to Anna Maria Luisa de' Medici (also known as Ludovica), princess, Elector Palatine and the last descendant of the Medici family, whose death marked the end of that prestigious dynasty. As can be seen from the letters in which Anna Maria berated her uncle Francesco Maria, cardinal and governor of Siena, for his dissolute lifestyle, this was a woman with a mind of her own, well capable of playing the role she had to adopt as the centuries-old history of the Medici came to an end. She herself had no children, left infertile by the syphilis caught from her husband, Johannes Karl Wilhelm, Elector Palatine. And she was no more successful in providing an heir for the dynasty when she arranged the marriage of her younger brother, Giovanni Gastone, the last grand duke: he quickly got rid of his wife to give free rein to his homosexuality. As there was to be no next generation of Medici, Anna Maria resigned herself to complying with the decision of the European powers of the day that her possessions should pass to the Habsburg-Lorraine

family. However, in doing so she imposed a condition that revealed her foresight: known as the "Family Pact", this forbade anyone to "remove from the capital of the State collections, paintings, statues, libraries, jewelleries and other precious objects", thus guaranteeing that these treasures would continue to adorn the Grand Duchy of Tuscany to the benefit of its inhabitants and the wonder of visitors.

And what an act of foresight it was! For the artistic heritage of the Grand Duchy would be the main resource of Tuscany and the city of Florence for centuries to come. Thus the honour that the city pays to Anna de' Medici each year is well deserved. What is rather less deserved is the rather casual siting of her monument.

INSCRIPTION TO GIOVANNI DELLE BANDE NERE

Piazza San Lorenzo

30

> *Pedestal that had to wait for its monument*

On the pedestal of the monument to Giovanni delle Bande Nere, around which tourists and market-traders swarm like so many bees, a side inscription that can be translated by: "A part of this monument, which Cosimo I had erected in honour of the memory of his father, Giovanni delle Bande Nere, stood here long neglected, so that the people named it the San Lorenzo Podium, until it was restored in 1850 and the statue of the great *condottiere* placed here, thus completing the fine work sculpted by Bandinelli."

The statue of this *condottiere* – here depicted seated rather than in a warlike posture because originally intended for the Negroni Chapel in the church of San Lorenzo – was to have been sited at Palazzo Vecchio, at the behest of Cosimo I. However, the pedestal was considered too massive for

that prestigious space so it was relegated to Piazza San Lorenzo – but without its statue.

It was not until 1850 – almost three centuries after its completion – that the statue was finally placed on the pedestal originally intended for it, which in the meantime the Florentines had nicknamed "the San Lorenzo podium" and used as a water trough for their horses.

Even today, Giovanni delle Bande Nere still struggles to be noticed amidst the numerous market stalls that crowd the space around him.

CANTO ALLE MACINE PLAQUE

Via Guelfa, at the corner of Via de' Ginori

> ## *Old traces of River Mugnone in the city centre*

The plaque here identifies this street corner as *CANTO ALLE MACINE*. In fact, an old water mill (*macine*) used to stand at the corner (*canto*) of these two roads. Nowadays there is no trace of the mill or of the water course – the Mugnone – that powered it. This tributary of the Arno used to run through the centre of the city along a course from Piazza della Libertà along Via de' Ginori to Via San Gallo. This would explain why the location of Calandrino's house in Boccaccio's *Decameron* (Day VIII, 3, 50) is given as just by the *Canto alle Macine*; it is here that this character returns from Porta San Gallo, convinced that he has found a stone that makes him invisible. But in Via San Gallo it is the Mugnone that has ended up invisible, having been rerouted each time Florence's city walls were expanded. At the time of the fourth ring of walls dating from 1078 – those which Dante describes as "the ancient ramparts" – the Mugnone flowed through Piazza San Marco then on to Via Cerretani, Via Rondinelli (its sharp angle favoured the drainage of the waters which here formed a marsh, recorded in the name of the present-day Via Panzani [*pantano* = marsh]), then along the route of Via Tornabuoni into the Arno. In 1175 the water course was rerouted towards Via San Gallo – hence the *Canto alle Macine* – from where it flowed towards Via de' Fossi (the name refers to the moats – *fossi* – of the former ramparts) and entered the Arno at a spot between Ponte alla Carraia and the church of Ognissanti. The course of the river was altered again in 1283 and in 1333, to follow the route of the present-day Viale Spartaco Lavagnini and Viale Strozzi; you can still see, spanning a dry river bed, the bridge of the old Porta Faenza city gateway, which was incorporated within the Fortezza da Basso in the sixteenth century. Nowadays, the course of the Mugnone lies even further west, along the route of Viale Milton and Viale Redi, emptying into the Arno near Ponte all'Indiano.

NEARBY

FARMACIA FRANCHI

Via dei Ginori, 65r • Tel: 055 210565

The gilded inscription on the pharmacy's inner door reads: *ANTICA FARMACIA AL CANTO ALLE MACINE FONDATA NELL'ANNO 1427*. And this venerable age is reflected in the interior, with double-door cabinets in unpainted wood extending round most of the walls and a large wooden counter richly adorned with pilasters. Was this the pharmacy used by the grandchildren of Calandrino, who in Boccaccio's *Decameron* lived not far from here, near the *Canto alle Macine* ?

SALETTA GONNELLI

Libreria Antiquaria Gonnelli
Via Ricasoli, 6
• Tel: 055 216835

First opened in 1875 and now exclusively dealing in rare books, Gonnelli's has always been more than an antique shop. Beyond the rooms of the bookshop itself – a temple to antique books – there

*Bibliophiles'
paradise*

is a real gem that is largely unknown to the non-bibliophile: the Saletta Gonnelli. Beneath elegant Renaissance vaults above simple columns, this small exhibition space is set back from the windows that give onto Via Ricasoli and is used solely for exhibitions of books, period prints and sometimes even paintings. It was thanks to this space that the bookshop, over time, became a key point of reference for the *Macchiaioli* group of Florentine and Neopolitan painters (*macchia* = patches – of colour). As well as exhibitions of work by such artists as Giovanni Fattori, Tito Conti and Giorgio de Chirico, the place also saw the launch of Futurist literary reviews and attracted such intellectuals as Benedetto Croce, Giuseppe Papini and Gabriele D'Annunzio, with publishing activities ranging over a variety of journals and scholarly works. Nowadays, the Saletta Gonnelli, within the shadow of the Duomo, remains dedicated to the enjoyment of books with its unique volumes of writing, pictorial and graphic arts. All in all, a museum for bibliophiles.

A BOMB AS A CREST

Teatro Niccolini
Via Ricasoli, 5 (theatre closed at present)

> **Symbol of the famous Accademia degli Infuocati**

A short distance from Piazza del Duomo, a small grille on the right-hand side of Via Ricasoli covers a doorway surmounted by two lanterns. This is the elegant entrance to a theatre that has been closed for some years now: Teatro Niccolini, which used to be called Teatro del Cocomero after the street (itself subsequently renamed Via Ricasoli). It was this earlier name that French writer Stendhal uses when discussing the theatre in his travel book *Rome, Naples et Florence en 1817*, mentioning in passing the peculiarity of Florentine pronunciation that turns "*cocomero*" into "*hohomero*".

At the centre of the façade, the entrance to the theatre is also marked by a decidedly unusual crest carved over the cornice. When you look closely, you see that this is not a watermelon as many Florentines claim – misled by the fact that *cocomero* in Italian means "watermelon" – but a sort of incendiary bomb, shown in the act of exploding. A rather incongruous presence in an age increasingly obsessed by the security of public places, this was the symbol of the famous Accademia degli Infuocati (Academy of the Enflamed) which was founded in 1652 after a split within the Accademia degli Immobili (Academy of the Immovables); after first being installed at the Teatro Cocomero, *Gli Infuocati* would transfer to the Teatro alla Pergola.

Unfortunately, the entrance and this bomb are all you can see of the theatre at present, financial difficulties having forced Teatro Niccolini, which in the 1980s was home to Carlo Cecchi's *Granteatro*, to close its doors. The building, which is privately owned, has occasionally been used for such special events as receptions or fashion shows, but it seems that the dilapidated state in which it now finds itself can only get worse. If you ever get the chance, don't hesitate to visit the interior, where a majestic staircase dominated by a huge mirror leads to a vast white auditorium adorned with stucco-work; there, the gently sloping stalls are surrounded by three ranks of boxes under a ceiling with a magnificent chandelier. The whole thing is now bathed in silence, the aftermath of a different sort of "bomb" to that depicted on the façade: the devastating effects of property speculation and inadequate funding for the arts.

WALLED-UP WINDOW IN PALAZZO PUCCI ㉟
Via dei Pucci, at the corner of Via dei Servi

> *Reminder*
> *of a failed*
> *assassination*
> *attempt against*
> *Cosimo I de' Medici*

In Florence as elsewhere there are numerous reasons for walling up a window. But that at the corner of Via dei Pucci and Via dei Servi was bricked up for a very special reason: to ward off evil and set an example.

The window is on the ground floor of the *palazzo* of the Pucci family, traditional allies of the Medici. This connection had brought the Pucci various important public offices in Florence, but then, in 1560, Pandolfo de' Pucci was banished from the court of Cosimo I for immoral behaviour.

He took the punishment so badly that he was soon planning an attempt on Grand Duke Cosimo's life, hiring two assassins to do the job. These murderers were expected to keep watch for the grand duke from this window in Palazzo Pucci, because Cosimo regularly passed by when going from his own palace to attend Mass in the basilica of the Santissima Annunziata.

However, as at the time of the Pazzi conspiracy, the gods smiled on the Medici, with the plot being discovered even before the conspirators could carry it out.

Both the assassins, Pandolfo himself and various members of other noble Florentine families (including some of the Ridolfi) who had joined the plot were all hanged from a window in Bargello prison. However, retaliation did not stop there: Cosimo, who it seems never entirely got over the conspiracy, ordered that Palazzo Pucci itself should be punished, by walling up the

window from which the two killers were to have fired on him.

The grand duke thus achieved various goals. First, he did not have to change his route to the basilica of the Santissima Annunziata; every time he passed by here, he was reassured by the fact that the window was no longer a source of possible danger. Secondly, that condemned window stood as a manifest sign of his power and vengeance. Indeed, the humiliation inflicted on the very fabric of the Palazzo Pucci would outlive the Medici dynasty itself, for no one has ever dared to reopen the window.

FLORENCE'S FINESTRELLE

Via del Corno, 3 - Borgo Santa Croce, 8 - Borgo San Frediano, 7r

Although easy to overlook, certain Florentine palaces have special little windows. These *finestrelle* ("little windows") were not intended just to allow light and air to enter corridors or storerooms but had a much more specific function: they were specially installed so that the children of the house could watch what was happening in the street without having to heave themselves up to a window-ledge from which they might fall. Set beneath the windows "for adults", these *finestrelle* were deliberately small and protected by a narrow mesh grille. You can see more than one example strolling around the streets of the old city centre, but if you want to be sure of finding one go to the back of Palazzo Vecchio, in Via del Corno; alongside Santa Croce, in Borgo Santa Croce (which is actually the building where Vasari had his studio); to the Borgo San Frediano in the Oltrarno district. By definition, these are mere details of Florentine architecture, but they reveal the care taken by architects and their clients when thinking about the needs of those who were going to live in the buildings.

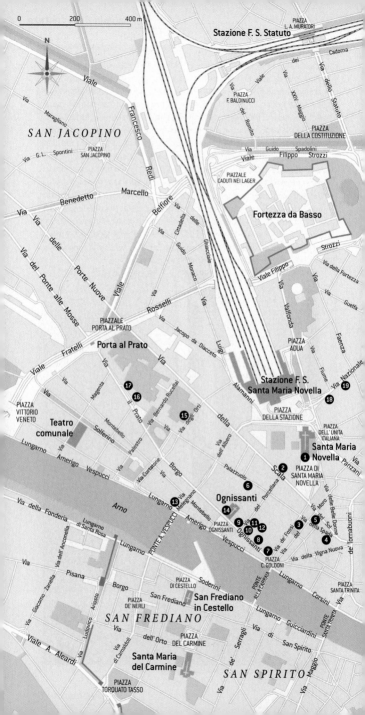

SANTA MARIA NOVELLA

ARMILLARY SPHERE IN THE CHURCH OF SANTA MARIA NOVELLA

①

Church of Santa Maria Novella
Piazza di Santa Maria Novella

> **The sphere at the origin of the Gregorian calendar**

Ignazio Danti, a Dominican monk who was also an astronomer and cartographer, included two astronomical instruments in the façade of the church of Santa Maria Novella. To the right of the entrance is a marble gnomon*, to the left a bronze armillary sphere (see below). It was with these instruments that Friar Danti calculated the discrepancy between the solar year and the Julian calendar, which had been devised by Julius Caesar in 46 BC, promulgated by law the following year and had remained in force ever since.

Having persuaded Pope Gregory XIII to recognise the importance of his calculations, the Dominican scholar then formed part of a committee of scientists (headed by Christophorus Calvius) which would successfully argue for the introduction of the new, "Gregorian", calendar. As already mentioned, the realignment involved skipping ahead ten days, so that one passed directly from 4 October 1582 to 15 October 1582.

THE JULIAN CALENDAR

The Julian calendar, developed during the reign of Julius Caesar (hence the name), remained in force until the reform introduced by Pope Gregory XIII in 1582. The Gregorian calendar which takes its name from that pope introduced a reform in the counting of leap years, which had previously meant that the date indicated by the calendar fell further and further behind the solar date. The most spectacular effect of the introduction of the new calendar was, in fact, the suppression of ten days. And this is why St. Theresa of Avila died on the night between 4 October and 15 October 1582...

ARMILLARY SPHERE

An armillary sphere or spherical astrolabe is a representation of the sphere of the heavens showing the movement of the stars around the Earth or sun. The name comes from the Latin for 'bracelet', given that such a sphere is made up of concentric calibrated circles which show the revolutions of celestial objects. Armillary spheres were developed by the Greeks and were already being used in the 2nd century BC, most notably by Ptolemy.

---

* A gnomon is the upright on a sundial whose shadow is cast onto a flat surface.

MUSEUM OF THE OFFICINA PROFUMO-FARMACEUTICA OF SANTA MARIA NOVELLA

❷

Via della Scala, 16
• Tel: 055 216276
• Pharmacy open all year round (except Christmas and two weeks in mid-August) from 9.30am to 7.30pm
• Visits, on request, to the pharmacy museum Monday–Friday between 10.30am and 5.30pm
• For guided tours, book at visteofficina@smnovella.com
• Admission free

> **Museum
> of a temple
> to body care**

The famous old pharmacy of Santa Maria Novella has a small and little-known museum that you can visit on request – an opportunity to see the sacristy frescoes by Mariotto di Nardo.

The museum has a library of specialist books: ancient volumes of recipes for the preparation of medicaments, botanical treatises and also richly illustrated volumes that bring home how harmoniously the sciences were once linked with the fine arts.

In the other rooms are collections of mortars, porcelain medicine jars and glass bottles of all sizes in which perfumes were mixed and preserved. There is also a curious collection of the apparatus for processing the herbs used in the preparation of essential oils.

All these articles reflect a period in the history of pharmaceutical sciences; authentic works of art, their splendour is in keeping with this wonderful historic pharmacy, which is one of the oldest in the world and has been in business for centuries.

First established in 1221 by the Dominican monks who had recently arrived in Florence, the pharmacy only began selling to the public in 1612. After a series of trials and tribulations in the nineteenth century – the refurbishment in a neoclassical style of certain rooms (for example, the one used for retail sales) and ultimate confiscation and nationalisation by the state in 1866 – the pharmacy was then sold into private ownership. The Officina has now transferred its production facilities to workshops in Via Reginaldo Giuliani. However, all its products are still made using traditional methods and natural oils, and bear such evocative names as *Alkermès*, *Acqua di Rosa*, *Elisir de Cina* and *Aceto dei Sette Ladri* (Seven Thieves Vinegar) – each of which sounds as if it could furnish the plot for an old and exotic movie.

FRILLI GALLERY

③

Via dei Fossi, 28r
• Tel: 055 210212
• www.frilligallery.com

Temple to the perfect copy

Housed in the six vaulted spaces of what used to be a stable for horse-drawn carriages, the Frilli Gallery provides a remarkable overview of the history of Florentine sculpture. The whole gallery, created with a refined clientele in mind, consists of copies of greater and lesser masterpieces. But these are not mass-produced copies, they are the product of a long tradition of craft skills applied to such fine materials as bronze and marble. The gallery not only works to commission for clients who want to embellish a garden or room with a copy of a famous sculpture, it also keeps a permanent exhibition of a range of famous masterpieces. For example, its workshops have produced perfect copies of the Porta Santa in St Peter's (Rome), the door to Santa Maria Maggiore (Rome) and even the door of the Florence Baptistery. Wandering around these rooms you encounter such works as Botticelli's *Venus* or Benvenuto Cellini's *Perseus*, all crowded together among the statues on display. If you look carefully you'll also see some columns that still bear the mark showing how high the waters of the Arno reached during the flood of November 1966.

REPRODUCTION OF THE HOLY SEPULCHRE ❹
IN JERUSALEM

Cappella Rucellai
Via della Spada
• Open Saturday at 5.30pm; closed July–September

" *Heart*
of Christian
Jerusalem
in Florence

This small chapel alongside the former church of San Pancrazio – which today houses the Museo Marini – contains a little-known reproduction of the Holy Sepulchre in Jerusalem.

The Rucellai family had close links with the Middle East (their family crest was a galleon with billowing sails) and the Holy Land was the source of the plant, subsequently cultivated in the Oricellai Gardens, which was used to obtain violet dye for wool.

These links with the holy places of Christianity were such that it was decided to reproduce within Florence the heart of the most important of all Christian sanctuaries: the Holy Sepulchre. While the atmosphere inside this chapel remains intimate and powerful, little trace of the solemnity within these old walls can be seen on the outside. The small doorway gives onto a narrow pavement in a street that has heavy through traffic, and it is from this inauspicious exterior that you enter a sanctuary of mystical harmony. The particular character of the interior owes a great deal to the architectural harmony of this small rectangular temple, which was completed by Leon Battista Alberti in 1467. The very proportions seem to be inspired by secret designs and an encoded language. The floor is a geometric carpet of marble, while the walls are covered with symbols and figures inspired by a happy blend of Florentine humanism and the art of the Middle East.

The entablature is engraved with a passage from St Mark's Gospel, while the upper part of the structure is enclosed by lily-shaped crenels and, as to be expected, the fifteenth-century ceiling is decorated with frescoes. This place is so small that it seems like a miniature temple fitted within the outer "box" of the chapel. The whole place is imbued with a kind of timeless gravity, and the fact that it is only open a few hours a week adds to the impression of a hidden jewel.

NEARBY

GALLI KNIFE SHOP, Via della Spada, 26r • Tel: 055 282410 ❺

If you have knives or other implements that need sharpening, this historic shop is the place to go. Its counter is lined with whetting wheels of various sizes that are always in use. The Galli knife shop, a father and son business, not only keeps up the vanishing craft of the knife-sharpener – much appreciated by hairdressers, gardeners and specialist craftworkers – it also sells top of the range knives for both professional and household use as well as being the only shop in Italy that still makes the palette knives used in restoring frescoes and paintings.

WINE BARS IN THE STREET

Via delle Belle Donne, 2
Via del Giglio, 2
Borgo Pinti, 27
Via Isola delle Stinche, 7r

> *It was forbidden to serve salted bread with wine to increase the customers' thirst*

Passing from Via Tornabuoni into the eloquently named Via delle Belle Donne (Street of Beautiful Women), you'll see, just above a closed window hatch, a plaque with a string of regulations on the consumption of wine. This hatch is one of the best preserved of Florence's *buche da vino* (literally "wine holes") and is inscribed with the opening hours for each day of the week and each season: during public holidays, the wine counter closed in the early afternoon and not in the evening, as it did on normal days.

If you keep your eyes peeled, you'll notice other such counters in the city centre. One is just a short walk away, in Piazza Strozzi, and another superb example is to be found at No. 2 Via del Giglio; there, the hatch is in the form of the doorway to a palazzo set within a miniature reproduction of the rustication that was so typical of numerous Florentine palaces. To the upper left of the doorway is a marble plaque that gives the wine counter's opening hours. These are slightly longer than those in Via delle Belle Donne, which is logical perhaps, given that the family that owned this palazzo had as its motto PER NON DORMIRE ("So as not to sleep"), which is actually engraved on their palazzo in Piazza Santa Trinità (see p. 43).

The hotel Monna Luisa at No. 27 Borgo Pinto also contains a *buchetta* within the foyer of the building (open to the public). Although the current owners have placed a large plant in front of the hatch, the opening with its two support ledges (for bottles) lets you see how these flourishing businesses actually worked. The *buchetta* in Via Isole delle Stinche, on the other hand, is now associated with ice cream rather than wine: it graces the façade of the famous Vivoli ice-cream shop.

The boom in such wine counters began in the seventeenth century, when Florence's commercial fortunes had gone into decline. Such outlets allowed families who owned vineyards to make extra money by selling their produce directly to the public. The trade was strictly regulated by the authorities – for example, it was forbidden to serve salted bread with the wine to increase a customer's thirst – and the wine was sold in the sort of straw-covered bottles still seen today (the straw protected the bottles when they were brought in by cart from the countryside). These drinks counters (*mescite*) were so popular because you could buy wine directly in the street, without having to pay the mark-up charged in inns and taverns; and, of course, the wine producers themselves benefited because they had another outlet for their produce.

Sometimes people also left a small pot of wine and some crusts of bread on the ledges of these wine hatches, so that the city's paupers could help themselves anonymously.

There are also some *buchetta* outside Florence: in Volterra (No. 6 Via Buonparenti) and at Colle Val d'Elsa (No. 14 Via Campana). See *Secret Tuscany* in this series of guides.

ORATORIO DEI VANCHETONI

6

Via Palazzuolo, 17
• For visits and information, call the Oratorio del Fuligno on 055 210232

> **Magnificent oratory for a paupers' banquet**

Walking down the narrow Via Palazzuolo you can't help but notice the façade of the Oratorio dei Vanchetoni. *Vanchetoni*, meaning "those who walk *cheto*" (Tuscan dialect for "humbly"), was the nickname given to the members of the Congregation of Christian Doctrine founded by Blessed Ippolito Galantini, a silk-weaver by trade. It was in the seventeenth century that he separated this structure from the adjoining complex of San Paolo, which no longer exists but was then famous for offering hospitality to St Francis of Assisi in 1221. The surviving rectangular structure is a fine example of Counter-Reformation taste, with its decorated ceiling and numerous paintings of the lives of saints (including Blessed Ippolito Galantini), as well as the Medici arms and superb marquetry-work cabinets in the sacristy. In this fine setting, the *Vanchetoni* dedicated themselves to various tasks: prayer and the teaching of Christian doctrine; assistance to the poor; and training youngsters in the art of silk-weaving. The most important event in the Congregation's calendar used to be a banquet held on the last Sunday of Carnival. The guests were one hundred people (over fifty years of age) in straitened circumstances, who instead of engaging in the fun and games of Carnival were given a rich meal in exchange for submitting to certain stringent conditions: their hair was cut

and they were required to don the robes of the Congregation, attend Confession and then receive Communion. The food was copious, but it had to be eaten in silence, listening to the reading of Holy Scripture. And all within the rich seventeenth-century decor of this oratory, which may have lost a number of its masterpieces to various different collections but still contains numerous works of art. The last of these paupers' banquets was held in the 1970s. Nowadays the oratory is used for concerts and plays, the traditions linked with the Congregation coming to an end because of a dispute with the City Council and the Regional Government of Tuscany. These two public bodies abolished the Congregation because it had failed to meet its statutory duties, apparently incapable of managing the considerable amount of property it possessed.

FARMACIA MÜSTERMANN

Piazza Goldoni, 2r
• Tel: 055 210660

T he history of Farmacia Müstermann, with its elegant period interior, reflects how the shifting moods of the time can make themselves felt. The pharmacy, founded by a German immigrant in 1897, is

Vicissitudes of a historic pharmacy

to be credited with having been the first to introduce homeopathic products to Florence when they were still little-known in Italy. In 1908 it was renamed Farmacia Anglo-Americana, with the clear intention of attracting custom among the sizeable Anglo-Saxon community in Florence. However, over twenty years later that name had become something of an embarrassment, not to say a real disadvantage, and thus in 1935 the original name of Farmacia Müstermann was restored, being more in keeping with the political alliances of fascism. Fortunately, after the Liberation no-one felt the need to change the shop sign once again, so the name of the original founder remains.

BAPTIST CHURCH

Borgo Ognissanti
• Worship at 10.30am every Sunday

> *Beatification of Stenterello*

Open only once a week, on Sunday morning, the Baptist Church of Borgo Ognissanti, a short walk from Piazza Goldoni, is unusual in being a theatre converted into a place of worship (unlike so many churches and oratories in Florence that have done the opposite and become theatres after deconsecration). Here, the altar has in a way got its own back, the crucifix standing on the spot once occupied by a stage. These secular origins are no secret, and the Florence Baptist Church retains all the characteristics of a theatre interior. However, as a recent plaque records, this wasn't just any old theatre: it was the birthplace of the variety character Stenterello.

At the time the small theatre was known as the Teatro Ognissanti (or Teatro Solleciti), and it was here that Luigi del Buono invented this cunning but ingenuous character, whose trademarks were his lanky form and stockings that didn't match. The theatre itself was founded in 1778 and remained in business until 1887. A few years after its closure it was bought (in 1895) by the Baptist Church, then funded by the sizeable British community in Florence.

A recent plaque commemorates the foundation of the theatre, even if perhaps the most important date associated with it is 16 February 1791, when Italy's first production of *Hamlet* was staged.

As in deconsecrated churches turned into theatres, here the original function of the building is clear, giving this church a rather theatrical air that makes it so much easier to conjure up the atmosphere of the performances at the Teatro Solleciti.

The first feature that immediately strikes you is the row of columns around the perimeter. These columns once supported the boxes and balcony, although now they support a sort of chancel. And if you look carefully at the polygonal apse, you can see how it echoes the form of an apron stage; in fact, the prompt box now leads to the baptismal fonts (in what used to be the actors' dressing rooms). The very place where Stenterello so often put on his costume and make-up is now where people are baptised! It's as if the Word of God had taken over where the tales of his adventures left off.

HOUSE OF GIOVANNI MICHELAZZI

9

Borgo Ognissanti, 26

Art Nouveau in Florence

Art Nouveau – known as *Stile Liberty* in Italian – never enjoyed great success in Florence. Its sinuous, free-flowing forms and plant-motif decorations may have been considered an affront to the linear rigour and elegant sobriety of the traditional Florentine style. However, not far from Florence in Borgo San Lorenzo, the heart of the Mugello, the Chini family founded a dynasty that became famous for its Art Nouveau work. Whereas in numerous other European countries, Art Nouveau resulted in swelling curved balustrades, oval windows and asymmetrical doorways, the Chinis in Florence were rather more restrained, working in a place which would have ridiculed the more extreme trends then in fashion.

Thanks to the architect Giovanni Michelazzi, there are at least some remarkable Art Nouveau buildings in Florence, beginning with No. 26 Borgo Ognissanti. A slim structure with large, very unusual windows flanked by stylised sculptures, this has a small main doorway that marks a felicitous break with traditional architectural canons. The numerous details may at first appear extravagant but they follow the criteria of a new code of aesthetics – and are certainly striking when seen in this street. Still, the Florentine bourgeoisie were clearly not great fans of such innovations, for the only other significant examples of Art Nouveau are outside the city centre: the building of the Galleria Carnielo in Piazza Savonarola and, above all, the Broggi-Carceni and Ravazzini villas at Nos. 99 and 101 Via Scipione Ammirato. Both villas are the work of Giovanni Michelazzi, with Villa Ravazzini decorated with ceramic tiles by Galileo Chini.

NEARBY

PALAZZO BALDOVINETTI: THE UPSIDE-DOWN HOUSE

10

Not far from here – at No. 12 Borgo Ognissanti – stands the curious *casa alla rovescia* (upside-down house). Palazzo Baldovinetti owes its nickname to the rather original architectural design: when you stand on the opposite side of the street and look at its window balustrades, balcony and the large consoles supporting it, you'll see that they're all the wrong way round. By some architectural wizardry, the design overburdens the façade while at the same time making it special. It's said that this "reversal" of the usual order of things was because of the narrowness of the city streets – the construction of houses with balconies was banned (it's true that an old building complete with balcony is rarely seen here). However, Baldovinetti did everything he could to obtain a permit for a balcony, convinced that Borgo Ognissanti was wide enough. In the end (around 1530) Alessandro de' Medici gave in to yet another application, but with the words: "Go on, you can build your blasted balcony! But upside down!" – never imagining that the architect would be able to meet that challenge to the letter.

MUSEUM OF SAN GIOVANNI DI DIO HEALTH CENTRE

Borgo Ognissanti, 20
• Open Monday–Friday from 8.30am to 1pm

> **Long history of a Florentine hospital**

A hospital is always at the very heart of a community, so it is generally a place of inexhaustible historical interest – especially if it has been in existence for six centuries. The hospital in Borgo Ognissanti, behind a rich façade that achieves a fine balance between monumental mass and elegant elevation, was for a long time the oldest in the city. Although the emergency rooms are closed and the place no longer takes patients, it is still a health centre – for the moment (it has been announced that even this last service is to be scrapped).

Dedicated to Santa Maria dell'Umiltà, this *spedale* (hospital) was founded by Piero Vespucci in 1382–1388, and on his death bequeathed to the Compagnia du Bigallo. The establishment took the name of San Giovanni di Dio in 1588, when its administration passed into the hands of the Augustinian congregation of Fatebenefratelli (Hospital Order of St John of God). In 1702 a church was added to the hospital, its façade – in a new style of Baroque – designed by Carlo Andrea Martellini; the vestibule, monumental double staircase and the various sculptures and frescoes date from 1735.

For some years now it has been possible to climb that spectacular double staircase in the main hall and visit a documentation centre covering the past activities of the Hospital of St John of God. Little-known and (despite its originality) not mentioned in any tourist leaflets, this small museum offers a good insight into various aspects of public health care in Florence over the centuries.

The collection includes surgical instruments from the hospital and other objects that bear witness to hospital life – for example, numerous scientific tomes – as well as material relating to the adjacent church. All in all, this is one of various institutions dedicated to the preservation of material reflecting aspects of everyday life in the city – in this case, health care, which was already one of the boasts of Florentine civic life by the end of the fourteenth century.

SAN GIOVANNI DI DIO CLOISTER

Borgo Ognissanti, 20
• Open Monday–Friday from 8.30am to 12.30pm

*Traces
of Amerigo
Vespucci*

I n 1454 the famous Florentine navigator Amerigo Vespucci was born a few steps from the Arno, in Borgo Ognissanti. The family home was just alongside the old hospital of San Giovanni di Dio (St John of God). On entering these premises now, you'll find a large marble plaque in the form of a giant parchment bearing the following inscription (in Latin): "To Amerigo Vespucci, a noble Florentine who, by the discovery of America, made famous his name and that of his fatherland, and extended the frontiers of the Earth. On this house, which formerly belonged to the Vespucci and was home to such an eminent man, the devout Fathers of St John of God placed this stone in 1719." In more recent times, this former hospice has been converted into a health centre. In the cloister is a series of twenty-nine panels in a rather neglected state which recount the whole story of the origins of the great Florentine traveller, his actual or supposed journeys, the links between exploration and trade at the time, and the respective claims of Amerigo Vespucci and Christopher Columbus. Curiously, although this series of panels forms a sort of permanent exhibition dedicated to the Florentine navigator, there is no mention of it either on the outside of the building or in tourist office information.

NEARBY

"AMERICAN PLAQUES" ON PONTE AMERIGO VESPUCCI
Lungarno Amerigo Vespucci and Lungarno Soderini

On the *lungarni* (Arno embankments) at opposite ends of Ponte Amerigo Vespucci are two bronze and concrete plaques with engravings evoking various countries of the American continent. The simple plaques list the names of various countries directly into the concrete, along with a few small drawings of vaguely traditional inspiration and rather original Latin American motifs. Among the countries of the New World listed there are obviously those which Amerigo Vespucci either discovered or visited, such as Brazil and Venezuela (so-named because Vespucci had found "something Venetian" about the houses of the Maracaibo region, which were raised on piles). There are also countries where Vespucci never set foot (for example, Bolivia and Chile). The choice is rather strange, given that the United States – the country which takes its very name from "Amerigo" – is not even included. Another curiosity is a hybrid nation identified as *Domicana*, which seems to conflate the two Caribbean nations of the Dominican Republic and Saint-Domingue (now Haiti).

VESPUCCI FAMILY FRESCO

Ognissanti church
Piazza Ognissanti
• Open for visits from 7.30am to 12 noon and 4pm to 7pm
• Closed Friday morning, and sometimes in the afternoon
• Tel: 055 2398700

An unsolved enigma

To the right as you enter the church of Ognissanti is a fresco by Ghirlandaio with a portrait of Amerigo Vespucci with the rest of the Vespucci family (who commissioned the work) praying at the feet of the Virgin. In this "group photo" the men are shown to the left of the Virgin, the women to the right. Reading from the left, therefore, are: Anastagio, Amerigo's great-grandfather; Stagio, his father; Giorgio Antonio, his uncle; Guido Antonio, another uncle and a monk at the monastery of San Marco; Amerigo the Elder, the explorer's grandfather, shown kneeling and from the back; and Antonio di Stagio, his brother. As for the women, they are, from the right: Caterina, Anastagio's wife; Caterina, Amerigo's sister; Lisabetta, Stagio's wife and mother of the explorer; Verdiana, Stagio's sister and Amerigo's aunt; Manna, seen kneeling and from the back, like her husband, Amerigo the Elder; Agnoletta di Stagio, his older sister. And the great Amerigo Vespucci himself? As he – together with Bernardo – was one of the two youngest members of the family, he is shown not as a worshipper in prayer but as a cherub: he is fluttering about top left, while Bernardo is on the right. However, this fresco is not only a family portrait, it is also a partly unsolved enigma. Note the distinctive way this depiction of the devout family is framed, defined by the Virgin's open arms and her cloak held aloft by the two cherubs. Far from Florence – in Castello di Teglio, in Valtellina – a frame of the same shape and size encloses a fresco on the ceiling of the Salone della Creazione in Palazzo Besta. The relation between the two frescoes is all the more striking because, unusually for an Alpine palazzo, the Teglio image depicts a mappemonde, a symbol of navigators and explorers. The composition of that mappemonde can be seen in relation to that of the posthumous 1570 edition of a geographical map drawn by the German mathematician Caspar Vopel in 1545. After the 1507 map by Martin Waldseemüller, that Vopel map was the most imitated of all the works that celebrated the voyages of Amerigo Vespucci. Furthermore, the Teglio image is a geographical fresco without equal; indeed it was unknown to specialists of ancient cartography until its discovery a few years ago. The relation between Valtellina and Florence has yet to be clarified, as has the relation between Amerigo Vespucci and the cartographer who painted this fresco mappemonde at Palazzo Besta. It is clear, however, that the author of that Teglio work knew the Ghirlandaio fresco in the church of Ognissanti, as he deliberately makes reference to it (and thence to Vespucci) in his own cartographical work.

SAN MARTINO DELLA SCALA CHURCH

Via Orti Oricellai, 18
• Tel: 055 267291
• Ring at the porter's lodge and ask for permission to visit, or book via fax (055 2672723) to the Director of the "Gian Paolo Meucci" Youth Penitentiary, either in the early afternoon of a weekday or on Saturday morning

> ## Church in a prison

San Martino della Scala is perhaps the least-visited church in Florence, but that doesn't mean it is not captivating nor central. The fact is that it is inside a prison for minors (Istituto Penitenziario Minorile), which explains why this is the best-hidden and least-known place of worship in Florence. However, it is open to the public.

This prison, housing around thirty juvenile offenders, has been part of the former premises of the convent of San Martino a Mugnone since 1873. That convent itself replaced the historic Ospedale della Scala (at the corner of the street you can still see traces of the old arcades).

Of the famous "staircase" (*scala*), which gave the hospital its name, there is no longer any trace. However, the cloister and church survive, well separated from the prison facilities themselves (two floors of cells, an auditorium, football pitch, library and a few workshops). To visit them, all you have to do is ring at the porter's lodge and ask for permission, which is usually readily given. From the lodge on the ground floor, you pass through into the elegant and peaceful cloister, a absolute haven of tranquility that is sometimes used as a concert venue. At the far end is a small doorway through one of the side walls of the church. The interior was reworked in the seventeenth century, with ostentatious stucco work by Giovan Martino Portogalli, and has various marble decorations and paintings; however, the Botticelli *Annunciation* which once hung there is now in the Uffizi. One of the rare examples in Florence of fully fledged Baroque art, the church is still in use, with Mass celebrated for the young prisoners. However, the large main door opening onto Via della Scala (No. 79), and thence leading into the city, is of course always kept locked.

"GARAGE" FOR *IL BRINDELLONE*

Quartiere del Prato, alongside No. 48
• The door can always be seen from outside
• Open only once a year, on Easter Sunday
Other, rare, opportunities to visit are the so-called "Open Door" days
organised by the City Council (dates from City Hall information offices)

> *A wooden
> door
> of unusual size*

Strolling through the Prato district, there's nothing of particular note until you reach No. 48. There, the sharp-eyed will spot a huge yet narrow wooden wall that stands as tall as the two buildings either side of it. Closer inspection reveals a double door of quite extraordinary size: in fact, this is the entrance to the space for storing what Florentines affectionately refer to as *Il Brindellone*, the wagon that is used during Easter Sunday celebrations.

Whereas everyone has heard of the *Scoppio del Carro* (Explosion of the Wagon) folk tradition that takes place on that day, most people are unaware of this "garage" – even if they have wondered what happens the rest of the year to this magnificently decorated three-tier wagon.

The famous *scoppio* takes up the tradition of the "holy fire" which in the Middle Ages was lit by rubbing together the fragments from the Holy Sepulchre which Godfrey of Bouillon (a medieval <u>Frankish</u> knight, one of the leaders of the <u>First Crusade</u>) had given to Pazzino de' Pazzi, who had distinguished himself in the assault on the walls of Jerusalem during that Crusade. The tradition survived even the disgrace into which the Pazzi family fell after their unsuccessful plot against Lorenzo de' Medici and his brother Giuliano. Over time, the celebration developed to include the use of this enormous three-tier triumphal wagon, lined with fireworks to be lit by the *columbina* – a rocket in the form of a white dove. The failure of the fireworks to ignite is seen as an omen of bad luck (for example, in 1966 – the year of the disastrous flood – that's what happened). The firework display lasts around twenty minutes in all and symbolises the flames of holy fire spreading around the city.

For the Easter celebration, *Il Brindellone* is drawn to the cathedral by two white cows; but for the rest of the year the enormous wagon is housed here.

The historic procession begins as soon as the wagon leaves its sanctum, whence it is returned after being escorted around the city. Apart from a few exceptional occasions, Easter morning is the only chance to witness the complex operation involved in throwing open these huge doors concealed between the two buildings and wheeling out the triumphal wagon.

GIARDINO CORSINI AL PRATO

Via Il Prato, 58
• Open all year from 8am to 12.30pm and 2.30pm to 6.30pm (in winter, until sunset); closed on Saturday afternoon and Sunday
• Admission: €7; group concessions
• To visit the garden when closed to the public, call 055 218994
• www.artigiantoepalazzo.it

> *One of Italy's finest privately owned gardens*

While the Prato district may have got its name from the term for meadow (*prato*), open expanses of grassland are a rarity here now. Still, the place does contain one of the finest privately owned gardens in Italy, concealed behind the walls of Palazzo Corsini. That garden is home to 130 tortoises, one for each of the lemon trees. And it is within that orchard that an exhibition entitled *Artigianato e Palazzo* (Craftwork and the Palazzo) is held every year in June. Devoted to the finest craftwork produced in Florence, this event offers food and wine tastings as well as practical demonstrations of such "minor arts" as decoration, bookbinding, locksmithery, marquetry, quality leatherwork and all the other trades in which ancient craft traditions are maintained and developed. The event is also one way for this garden and palazzo to keep abreast of the times – even if over the centuries they have already had to adapt to changing circumstances and tastes. When Bernardo Buontalenti designed the building in 1572, he envisaged a garden of geometrical paths outlined by hedges, with the greenery completing his own architectural designs. About 50 years later (in 1624), that geometrical layout was altered by the addition of various Baroque features designed by Gherardo Silvani. One of the special features of this garden is

its central avenue flanked by statues of decreasing size meant to create the illusion that the perspective runs much deeper than it actually does. In the 18th century, when one of the Corsini family became pope (Clement XII), the loggia was adorned with numerous plaques bearing inscriptions in Latin, Greek and even Etruscan. Around 1860, the garden underwent another substantial change, when it was adapted to meet Romantic canons of taste; on that occasion, for example, the old *ragnaie* (nets spread to catch insects) were replaced by two copses of tall trees. Today, with its avenue of Roman statues, Teatro di Verzura (an open-air theatre currently being restored), famous lemon trees and tortoises, this wonderful garden is a secret haven in the heart of the city.

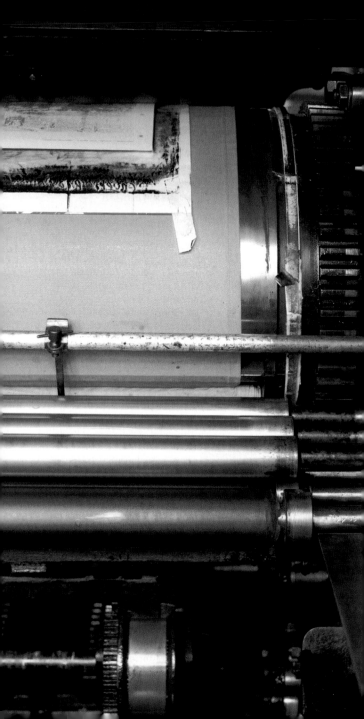

LITTLE-KNOWN TREASURES OF THE FRATELLI ALINARI COMPANY

Fratelli Alinari
Largo Fratelli Alinari, 15
• Tel. 055 23951 • Stamperia d'Arte Alinari: visits on request by writing to negozio@alinari.it • Biblioteca Alinari: visits on request by writing to biblioteca@alinari.it • Archives consultable online at www.alinari.com or via fototeca@alinari.it

> **Art printworks, library and archives ...**

T he location of Fratelli Alinari, not far from the Alinari National Museum of Photography in Piazza Santa Maria Novella, is no coincidence, for these are the historic premises of the Alinari brothers photography workshop, a pioneer of its kind in Europe. Besides the offices and other administrative services, there are art printworks, a library and archives.

The printworks and the library are a continuation of the museum tour. In the former you can discover the wonders of collotype, an early procedure for reproducing photographic images on paper using a glass plate. The Alinari photography works is the only one in the world that still has the equipment – and, above all, the technical expertise – to carry out this work, using collotype to reproduce: photographs and daguerreotypes; images of old or contemporary works of art, pictures of frescoes, paintings, sculpture and buildings; and two-colour drawings – all without the inevitable "hallmarks" of industrially produced images.

The library not only contains thousands of books on photography but also rare complete editions of the magazines that are themselves part of the history of this artistic discipline – for example, *Camera Work*, edited in New York by Alfred Stieglitz from 1903 to 1917, or the *Bollettino della Società Fotografica Italiana*, published in Florence from 1889 to 1912. The archives (which can be consulted online) contain 4 million images: the sum of the Alinari collections and of the collections put together by numerous other art or photographic historians. There are also 45 million photographs from archives in Italy or abroad that are represented (or administered) by the Fratelli Alinari company. Even though they have never left the *largo* (square) at the end of Via Nazionale which now bears their name, the Fratelli Alinari have clearly come some way since they first set up shop.

WHAT IS COLLOTYPE?

This technique consists in coating a glass plate with a special layer of dichromated gelatine and then dried carefully in an oven for a few hours. The negative is then applied to this plate, which is immediately inked by hand and then pressed onto paper using a hand press. The care needed for each phase of this process is so meticulous that a collotype plate produces only a limited number of reproductions – 500 at most; any more and the layer of gelatine is damaged. Each numbered collotype image is thus one of a limited series.

STAVINI, A CONTRACTION OF *STA FRA I VINI*

Stavini - Viale Fratelli Rosselli, 22–26r • Tel: 055 211488

In business since 1940, this motorcycle parts shop in Piazza Ognissanti is special because of the name of the owner: Roberto Stavini, whose own father, Amadeo, was the first and only person in Italy with this surname. A contraction of *sta fra i vini* (he lives among wines), the name was chosen by the Corsini family of San Piero a Sieve for an abandoned child they brought up. The family were in fact dedicated to viticulture and the production of wine, and this foundling became their chauffeur. Perhaps it is this association with motor vehicles that led his own son, Roberto, to open a motorcycle parts shop.

FRESCOES IN GARAGE NAZIONALE

Via Nazionale, 21
• Tel: 055 284041
• Open 6am to midnight Monday–Saturday; from 7am to 1pm and from 3pm to 10pm Sundays and holidays
• Charges vary, according to type of vehicle, from €23 to €33 per day or €3.70 to €5.20 per hour

The car park in Via Nazionale is worth a stop, if only for an hour, partly because it is like no other garage in the city, partly because it is in a street that is always crowded with traffic.

"Automobile" frescoes in an art garage

In 1987 the Garage Nazionale decided to enliven the daily life of the city's motorists by commissioning Carlo Capanni to paint two remarkable frescoes of vintage and modern Italian cars alongside the access ramps.

Along with filling stations decorated with ceramics, this is yet another example of how art can be applied in an everyday context – a modern expression of that great Florentine tradition of beauty "accessible to all".

DESIGNER TO THE PUMPS

Piazza Donatello · Piazza Ferrucci

Nothing could be more anonymous than a filling station. Florence, however, has succeeded in enlivening some of them – even if passing motorists rarely pay attention to the results. No one knows who was the first to suggest decorating them with ceramic tiles. Whoever it was, the idea has borne fruit and motorists can now refresh their aesthetic sense at these three garages:

Agip in Piazza Donatello;

Esso in Piazza Donatello;

Api in Piazza Ferrucci.

In the two Piazza Donatello stations, the walls facing the traffic have been decorated with pictorial ceramics; the tiles in the Agip station are even signed (*B. Lucchesi*). The inspiration for the decoration is the two themes of travel and fuel. You can, for example, see St Christopher (the patron saint of travellers) and an oil well alongside an avenue bordered with trees and various monuments; other features include a petrol lamp and the famous Agip symbol of a six-legged dog spitting fire. A short distance away, the Mobil-Esso station is decorated with a single vast image in ceramic tiles depicting the union of water and sky, complete with fishes and birds, sun and moon. The signature is hieroglyphic, with the date 1954.

In Piazza Ferrucci, the elegant modern filling station in red brick is decorated on various sides with Florentine themes rendered in contemporary ceramics, all signed *Mario Dal Mas Fecit 1961*.

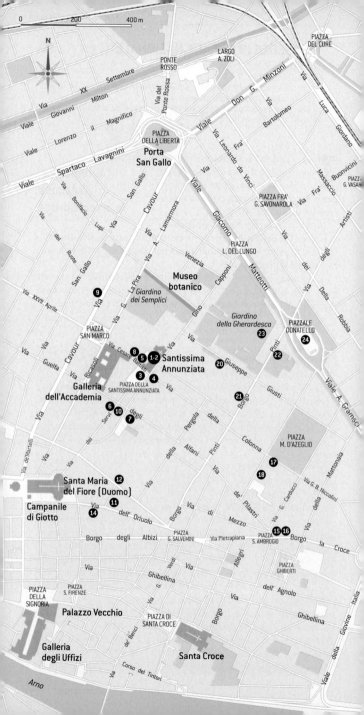

SS ANNUNZIATA

THE CLOISTER OF THE DEAD

Church of La Santisssima Annunziata
Piazza Santissima Annunziata
• Open from 7am to 1pm and 4pm to 7pm
Considering when masses are celebrated, it is better to visit the church
between 4pm and 5pm
• To reach the Cloister of the Dead, go to the far end of the church; the
entrance is on the left behind a red curtain.

> **A secluded cloister in the church of the painters**

One can end one's visit to the architectural complex of La Santissima Annunziata by visiting a little known part of the church: the Cloister of the Dead, which is reached from the side aisle on the left. This secluded part of the monastery not only contains numerous tombstones but also – above the doorway into the church – a magnificent *Madonna del Sacco* by Andrea del Sarto and a cycle of eighteenth-century frescoes depicting various scenes in the history of the Servites (*I Servi di Maria*). From the other side of the cloister one gains access to the Chapel of the Company of Saint Luke, the confraternity of Florentine painters and the precursor of the *Accademia delle Arti e del Disegno* created by Cosimo I. In effect, this – the most important Marian sanctuary in the whole of Florence – would during the course of the sixteenth century be the workplace of such great artists as Andrea del Sarto, Pontormo, Rosso Fiorentino, Luca Giordano, Bronzino, Perugino, Vasari and many others (including artists from Flanders and Germany). Within the Santissima Annunziata, these artists would paint religious scenes or specific episodes of religious life, their activities here being reflected in the legend surrounding the image of the Virgin by Frà Bartolomeo (see double page overleaf). Certain artists – for example, Baccio Bandinelli, the Flemish artist Jan van der Straet and the Frenchman Giambologna – are buried here; Domenico Passignano actually painted his own tomb within the monastery. Amongst the figures which appear in *The Coming of the Magi* in the Ex-Voto Cloister one can recognise a self-portrait of Andrea del Sarto and a portrait of his friend Jacopo Sansovino.

DELIBERATE DAMAGE TO A PAINTING

One part of the painting entitled *The Marriage of the Virgin* is damaged. This mutilation is said to be due to the artist himself, Franciabigio, who was angered by the fact the monks were always looking over his shoulder as he worked.

FRA BARTOLOMEO'S PAINTING OF THE VIRGIN ❷

Church of La Santissima Annunziata
Piazza Santissima Annunziata
• Open from 7am to 1pm and 4pm to 7pm
• Considering when masses are celebrated, it is better to visit the church between 4pm and 5pm

" A rare
acheiropoieton

The church of La Santissima Annunziata (The Blessed Virgin Annunciate) contains a painting that is the object of a famous legend: Fra Bartolomeo's Virgin. During the period of the first religious foundation here, around 1252, this monk (not the famous one of the 16th century) was said to have fallen asleep whilst completing the face of the Virgin in a painting, and when he woke up he found the picture finished; however, the actual painting dates from the fourteenth century and was partially repainted in the fifteenth. Such images are referred to as *acheiropoieta* (see opposite). It is perhaps a unique example of such a religious image in Florence. In this particular case, the *acheiropoieton* could be said to confirm the very special link there has always been between the church of La Santissima Annunziata and the art of painting.

ACHEIROPOIETIC WORKS OF ART

In the Christian tradition, the term *acheiropoieton* refers to works of art "not made by the hand of man". Thus it relates to images created either by transposition from direct contact (as with the Shroud of Turin and the Veil of Veronica) or by divine intervention.

This term was apparently coined by St. Paul himself in a particular context: during a stay at Ephesus, he rose up against pagan idolatry and especially against the numerous many-breasted statues of Artemis, mother of the gods. He declared that the "gods made by the hand of man are not gods". With the use of this term *acheiropoieton* he showed respect for the Judaic prohibition of images, attacked pagan idols by setting the actual body of Christ against them, and limited eventual abuse by also claiming that this body of Christ was exclusively in the form it took after the Transfiguration (see p. 21), in other words after an event that followed the Resurrection.

Besides the celebrated Shroud of Turin and the Veil of Veronica (see Secret Rome in this series of guides), tradition holds that a few other rare *acheiropoietic* images still exist today. One example is to be found at Mount Athos in Greece: this theocratic monarchy, isolated on a peninsula in northeastern Greece since the 11th century and out of bounds to women, children and female animals, is home to two *acheiropoietic* icons. One is in the monastery of the Great Lavra and the other in the monastery of Iviron. In France, there is also an *acheiropoieton* in the church of Notre-Dame-des-Miracles at Saint-Maur near Paris (see our guide *Banlieue de Paris Insolite et Secrète*, not yet available in English).

Similarly, the Holy Visage of Edessa, now in the Bartholomite Church of Genoa, is said to have been painted by Christ himself.

The painting of Christ in the Sancta Santorum of the Lateran in Rome is said to have been drawn by St. Luke and then completed by angels, and the famous sculpture of the Holy Visage in Lucca (Tuscany) is said to have been started by Nicodemus (who, together with Joseph of Arimathea, was present at Christ's crucifixion), but then completed by angels (see our guide *Secret Tuscany*).

In Venice (see our *Secret Venice*), the chapel of Saint Lucy in the church of Santi Geremia e Lucia contains a miraculous sculpture of Christ which was inexplicably "completed" after the death of the Capuchin friar who had begun the work and yet had never been able to model the face to his satisfaction.

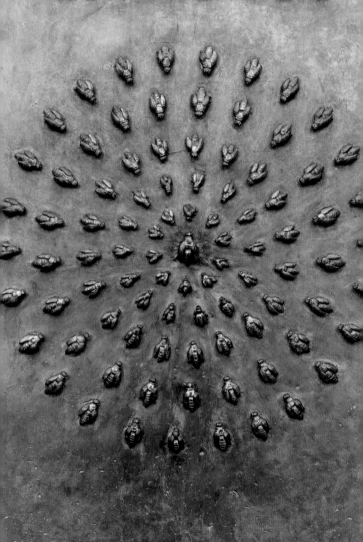

THE BEES ON THE EQUESTRIAN MONUMENT OF FERDINANDO I ❸

Piazza Santissima Annunziata

> *A symbol of power become a game for children*

This must be the most stylised depiction of insects in the whole world. Indeed, at first glance one cannot even identify this motif on the bronze pedestal of the equestrian monument to Ferdinand I de Medici, grand duke of Tuscany from 1587 to 1609.

Designed by the Mannerist sculptor Giambologna but actually cast by his pupil Pietro Tacca (in 1608), the statue was made from the bronze cannons on Turkish ships seized by the Order of the Knights of Santo Stefano.

If one looks closely at the plinth, one sees what at first sight looks like a circle dotted with balls; however, this is not just a circular decorative motif but a swarm of bees, surmounted by the significant inscription *Maiestate Tantum* [meaning that for Ferdinando to govern "his Majesty sufficed"].

These insects are intended as a symbol of power, to be read in various ways. Not only do they refer to the State as a community, as a place of industry and disciplined organisation, but also to the supremacy over the whole of the queen bee (a symbol of the authority of the grand duke).

Such an unusual depiction of a swarm of bees has spawned urban legends. Both children and adults play the game of trying to count all the individual bees. But it is said that, after a certain number, one inevitably loses count because of the irregular concentric arrangement of the swarm. This little

puzzler was perhaps intended, both the grand duke and Tacca wanting to illustrate to the populace that they were incapable of grasping the full sense of supreme power.

It is said that parents nowadays use this swarm to test their children's power of concentration, rewarding them if they manage to count up the exact number of bees. It is also said that if you do count them – without touching or pointing – then you will enjoy good luck.

For those who do not want to take this opportunity to put themselves to the test, the answer is that there are 91 bees. But does that total include the queen bee or not?

THE "FOUNDLING WHEEL"

❹

Ospedale degli Innocenti
Piazza della Santissima Annunziata

From 1445
to 1875

This *Ospedale degli Innocenti* is famous for its museum (which contains various fine works of art), for the fact that it houses the UNICEF Innocenti Research Centre concerned with children's rights, and for one very special historic artefact: its famous "foundling wheel", where families – or single mothers unable to raise their child – abandoned unwanted infants.

This apparatus made it possible to commit this desperate act anonymously without leaving the child to die. It took the form of a sort of "baby hatch", located under the arcades to the left of the hospital entrance. Alongside was a string attached to a bell used attract attention, so that the abandoned infant would not be left out in the open air for too long. The rotating cylinder is no longer extant, but the hatch itself has not changed since 5 February 1445, when it received its first "innocent", a girl who was named Agata after the saint whose feast day was celebrated on that date. The system itself was not abolished until 1875, some time after the unification of Italy and Florence's period as capital of the kingdom. A plaque now commemorates its use.

However, the orphanage of the Innocenti was not always the final destination of these abandoned infants. When they had been gathered

in from the "wheel", they were sent to the Loggia del Bigallo, near the Duomo, where they were put on public display, hoping either that they would be adopted or that their repentant parent(s) would come back and claim them.

What is most striking nowadays is the actual beauty of the foundling wheel, which gives the impression of being a fine example of the applied arts rather than an instrument of social assistance. The Florentines affectionately refer to it as *la mangiatoia* [the manger], a term which conjures up thoughts of Christmas and the nursery. The truth is that the word here designates a mechanism that was far from cosy, yet did mark an advance in levels of social assistance.

THE FOUNDLINGS' WHEEL

It is said that in 787, Dateus, a priest in Milan, began placing a large basket outside his church so that abandoned infants could be left there. More organised initiatives for the reception of abandoned children were begun by the Hospice des Chanoines in Marseilles from 1188 onwards, with Pope Innocent III (1198-1216) later giving the practice the Church's benediction; he had been horrified by the terrible sight of the bodies of abandoned infants floating in the Tiber and was determined to do something to save them.

So the doors of convents were equipped with a sort of rotating cradle which made it possible for parents to leave their children anonymously and without exposing them to the elements. The infant was left in the outside section of the cradle, and then the parent rang a bell so that the nuns could activate the mechanism and bring the child inside. Access to the "turntable" was, however, protected by a grille so narrow that only newborn infants would fit through ...

Pope Gregory VII, Genghis Khan and Jean-Jacques Rousseau are some of the famous personalities who were abandoned as babies.

Abandoned during the 19th century, the system had to be readopted after some twenty years at various places in Europe due to the sharp upturn in the number of infants abandoned.

Foundlings' wheels of historical significance can be seen at the Vatican and in Pisa and Florence (see *Secret Tuscany* and *Secret Rome* in this series of guides), Bayonne (France) and Barcelona (see *Secret Barcelona*).

THE OPEN WINDOW IN PALAZZO GRIFONI   ❺

Piazza della Santissima Annunziata

A haunted room?

This is one of the enigmas of Florence: the second-floor window on the left-hand side of the façade of Palazzo Grifoni is said to be "always open", its shutters ajar.

The story goes that it was from here that a member of the Grifoni family bid farewell to her husband as he set off for war. Thereafter, she languished at the window, waiting in vain for his return. When she herself died, it was decided to finally close the window. But then, some say, the room seemed to become haunted: paintings came away from the walls, lights went out for no apparent cause and furniture mysteriously shifted from one place to another. Once the window was re-opened, everything went back to normal.

Other sources have it that the inhabitants of the area demanded that the window stay open because they had become so used to seeing it like that.

Whatever the truth, those half-open shutters can have a strange effect upon the passers-by who cross Piazza Santissima Annunziata every day, suggesting that one has yet to resolve the "Mystery of the Open Window".

NEARBY

RIGACCI   ❻

Via de' Servi, 71 red • Tel: 055 216206

Entering this "stationer's" for painters is like making one's way into a forest of easels, paintbrushes, paint pots and – above all – canvases of every size (some made to measure for clients, others prepared using a secret recipe that includes rabbit glue, honey and plaster). But for the non-painter, who isn't looking for art supplies, the most striking thing about the interior is the numerous marks of affection left by artist/clients: a precious selection of these works hangs from the lintel between the shop proper and the backroom. Exhibited without the least pomp, one can see paintings by some of the great names of twentieth-century Italian art: Annigoni, Bartolini, Landi, Bausi and the various figures associated with the *Manifesto dell'Astrattismo Classico* (Berti, Brunetti, Monnini, Nuti), of which Rigacci himself was one of the original promoters. Associated with most of these paintings is a story related to the family which has owned this "artists stationer's" for four generations – for example, the birth in 1934 of a son to the then owner Mario Rigacci (that son, together with his brother Rolando, is the current owner of the business).

ROTONDA DEGLI SCOLARI OR DEL BRUNELLESCHI

❼

Via degli Alfani, corner of Via del Castellaccio
• Open Monday to Friday from 8am to 7.30pm; closed on Saturday, public holidays and two weeks in mid-August.
• Admission free

The Temple of the Ideal City

You have to be sharp-eyed to see this, tucked away amidst the buildings at the corner of Via degli Alfani at the far side of Piazza Brunelleschi. Indeed, the geometric perfection of Brunelleschi's famous Rotonda seems out of place here. One gets the impression that it has been set aside for a moment to await a more suitable setting – perhaps in the middle of a city square that is not used as a car park, or as the culmination of a fine perspective. Currently home to the University Language Centre (*Centro Linguistico d'Ateneo*), it is frequented by numerous students, but no one else seems to think it worth a visit.

However, this is a historic building of great originality. The project was itself financed by a fittingly original character: Filippo Scolari, a Florentine *condottiere* in the pay of Sigismund, Emperor of Hungary, who heaped wealth and honours on this captain of arms, bestowing upon him the title of *Ispàn* in recognition of his victories over the Turks (an honour that led to him being known to his fellow Florentines as *Pippo Spano*). Scolari – together with his brother, Matteo – died in 1426, leaving a bequest for the building of a church at the monastery of Santa Maria degli Angeli. In 1434, Brunelleschi drew up a design for the building, which would seem to have been inspired by models to be seen in Renaissance images of ideal cities (images that would then figure in twentieth-century Metaphysical painting). The central-plan church has an octagonal interior with eight identical side chapels, whilst the exterior is made up of sixteen façades with alternating walls and niches. Indeed, it is as a perfect structure that reflects the laws of universal harmony. However, perfection is not for this world, and in 1437 the Florentine Republic suspended work on the church, using the Scolari legacy to finance its war against Lucca; thus, the rotonda was left unfinished. Roofless and with walls reaching up to seven metres from the ground, the structure was left looking rather like a symmetrical miniature of the Abbey of San Galgano set right in the heart of Florence; it even acquired the nickname *Il Castellaccio* [The Broken-Down Castle]. Long abandoned, it was only in the seventeenth century that anyone took the trouble to raise a provisional roof over it, and it was not until 1937 that the architect Rodolfo Sabatini completed the structure, faithfully following Brunelleschi's own drawings.

So, a full five centuries were needed to complete a building of quite unique layout.

ISTITUTO GEOGRAFICO MILITARE

Via Cesare Battisti, 10
• Admission by appointment from Monday to Friday 9am to 1pm
• Tel: 055 2732244

> **The Headquarters of Italian Cartography**

A simple phone appointment will allow you to visit a place which is set within the old city centre and yet is itself an entire world – indeed, universe. Concealed between Piazza San Marco and Piazza della Santissima Annunziata, the Istituto Geografico Militare is a true national treasure, set up here when Florence was capital of the Kingdom of Italy (from 1865 to 1870). Indeed, one of the first tasks undertaken by the new institute was the production of the first topographical map of a united Italy; to a scale of 1:100,000, this was an immense project that took more than thirty years' work to complete.

The Institute is fascinating not only for those with a passionate interest in cartography, but also for those who are merely curious about antique planispheres and atlases; the wonderful examples here have been housed in the magnificent rooms of this seventeenth-century *palazzo* for almost 150 years now. The collection also contains 200,000 books and a substantial body of photographic material, as well as geographical, chorographical, hydrological and geological maps of Italy, Europe and the entire world.

The large salon, which used to be the meeting-place of a famous cenacle, is magnificently decorated with seventeenth-century frescoes and lined on two sides with monumental bookcases; the space in the middle of the room is occupied with various globes.

Whilst housing a historic library and museum of cartography, the place is also a fully functional scientific institution, whose task is to constantly update cartography on the basis of the scientific instruments available. The military personnel are friendly and helpful; and whilst the silence of these vast rooms reveals that they attract few public visitors, one somehow gets the impression that the whole of the world is gathered about one.

CHIOSTRO DELLO SCALZO

Via Cavour, 69
• Tel: 055 2388604
• Open Monday, Thursday and Saturday from 8.15am to 1.50pm; closed on public holidays (except when they fall on the above-mentioned days) and for two weeks before and after 15 August.
• To visit the cloister at other times, write to museo.davanzati@polomuseale.fi.it
• Admission free

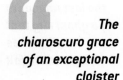

The chiaroscuro grace of an exceptional cloister

This small *Chiostro dello Scalzo* [Cloister of the Discalced] is like no other art treasure in Florence – indeed, in Italy. From outside one might barely notice it behind the simple and elegant façade which once gave access to the (now destroyed) church of the *Compagnia dei Disciplinati di San Giovanni Battista*. The name now associated with the cloister comes from the fact that the confraternity was also known as the *Compagnia dello Scalzo*, because the bearer of the cross in their religious processions went barefoot (discalced). Once across the threshold one encounters a veritable jewel, exceptional because here the Renaissance love of colour gives way not to black and white but rather to orange and white. The frescoes in the cloister are almost entirely the work of Andrea del Sarto and comprise sixteen distinct works in chiaroscuro that depict the Life of St. John the Baptist, the patron saint of Florence. The painter worked on this cycle for ten years (from 1514 to 1524); the two frescoes not by him are the work of Franciabigio, who replaced his master while he was in Paris. The light colours and nuanced draughtsmanship of these works totally transforms the walls, suggesting comparisons with Japanese painting, where colour and line are less sharply defined. The use of monochrome heightens the lightness of touch in this account of the life of the Baptist, with the graceful quality being particularly notable in the scenes of the Baptism of Christ.

This cloister is the last extant trace of the Confraternity of the Disciples of Saint John the Baptist, which was abolished in the eighteenth century by Grand Duke Pietro-Leopardi I; this wonderful cloister was the one thing to escape his seizure of their church.

NEARBY

FARMACIA DELLA SANTISSIMA ANNUNZIATA
Via dei Servi, 80 red • Tel: 055 210738

This is one of the oldest pharmacies in Florence, first opened by the Benedictine nuns of San Niccolò and then taken over in 1561 from the *speziale* (apothecary) Domenico di Vincenzo by Domenico Brunetti. Unfortunately, the famous shop counter was destroyed during the disastrous 1966 flood, though there are still some quality furnishings. Worthy of figuring in a museum, these include: three glass-fronted seventeenth-century cabinets, whose delicacy of appearance is enhanced by wonderfully decorative sprays of gilded flowers, and a collection of pharmacy jars made by Ginori.

JOURNEY AROUND ROMAN FLORENCE

Guided tours first Sunday of each month
• Tours begin at the Firenze com'era museum in Via dell'Oriuolo, 24
• Tour times: 10am–11.30am, 11am–12.30pm and 12 noon to 1.30pm
• Tel: 055 2768224

> *Florentia:*
> *the last remnants*
> *of a ghost city that*
> *still makes*
> *its presence felt*

Some of the Florence that was known as *Florentia* still survives; now hidden and underground, these remnants sometimes re-emerge, sometimes call upon us to rediscover them. On the first Sunday of each month, Florence City Council organises a tour around Roman Florence, which begins with a clear and instructive lecture in the rooms of the *Firenze com'era* (Florence as it was) museum in Via dell'Oriuolo, where a model of the Roman Florence shows it to be much larger and more magnificent than you might have thought. This combination of visual illustrations and commentary gives a real idea of the urban development of Roman *Florentia*, locating its boundaries and main buildings in relation to the present-day urban fabric. But then you move on from models to the real thing, leaving the museum to walk to Piazza San Giovanni, where there was a city gateway with the rather splendid name of Porta contra Aquilonem (Gate against the North Wind). The tour continues along Via Roma (the *cardus* – that is, the north-south axis – of the Roman city) to what was the heart of Roman Florence: the present-day Piazza della Repubblica, which was once

the site of an imposing temple to Jupiter, Minerva and Juno, of which no trace survives. A little farther on – between Via del Proconsolo and Piazza San Firenze – work is still ongoing at the archaeological site around the ancient temple of Isis which was first uncovered at the end of the eighteenth century. Recent finds here include various tombs (other remains of Roman Florence to be seen in the Torre della Pagliuzza museum at the Hotel Brunelleschi, in Piazza Elisabetta). Nearby, the cellars of the restaurant *Alle Murate* also contain remains of Roman buildings, and the tour ends in the cellars of Palazzo Vecchio, where excavations have revealed fragments of a Roman theatre.

"THE STENDHAL SYNDROME IS NO AESTHETIC ECSTASY BUT RATHER THE RESULT OF A TILTED HEAD RESTRICTING BLOOD FLOW"

Hospital of Santa Maria Nuova • Piazza Santa Maria Nuova • Tel: 055 27581
• Emergency number: 118

When visiting Florence, *Homo turisticus* has so much to see that he feels he must carry on relentlessly. As soon as he arrives by train or plane, he finds himself immersed in a cultural heritage whose wealth has no equal in the world; wherever he goes in the city centre, art is on his heels, reminding him of his duty. And forced into contemplation, he ends up having hallucinations: too much beauty, too much happiness, too many emotions – all these go to reinforce the sense of displacement resulting from the loss of habitual points of reference and continual encounters with the sublime. This can produce a certain malaise, a sudden need to rest and drink something. And in the worst cases, one ends up not in a street-side café but in an ambulance, suffering from more extreme symptoms: dizziness, heart flutters, black-outs.

These are the classic symptoms of what for the past thirty years or so has been referred to as the "Stendhal Syndrome", and the hospital of Santa Maria Nuova has a department that specialises in this psycho-somatic affliction suffered by over-enthusiastic tourists.

The name comes from the fact that Henri Beyle, better known as Stendhal, records suffering from just such symptoms when, in 1817, he visited the church of Santa Croce to see the tombs of Michelangelo, Galileo and Alfieri, as well as the ceiling frescoes by Volterrano. In his *Rome, Naples et Florence*, he writes: "I was already in a sort of ecstasy at the mere idea of being in Florence [...] Absorbed in the contemplation of sublime beauty, I saw beauty close-to; I might be said to be touching it. I had got into that state of feeling in which the celestial sensations resulting from the fine arts overlap with the passions. Upon coming out of Santa Croce, my heart was pounding [...] I walked as if I were afraid of falling over."

These symptoms have been known to affect travellers to other cities – in particular, Jerusalem and Paris: in one due to the overwhelming religious presence of the place, in the other due to the rhythm and majesty of the urban fabric. But it would seem that in Florence the sole cause is beauty alone.

For certain physicians, "the Stendhal Syndrome" has a much more prosaic explanation: it is due to the circulatory problems caused by continually holding the head tilted to look up at cupolas, bell-towers and frescoes. The admiration of beauty, it seems, stops an adequate flow of blood to the brain.

THE CRUCIFIX OF THE HOSPITAL OF SANTA MARIA NUOVA

Piazza Santa Maria Nuova
• Currently undergoing restoration, the Salone Martino V usually houses the management offices
• It is advisable to apply for information to 055 27581

> *A few secrets of Florence's oldest hospital*

A veritable microcosm of the community it serves, any hospital contains secrets and surprises – all the more so if, as is the case with Santa Maria Nuova, it is an ancient foundation.

The founder of this hospital was actually the banker Folco Portinari, the father of Dante's Beatrice. However, it was only with some difficulty – and the essential intervention of Pope Boniface VIII – that he managed to acquire the land here, given that the Carmelites had wanted it as the site of their new monastery. Of course, that first hospital was much smaller: when it opened its doors in 1288, it had beds for just seventeen patients. That initial foundation is also famous because it was here that Monna Teresa, Beatrice's nurse, founded the Oblates, a nursing order of nuns.

Over the centuries, the hospital acquired numerous works of art, enough to form a museum. There are still plans to do so, particularly with regard to the *salone* named after Pope Martin V, which is decorated with a 1420 fresco by Bicci de Lorenzo. However, the real masterpiece in the hospital is the powerful *Crucifix* by Francesco da Sangallo. This life-size sculpture in wood has been put to a rather exceptional use for a work of art: laid out on a bed like a patient, this expressive rendition of the suffering Christ was used to test the scanner in the hospital's tomography department.

NEARBY

THE GRATING OVER THE SECRET PASSAGEWAY AT THE HOSPITAL OF SANTA MARIA NUOVA

Another special feature of this hospital is the secret passageway that links the main courtyard to the Oblates Convent, which now houses the City Library. One end of this three-metre high passageway has been bricked up. However, in the hospital courtyard one can still see the vent to let in air and light; it is recognisable by its long narrow grating. Perhaps this historic underground passageway might one day be re-opened to spare pedestrians the need to dodge the traffic.

...lo dell'Anno 1793.

Dazzaiolo ... 1793

...IIII. 32

12

ARCHIVIO STORICO DI FIRENZE

Palazzo Bastogi Bastoni
Via dell'Oriuolo, 33
• Tel 0552616527
• Free admission upon prior booking at archstor@comune.fi.it
• Visits must be at the following times: Monday and Friday 9am to 3.30
pm and Tuesday, Wednesday and Thursday 9am to 6pm

**Annals
and Archives**

The historical archives of Florence are an inexhaustible mine of wealth, a labyrinth of documents wherein one event summons up reference to others. One could spend one's whole life here without ever getting bored – or perhaps just spend fifteen minutes or so relaxing in a most unusual and most educational manner. There are not many cities where the historical archives are so readily accessible, and also serve to house interesting temporary exhibitions. Located in Via dell'Oriuolo, the Archives occupy rather narrow premises that are ideally located: they stand opposite the former Oblate Convent that now houses the City Library. There are tens of thousands of documents, all divided into different collections. The material covers all aspects of social life in the city, from dossiers on the bodies involved in public assistance and the proceedings of the City Council, to records of the financial and artistic affairs of the Teatro Niccolini (1699-1932) or documents regarding the four-century-long history of the Ospedale di San Giovanni di Dio (1604- 1968). Each of these collections casts new light on a specific aspect of the city's history – ranging from the fairly brief

period when Napoleonic Florence was governed by a French-style *mairie* to the records of the *Scuole Leopoldine*, where the individual histories of the pupils illustrate the position of women in the worlds of work and education over a period of around two centuries. As for the collections of drawings, these comprise some 40,000 documents that date from the period ranging from the end of the eighteenth century to the 1960s. There are, for example, the plans relating to the rebuilding of Florence after the Second World War, with various unpublished architectural designs.

Along with any temporary exhibitions being held, do not omit to visit the elegant study room, which is open to the general public. This is a pleasant place to spend half a day searching through the documents and chronicles that record the "everyday" history of the city.

TABERNACOLO DEL MIRACOLO DEL SANGUE ⓯

Church of Sant'Ambrogio
Piazza Sant'Ambrogio
• Open daily from 8am to 12 noon and 4pm to 7pm

> *Where the feast of Corpus Domini originated: the Sant'Ambrogio Miracles*

To the left of the high altar in the church of Sant'Ambrogio (St. Ambrose) is a chapel that commemorates the miracle which took place here on 30 December 1230, when the surrounding area was still countryside. Also mentioned in the *Chronicles* of Giovanni Villani, the story goes that the parish priest, Ugoccione (or Uguccione), discovered a few drops of blood within the chalice he had used in celebrating mass. He declared it a miracle, a claim which was sanctioned by the bishop after a day of strict observation. It was this event – together with another of the same kind which took place a little later in Bolsena – that would lead to the institution of the Feast of Corpus Domini in 1264.

The miraculous blood of 1230 was regularly carried in ritual procession, and over a century later – in 1340 – it would cause another miracle, which spared Florence from the plague. In 1595, there was yet another miraculous escape. When a fire broke out around the altar, the flames reached the tabernacle where the ciborium was kept but did not damage the consecrated hosts; indeed, when the water used to quench the fire touched the hosts, they took on a circular form and were thereafter kept as holy relics.

Over time, Sant'Ambrogio was adorned with various art works recounting

these miracles. In the fifteenth century, the relics were transferred from the high altar to the chapel on the left; the marble tabernacle is the work of Mino da Fiesole and shows Ugoccione handing over the blood he had discovered to the Mother Superior of the nuns attached to the church. As for the second miracle, it is depicted in a fresco by Cosimo Rosselli showing the procession in Piazzetta de Sant'Ambrogio (which serves as the church parvis). The artist included a self-portrait amongst the crowd of the faithful.

NEARBY

THE BLAZON OF "THE RED CITY"

Another curiosity at Sant'Ambrogio is to be noted upon leaving the church. On the outer pier at the corner of the façade is a small blazon of the "red city" (*Città Rossa*), and at the corner of Via de' Macci are sixteenth-century plaques referring to "The Great Monarch of the Red City" (also mentioning the tabernacle of Sant'Ambrogio). These were the heraldic devices of a local student confraternity founded at Sant'Ambrogio in the fourteenth century.

THE STAIRCASE OF PALAZZO BUDINI-GATTAI

Piazza D'Azeglio, 28
• Visits by appointment, telephone 368 787 6962 or writing to claudio. screti@iol.it
• There are public toilets in this square open Monday to Saturday from 10am to 1pm and 3pm to 7pm

> *A city square that reflects "Florence the Capital"*

Apparently modelled on a British city square – with tall trees and vast lawns – Piazza D'Azeglio was, until the end of the Second World War, enclosed by a metal gate for which only the residents had a key. All around this *piazza* are buildings that reflect the type of appearance which the city wished to assume when it became the capital of Italy (for the period 1865 to 1870). One of these is the small private residence of the Palazzo Wilson-Gattai. Designed by the first owner, Frederick Wilson, this hybrid was inspired by the architecture of the Renaissance but reveals a clear delight in opulence – note, for example, the use of Carrara marble. When Gaetano Gattai became owner of the building in 1892, the *palazzo* underwent some changes; the most important of these was undoubtedly the daringly helicoidal external staircase – a rare example of such a feature in Florence, it makes the *palazzo* particularly spectacular. The various rooms that overlook the *piazza* also have their charm, as they are decorated with a series of nineteenth-century frescoes; they can only be visited when they are not rented out. There is also a romantic-inspired garden of dense greenery.

NEARBY

"1865": A PERIOD RESIDENCE

Via Luigi Carlo Farini, 12
• www.1865.it • Admission free by appointment: call 055 2340586, or e-mail cinzia@auxe.net

The period residence "1865" is located in a neoclassical building commissioned for the Orsini family in the very year that Florence became capital of Italy, hence its name. The main salon, whose ceiling is frescoed with allegories of the various arts, contains a small library of precious texts relating to the cultural history of the day: there are works on the local area as well as books by writers from Italy and abroad who lived in "Florence the Capital". The polyglot owners receive visitors by appointment, as was common in the past. On occasion, these meetings can develop into a concert in the salon itself or into conversations over tea and cake.

FONDAZIONE SCIENZA E TECNICA

Via Giusti, 29
• Planetarium: visits on Sunday afternoon, by appointment. Telephone some days in advance, Monday to Friday from 9am to 3pm: 055 2343723 (www.planetario.fi.it)
• Physics Laboratory: guided tours on Sunday, by appointment. Telephone from Monday to Saturday from 9am to 7pm: 055 2346760
• Tours only in Italian

> **A little-known temple of science**

The *'Gaetano Salvemini' Istituto Tecnico per Geometri* (Technical Institute for Land Surveyors) is home to a fascinating science museum that is little known to visitors and locals alike. Not part of the usual circuit of the city's natural history museums, the *Fondazione Scienza e Tecnica* is one of the hidden centres of Florence's scientific establishment, whilst its 53-seater planetarium, laboratory and teaching materials are well-known to generations of students.

A visit here is both instructive and, in some ways, spectacular, for this is a craft museum that has few equals in Italy. Unfortunately, one can only see a part of the collection, which totals more than 50,000 manufactured objects, ranging from astonishing models used in teaching the laws of dynamics and mechanics to scientific instruments that illustrate the history of scientific experimentation and teaching. There are also remarkable collections of books, as well as collections of natural-history samples and industrial products.

Here one breathes the air of an age-old temple of learning, where generations of students have been trained and educated amidst botanical charts, mineral samples, wax anatomy models and zoological specimens.

Far from being a mere pile of bric-a-brac, this is a collection that illustrates developments in the applied sciences and their reflection in technological advances.

FAÇADE OF PALAZZO ZUCCARI

Kunsthistorisches Institut
Via Giusti, 44

> **The preposterous façade of the German Art Institute**

L
ocated between Piazza D'Azeglio and Piazza Santissima Annunziata is a *palazzo* that is unique in Florence - a spectacular demonstration of how aesthetic canons can change. During the Renaissance no-one would ever have thought of creating so eclectic and idiosyncratic a façade for a *palazzo*, but by the end of the sixteenth century adherence to the rules was obviously much less strict. The Mannerist painter Federico Zuccari did not stay in Florence a long time, though he did paint the huge (recently restored) fresco of *The Last Judgement* in the cupola of the Duomo. For some time, he lived not far from here – in Via Capponi, next-door to the house occupied by Andrea del Sarto (whose residence here is now commemorated by a plaque). However, Zuccari then decided to build himself a home, in a Mannerist style that would be a public affirmation of his personality as an artist. Thus, in the years 1578-79 he created this house, with a façade that is more like a pastiche than a composition, as its various components are organised in a very theatrical manner: panels of bare brick and blocks of unfinished rock alternated with polished blocks of stone, bas-reliefs depicting the symbols of Painting, Architecture and Sculpture (re-worked in 1920), windows with opulently decorated gratings, two niches, stone benches at pavement level and a cartouche (now covered with roughcast) which Zuccari was to have adorned with a fresco. This whole façade is the frontage to a tall narrow building that appears even more incongruous when one looks at the other structures in this quiet street. If Zuccari aimed to leave some unusual and indelible record of his passage through Florence, then he certainly succeeded. Today, the Palazzo Zuccari houses the *Kunsthistorisches Institut*. At present Florence's most influential foreign-run institute for art history studies, it has one of the best specialised libraries on this subject – with more than 300,000 books and a thousand or so specialist magazines that would be difficult to find elsewhere. There is also an immense collection of photographs of Italian art. A highly-esteemed centre of research, this institute has been in existence since the end of the nineteenth century, its academic rigour in a sense counterbalanced by the sheer exuberance of Zuccari's façade.

Zuccari was also responsible for another eccentric house, this time in Rome, in Piazza di Spagna. That structure has windows in the form of large open mouths, giving the impression of monstrous gaping jaws. (See our *Secret Rome*.)

STROLL ALONG THE HISTORIC BORGO PINTO ㉑

Borgo Pinto and surrounding streets

An artists' street

Narrow and winding, the irregular course of Borgo Pinto is lined with various fine buildings. It is also the site of Santa Maria Maddalena dei Pazzi church, which houses Perugino's sublime *Crucifixion*.

For some mysterious reason, this street has always been a gathering-place for painters, sculptors and architects, who – right in the heart of this area of Florence – seem to draw inspiration from the place. Porta dei Pinti itself, one of the old city gateways, was however one of those Giuseppe Poggi demolished to make way for the ring-road boulevards, its place now being taken by Piazzale Donatello.

For centuries, great artists chose to live in this street, one of the last being Lorenzo Barolini (1777–1850), a neoclassical sculptor who lived at No. 87, just opposite the palazzo that Antonio and Giuliano da Sangallo had had built for themselves.

Perugino lived on the corner of Via Laura, while at No. 26 were studios and living accommodation which the Grand Duke made available to his court artists; thus, from the end of the sixteenth to the eighteenth centuries, this place was home to such figures as Giambologna, Pietro Tacca and Giovanni Battista Foggini. Parallel to Borgo Pinto runs Via della Pergola,

where, at No. 59, lived Benvenuto Cellini; while at right angles is Via della Colonna, which was home to Pontormo (at No. 23) and Niccolò Tribolo (No. 13). In the nearby Via Giusti you can see the palazzo with the extravagant façade built by Zuccaro in the sixteenth century.

At the end of the nineteenth century the "artists' quarter" shifted to the far end of Borgo Pinto, where the elegant buildings on the northern side of Piazzale Donatello were occupied by numerous artists' studios. The area became such a centre of the creative arts that it gave rise to the so-called "Gruppo Donatello", which still exists today.

THE BORGO PINTI GARDEN

㉒

Borgo Pinti, 76
- Free admission
- Open throughout the year from 1.30pm to 4.30pm in the winter and 1.30pm to 6pm in summer; closed on public holidays and Sundays.
- Dogs must be on a leash

A small Romantic garden

Without any sign to announce its existence, a small garden of great charm and long history is tucked away behind railings in peaceful Borgo Pinti, right in the heart of the city.

In the sixteenth century, when this entire district was enclosed within a crenellated wall, Alemanno Salviati created a garden of simples here, cultivating Tuscany's very first Catalonian Jasmin (imported from Greece) and other rare plants – for example, the Muscat grape. A century later various citrus plants were introduced, along with a number of prestigious shrubs and trees. However, it was Camillo Borghese who, at the end of the eighteenth century, would give the garden its present appearance, undertaking important changes: two knolls were raised, the medicinal plants were removed and the parterres were modified in line with the

Romantic tastes of the day.

Now administered by the Barbieri Cooperative, which provides training and assistance for people of restricted mobility, this charming area of greenery has a sports ground and running track, a vegetable garden and small shaded alleys lined with benches (complete with ashtrays of different colours).

Unlike other old patrician gardens in the centre of Florence, there is nothing monumental about this place. Quite the opposite, the garden has the convivial air of a place where one might encounter young lovers, mothers pushing prams or local pensioners.

THE EGYPTIAN VICE-REGENT SELLS HIS GARDEN BECAUSE HE WAS DENIED PERMISSION TO INSTALL HIS PRIVATE HAREM

Various panels here provide interesting historical information about Borgo Pinti. One learns that along the garden is a collection of buildings meant to serve a special purpose. In 1880 they were bought by the Egyptian vice-regent, Ishmail Pasha, but were quickly sold on to the much less exotic *Società Strade Ferrate Meridionali* [Southern Tram and Rail Company] : the Florence City Council had prohibited the vice-regent from installing his private harem here.

THE GARDEN OF PALAZZO DELLA GHERARDESCA

Access via the Four Seasons Hotel
Borgo Pinti, 99
• Tel: 055 2626
• The public is admitted to the cafés and restaurants inside
• The 'Al Fresco' café is open 12 noon to 7pm from May to October and is located in the middle of the garden

> **The largest private garden in Florence**

On any map of Florence you immediately notice a large patch of green just to the north of the city centre, near Viale Matteotti. This is the garden of Palazzo della Gherardesca (access from Borgo Pinti) and is the largest private area of green in Florence; it is even bigger than the Torregiani Garden in Via dei Serragli.

After being closed for years, this vast open space has become the grounds of a luxury hotel, whose opening gave rise to a well-publicised public debate: the redevelopment of a long-neglected area *versus* the cession to private ownership of an important environmental resource. The garden itself has a long history: the *Arte Della Lana* [Wool Guild], one of the seven original craft corporations in Florence, used this area for a vegetable garden, a plant nursery and even for a *ragnaia* (a system of nets spread to catch insects).

After the site became the property of the della Gherardesca family, the inevitable Giuseppe Poggi – the architect most typically associated with the redevelopment of Florence after it became the capital of the kingdom of Italy – created a monumental entrance onto Viale Matteotti, consisting of a gate set within an archway and flanked by two smaller side entrances.

Upon entering, one immediately sees a fountain adorned with a *putto*, beyond which is a garden laid out according to the aesthetic canons of the nineteenth century. Restored after the Second World War, it has more recently been modified by the hotel that now occupies Palazzo della Gherardesca. The Romantic layout of the garden comprises small temples, side alleys, water basins, artificial knolls and other decorative 'follies'. As for the plants themselves, there are magnificent azaleas and various remarkable shrubs and trees – including a giant thuja, a sequoia, a large maple tree and numerous cypresses. The magnificence of the plants and the very scale of the garden somehow seem out of proportion for a space reserved for use by a single hotel. However, while one may have no illusions regarding the possibility of the place becoming a public park, the presence of small cafés within the grounds means that the public does get the chance to visit it – and thus discover this far from negligible part of Florence's past.

UNUSUAL TOMBS IN THE ENGLISH CEMETERY ❷❹

Piazzale Donatello, 38
• Winter opening hours: Monday 9am to 12 noon; Tuesday to Friday from
2pm to 5pm • Summer opening hours: Monday 9am to 12 noon; Tuesday
to Friday 3pm to 6pm • Closed Saturday and Sunday
• A donation is welcome

*Cosmopolitan
Romanticism in the
"Island of the Dead"*

Set amongst the avenues that form ring-roads around the city centre, the *Isola dei Morti* [Island of the Dead] is a very distinctive green knoll known to all Florentines by sight. Though few venture inside, the English cemetery here is one of the most fascinating cemeteries in Europe. Indeed, quite soon after it was opened (in 1827), its reputation was already beginning to outshine that of the older English cemetery in Livorno (see our *Secret Tuscany*). For a long time, this was the only cemetery within the Grand Duchy where Jews and other non-Catholics could be buried, becoming known as "The English Cemetery" because the sizeable British community in Florence provided a substantial proportion of its population; however, Greek Orthodox, Russian Orthodox and Jews were also buried here. One community which did not bury its dead here was the Swiss Evangelical Church, which chose instead to purchase its own plot of burial ground, just beyond Porta a Pinti and thus outside Florence's city walls. However, it was so close to those walls that when they were demolished fifty years later, the cemetery itself had to be closed (in 1877): it was by then right in the middle of the urban expansion resulting from Florence's role as capital of the Kingdom of Italy. That urban expansion also saw Giuseppe Poggi, the architect behind the redevelopment of the new capital, redesign the original polygonal boundary of the English Cemetery to create an oval that would stand in the centre of Piazzale Donatello. That change – in 1865 – resulted in this knoll of trees and tombs becoming isolated within a defined perimeter. Hence, without intending to, Poggi had transformed a cemetery into an "island of the dead". And if the external appearance of the cemetery is already exceptional, its interior is even more remarkable: a visit to its labyrinth of alleys is as rewarding as that to a museum, even if the constant noise of traffic is annoying. The tombs here include those of: the last known descendants of Shakespeare, Beatrice and Edward Claude; the poet Elizabeth Barrett Browning (a sarcophagus borne up on six slim columns); Giovan Pietro Viesseux, a Swiss national who made an important contribution to Florentine literary history and founded the famous Cabinet Viesseux in Palazzo Strozzi; the sculptor Hiram Powers, who lived in Via de' Serragli. The fame of the cemetery then spread beyond Florence, becoming a source of inspiration that found echo in European culture as a whole. For example, Louise Adams, whose death is featured in *The Education of Henry Adams*, her brother's autobiography, is buried here. And the above-mentioned tomb of Elizabeth Barrett Browning inspired a poem in which Emily Dickinson included lines written by the earlier poet (who herself had written a poem inspired by a sculpture by Hiram Powers). A further link can be seen in the fact that Casa Guidi, where Robert Browning and Elizabeth Barrett Browning had lived, was itself immortalised in a work by the Greek-born painter Robert Mignaty, who, together with his brother, is also buried in this "Island of the Dead". Walking around the cemetery, one encounters tomb inscriptions in English, Hebrew, Russian, German and other languages – a polyglot anthology of Romanticism and biblical quotations (such quotations were then forbidden in Catholic cemeteries). If one follows the winding paths right up to the summit of the hill, one comes to a column which itself has a special history, given that it was a gift from Frederick-Wilhelm IV of Prussia. However, do not leave without placing a flower on the grave of the cemetery's most exotic occupant: Nadezhda De Santis, a girl who, at the age of fourteen, arrived in Florence from Sudan following the Champollion and Rossellini expedition to Nubia. In effect, she was one of the last slaves to be brought to Europe – and she is certainly one of the first Africans to be buried in Florence.

A PAINTING, OF WHICH ADOLF HITLER POSSESSED A VERSION

One of Arnold Böcklin's daughters is buried here, and his painting *Island of the Dead* contributed to the fame of this amazing cemetery. When he visited Florence, Adolf Hitler – who owned the third version that Böcklin painted of this subject – wanted to see the English cemetery. He was not the only one to be struck by the painting: it had also made a powerful impression on both Freud and Lenin.

The cemetery was also the inspiration for Sergei Rachmaninov's symphonic poem (opus 29), which is entitled *The Island of the Dead*.

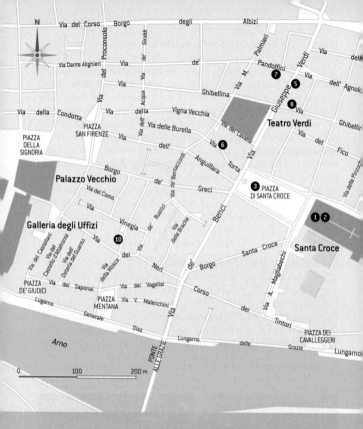

SANTA CROCE

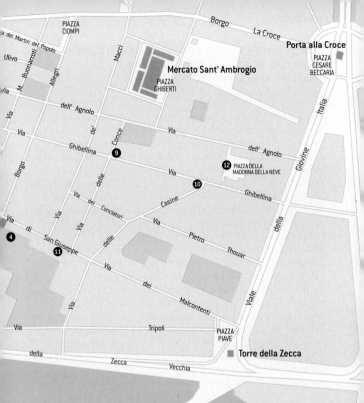

PEREGRINATIONS OF DANTE'S MONUMENT: A VERY FLORENTINE WAY OF HONOURING THE AUTHOR OF *THE DIVINE COMEDY*

Monuments to Dante in the Basilica of Santa Croce
Piazza Santa Croce and the Uffizi Loggia

When Santa Croce was finally consecrated as the mausoleum for the nation's famous sons, a large monument was erected for the tomb of the great Florentine poet Dante Alighieri. However, that tomb is now only a memorial, for Ravenna refused to give up the body of the poet whom Florence had condemned to exile. Anxious to make amends to this favourite son – and perhaps feeling a little guilty about the treatment he had received – Florence then honoured him with various gestures that were not always well thought out. For example, Via Dante may well be where the Alighieri family home once stood but it is just a minor side street – and the Casa di Dante museum is just a reconstruction.

As for the most visible monument to the poet – the one in Piazza Santa Croce – that was initially a monumental gaffe: at first it was raised in the very centre of the square but then, not without some embarrassment, had to be moved to the left of the church's main doorway so as to allow cameras to film the games of "historic football" played here (see p. 216).

The statue of Dante in Santa Croce shows the poet seated and leaning forward; the one in front of the church shows him standing with his right arm dangling at his side and his left wrapped in his gown; in the Uffizi Loggia, he is again shown standing but with his arm raised and his index finger near his nose.

"IN THE CHURCH, DANTE'S HAVING A DUMP, IN THE SQUARE HE'S WIPING HIMSELF AND IN THE LOGGIA HE'S SNIFFING HIS FINGER"

The Florentine delight in earthy wit has seized upon the chance to ridicule these rather unfortunate poses, coming up with the observation: "In the church Dante's having a dump, in the square he's wiping himself and in the loggia he's sniffing his finger" – a dictum mentioned by the early-twentieth-century poet Venturino Camaiti, who wrote parodies of all 100 cantos of *La divina commedia*.

Sharp-eyed visitors can decide for themselves if this brief description of the three statues is accurate. They might also ponder whether Ravenna, which boasts of having received Dante in the way he deserved, actually measures up to all these gestures of respect with which Florence the Incorrigible still commemorates its great poet. Perhaps the irreverence, though, is a form of popular affection, an expression of the fellow-feeling between the city and its most famous son. The familiarity may not be subtle, but it is undeniably a measure of the poet's prestige.

FAÇADE OF THE BASILICA DI SANTA CROCE ❶

Piazza Santa Croce

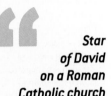

> **Star of David on a Roman Catholic church**

Until the nineteenth century, the façade of Santa Croce (Basilica of the Holy Cross) was left in undressed *pietra forte* (sandstone). The neo-Gothic design seen today was the work of the Ancona-born architect Niccolò Matas, who included in his designs a sign that bears witness to his own religious creed: the Star of David on the tympanum. Matas was also the architect of the monumental Porte Sante cemetery; however, for his own burial place he chose a plot directly opposite the main entrance to the basilica. This story has a curious antecedent in that, in the fifteenth century, the Franciscan monks of Santa Croce had rejected the designs by the architect Pollaiolo precisely because he wanted to include the family symbol of his patrons, the Quaratesi.

THE STAR HEXAGRAM: A MAGICAL TALISMAN?

The hexagram – also known as the Star of David or the Shield of David – comprises two interlaced equilateral triangles, one pointing upwards and the other downwards. It symbolises the combination of man's spiritual and human nature. The six points correspond to the six directions in space (north, south, east and west, together with zenith and nadir) and also refer to the complete universal cycle of the six days of creation (the seventh day being when the Creator rested). Hence, the hexagram became the symbol of the macrocosm (its six angles of 60° totalling 360°) and of the union between mankind and its creator. If, as laid down in the Old Testament (*Deuteronomy* 6:4–9), the hexagram (*mezuzah* in Hebrew) is often placed at the entrance to a Jewish home, it was also adopted as an amulet by Christians and Muslims. So it is far from being an exclusively Jewish symbol. In both the Koran (38:32 et seq.) and *The Thousand and One Nights*, it is described as an indestructible talisman that affords God's blessing and offers total protection against the spirits of the natural world, the djinns. The hexagram also often appears in the windows and pediments of Christian churches, as a symbolic reference to the universal soul. In this case, that soul is represented by Christ – or, sometimes, by the pair of Christ (upright triangle) and the Virgin (inverted triangle); the result of the interlacing of the two is God the Father Almighty. The hexagram is also found in the mediated form of a lamp with six branches or a six-section rose window.

Although present in the synagogue of Capernaum (third century AD), the hexagram does not really make its appearance in rabbinical literature until 1148 – in the *Eshkol Hakofer* written by the Karaite* scholar Judah Ben Elijah. In Chapter 242 its mystical and apotropaic (evil-averting) qualities are described, with the actual words then often being engraved on amulets: "And the names of the seven angels were written on the *mezuzah* & The Everlasting will protect you and this symbol called the Shield of David contains, at the end of the *mezuzah*, the written name of all the angels."

In the thirteenth century the hexagram also became an attribute of one of the seven magic names of Metatron, the angel of the divine presence associated with the archangel Michael (head of the heavenly host and the closest to God the Father).

The identification of Judaism with the Star of David began in the Middle Ages. In 1354 King Karel IV of Bohemia granted the Jewish community of Prague the privilege of putting the symbol on their banner. The Jews embroidered a gold star on a red background to form a standard that became known as the Flag of King David (*Maghen David*) and was adopted as the official symbol of Jewish synagogues. By the nineteenth century, the symbol had spread throughout the Jewish community. Jewish mysticism has it that the origin of the hexagram was directly linked with the flowers that adorn the *menorah***: irises with six petals. For those who believe this origin, the hexagram came directly from the hands of the God of Israel, the six-petal iris not only reassembling the Star of David in general form but also being associated with the people of Israel in the *Song of Songs*.

As well as offering protection, the hexagram was believed to have magical powers. This reputation originates in the famous *Clavicula Salomonis* (Key of Solomon), a grimoire (textbook of magic) attributed to Solomon himself but, in all likelihood, produced during the Middle Ages. The anonymous texts probably came from one of the numerous Jewish schools of the Kabbalah that then existed in Europe, for the work is clearly inspired by the teachings of the Talmud and the Jewish faith. The *Clavicula* contains a collection of thirty-six pentacles (themselves symbols rich in magic and esoteric significance) which were intended to enable communication between the physical world and the different levels of the soul. There are various versions of the text, in numerous translations, and the content varies between them. However, most of the surviving texts date from the sixteenth and seventeenth centuries – although there is a Greek translation dating from the fifteenth.

In Tibet and India, the Buddhists and Hindus read this universal symbol of the hexagram in terms of the creator and his creation, while the Brahmins hold it to be the symbol of the god Vishnu. Originally, the two triangles were in green (upright triangle) and red (inverted triangle). Subsequently, these colours became black and white, the former representing the spirit, the latter the material world. For the Hindus, the upright triangle is associated with Shiva, Vishnu and Brahma (corresponding to the Christian God the Father, Son and Holy Ghost). The Son (Vishnu) can be seen to always occupy the middle position, being the intercessor between things divine and things earthly.

qara'im or *bnei mikra*: "he who follows the Scriptures". Karaism is a branch of Judaism that defends the sole authority of the Hebrew Scripture as the source of divine revelation, thus repudiating oral tradition.
**Menorah – the multibranched candelabra used in the rituals of Judaism. The arms of the seven-branched menorah, one of the oldest symbols of the Jewish faith, represent the seven archangels before the Throne of God: Michael, Gabriel, Samuel, Raphael, Zadkiel, Anael and Kassiel.

"HERMETIC" SKY OF THE PAZZI CHAPEL

Basilica di Santa Croce
Piazza Santa Croce
• www.santacroceopera.it
• Open Monday–Saturday from 9.30am to 5.30pm; Sunday and Holy Days of Obligation (6 January, 15 August, 1 November, 8 December) 1pm to 5pm; open Easter Monday, 25 April, 1 May and 2 June; closed 1 January, Easter Sunday, 13 June, 4 October and Christmas Day
• Admission: €5 (full price); €3 (concessions); families: parents €5, children free

> *The same night sky as San Lorenzo sacristy*

The frescoed cupola in the Pazzi Chapel alongside Santa Croce is painted with exactly the same star-studded sky as appears in the old sacristy of San Lorenzo (see p. 127). This is unique: two frescoes commissioned from two different artists by two different patrons in two different parts of the city, yet both depicting the same – very significant – night sky.

Like the Medici, the Pazzi family maintained close relations with René of Anjou, the titular "King of Jerusalem", who during his stay in the city knighted one of the Pazzis and was present at the baptism of a child recently born to these aristocratic Florentines.

HERMES TRISMEGISTUS AND HERMETISM: ATTRACTING CELESTIAL ENERGY TO EARTH BY REPRODUCING THE COSMIC ORDER

Hermes Trismegistus, which in Latin means "thrice-great Hermes", is the name given by the neo-Platonists, alchemists, and hermetists to the Egyptian god *Thot*, *Hermes* to the Greeks. In the Old Testament, he is also identified with the patriarch Enoch.

In their respective cultures, all three were considered to be the creators of phonetic writing, theurgical magic, and messianic prophetism.

Thot was connected to the lunar cycles whose phases expressed the harmony of the universe. Egyptian writings refer to him as "twice great" because he was the god of the Word and of Wisdom.

In the syncretic atmosphere of the Roman Empire, the epithet of the Egyptian god *Thot* was given to the Greek god *Hermes*, but this time was "thrice great" (*trismegistus*) for the Word, Wisdom and his duty as Messenger of all the gods of Elysium or Olympus.

The Romans associated him with *Mercury*, the planet that mediates between the Earth and the Sun, which is a function that Kabbalistic Jews called *Metraton*, the "perpendicular measure between the Earth and the Sun".

In Hellenic Egypt, *Hermes* was the "scribe and messenger of the gods" and was believed to be the author of a collection of sacred texts, called *hermetic*, that contained teachings about art, science, religion and philosophy – the *Corpus Hermeticum* – the objective of which was the deification of humanity through knowledge of God.

These texts, which were probably written by a group belonging to the *Hermetic School* of ancient Egypt, thus express the knowledge accumulated over time by attributing it to the god of Wisdom, who is in all points similar to the Hindu god *Ganesh*.

The *Corpus Hermeticum*, which probably dates from the 1st to the 3rd

centuries AD, represented the source of inspiration of hermetic and neo-Platonic thought during the Renaissance.

Even though Swiss scholar Casaubon had apparently proved the contrary in the 17th century, people continued to believe that the text dated back to Egyptian antiquity before Moses and that it announced the coming of Christianity.

According to Clement of Alexandria, it contained 42 books divided into six volumes. The first treated the education of priests; the second, the rites of the temple; the third, geology, geography, botany and agriculture; the fourth, astronomy and astrology, mathematics and architecture; the fifth contained hymns to the glory of the gods and a guide of political action for kings; the sixth was a medical text.

It is generally believed that Hermes Trismegistus invented a card game full of esoteric symbols, of which the first 22 were made of blades of gold and the 56 others of blades of silver – the *tarot* or "Book of Thot". Hermes is also attributed with writing the *Book of the Dead* or "Book of the Exit towards the Light," as well as the famous alchemy text *The Emerald Table*, works that had a strong influence on the alchemy and magic practised in medieval Europe.

In medieval Europe, especially between the 5th and 14th centuries, hermetism was also a School of Hermeneutics that interpreted certain poems of antiquity and various enigmatic myths and works of art as allegorical treaties of alchemy or hermetic science.

For this reason, the term *hermetism* still designates the esoteric nature of a text, work, word or action, in that they possess an occult meaning that requires a hermeneutic, or in other words a philosophical science, to correctly interpret the hidden meaning of the object of study.

Hermetic principles were adopted and applied by the Roman *Colegium Fabrorum*, associations of the architects of civil, military and religious constructions. This knowledge was transmitted in the 12th century to the Christian *Builder-Monks*, the builders of the grand Roman and Gothic edifices of Europe, who executed their work according to the principles of sacred architecture, true to the model of sacred geometry.

It is the direct legacy of volumes three and four of the *Corpus Hermeticum*, according to which cities and buildings were constructed in interrelation with specific planets and constellations, so that the design of the Heavens could be reproduced on Earth, thus favouring cosmic or sidereal energies. All of this was done with the purpose of achieving the hermetic principle that states: "Everything above is like everything below".

During the European Renaissance (16th and 17th centuries), hermetism was replaced by humanism. Forms were rationalised and the transcendental ignored.

It was the end of the traditional society and the beginning of a profane, Baroque and pre-modernist society, paving the way for the arrival of the materialism and atheism that dominates the modern world. There were, however, some exceptions to this predominant rule in Europe. In Portugal, in the 16th century, the *Master Builders*, the heirs of the Builder-Monks, founded the Manueline style according to the hermetic rules of sacred architecture.

MARKINGS FOR A "FLORENTINE FOOTBALL" PITCH ❸

Palazzo degli Antellesi
Piazza Santa Croce, 20 and Piazza Santa Croce, 7

> **Traces of the sport of yesteryear**

Played in period costume, *calcio storico* (literally, "historic football") is one of the curiosities of Florence. And that it is "historic" is evident in Piazza Santa Croce, where there are authentic traces of the Renaissance: the end markers of the halfway line across the pitch where the matches used to be played.

The first of these markers is a marble disk set within the façade of Palazzo degli Antellesi, which stands to the left of a jewellery shop (on the right-hand side of the piazza as you look towards the church). The date "10 February 1565" is carved in the stone. Directly opposite, on the façade of the building at No. 7, is the second marker. This smaller disk depicts a ball and is divided into four quarters: two red and two white.

Before matches, a white line was traced across the square from the centre of one disk to the other; this marked the halfway line of the pitch where the two teams competed. At the centre of that line the *pallaio* (ball holder) would throw the ball into play by hurling it against one of the two disks; when it bounced back onto the pitch, the game had started. The matches were, however, sometimes played elsewhere: for example, in 1491 and 1605 they were held on the frozen surface of the Arno.

In 1530, when papal forces were besieging Florence, the city decided to show its contempt for the threat by sticking to their Carnival calendar, despite the shortage of food. Thus the traditional match of *calcio fiorentino* took place right under the eyes of the besiegers, camped on the hills around Florence. Unsportingly, the enemy even fired a cannon ball during play, which was greeted with vociferous booing from the Florentines.

In 1575, Florentine merchants in the French city of Lyon decided to organise a match of *calcio fiorentino* – an event commemorated during the 1998 World Cup by a match between Florence and Lyon. It is even said that the development of the modern game in England is due to the fact that, in 1766, the English Consul witnessed a match of *calcio storico* played in Livorno.

The famous players of *calcio fiorentino* included several members of the de' Medici family, as well as three future popes: Clement VII, Leo XI and Urban XIII (the latter was even born at No. 5 Piazza Santa Croce). The game, however, lost popularity in the seventeenth century, with the last known match being played in 1739.

Then, in 1930, the first match of modern times was played – to commemorate the 400th anniversary of the papal siege. Nowadays, a tournament is held every June between teams representing the four historic districts of Florence; the two elimination rounds and the final are played on a sand-covered Piazza Santa Croce.

Often considered the ancestor of modern football, *calcio storico fiorentino* might just as readily be compared with rugby, given its rules and the robust physical contact that forms part of the game. Each match lasts fifty minutes and is played on a sand-covered pitch. For the modern tournament, the twenty-seven players are dressed in white (Santo Spirito), red (Santa Maria Novella), green (San Giovanni) and blue (Santa Croce). Once chosen from among the local nobility, the players representing the four districts these days are simply powerful – and ruthless – young men: the fact that you play (or used to play) *calcio storico* is a boast, a sign that you're tough, someone not to mess with. Even if the basic aim is to get the ball in the other team's net – and the game is not exactly "no holds barred" – this is a violent sport, and the games commonly end as they used to: in a general punch-up. All this is in stark contrast to the traditional costumes worn by the players, which are often in shreds by the end of a game. The name of the game may suggest some sort of pageant, but people still remember one match in which a player's ear was bitten off. Some of the rough stuff is even politically motivated, at times requiring the police to intervene; in fact, for a few years the matches in Santa Croce were banned.

DIVINE COMEDY PLAQUES ON BUILDINGS THROUGHOUT THE CITY

" A real treasure hunt?

In the streets of central Florence you'll find a total of thirty-four plaques with quotations from the *La divina commedia*: nine from *Inferno*, five from *Purgatorio* and no less than twenty from *Paradiso*. The latter are primarily related to the Florentine families that Dante mentions in the sixteenth *canto* of that work. Given their number and unity of form, these plaques form a sort of unfolding poetic mural that is unique in the world. However, although they are now considered to be an integral part of the "Stones of Florence", they actually date from a project initiated in 1900, when the City Council appointed a committee of three Dante experts (including Isidoro del Lungo) to identify: (1) lines within the

poem that are in direct relation to the city, either place names and geographical locations or with respect to the characters depicted; (2) the most suitable – and most accurate – places to site such plaques. Seven years were enough for the entire project to be completed, thus setting the seal on the relationship between the poet and the city which raised and then exiled him.

WHERE ARE THE THIRTY-FOUR PLAQUES WITH QUOTATIONS FROM *LA DIVINA COMMEDIA*?

You could undertake a sort of treasure hunt to identify the various locations. Most plaques are clearly visible from public areas: in Via dell'Oca, the courtyard of Palazzo Vecchio and along the Corso there are a good twelve of them. Others, however, are located in more out-of-the-way places. One, for example, is on the tower of the Zecca Vecchia (Old Mint), which is now encircled by outer city boulevards, another is at the foot of the steps leading up to San Salvatore al Monte, and another is even farther out in Piazza San Salvi. For those who can't be bothered to search for all thirty-four, here is a list of all the locations and quotations:

Inferno VIII, 61–63 (Filippo Argenti): Via del Corso, location of the home of the Adimai, parents of Filippo Argenti;

Inferno X, 58–63 (Guido Cavalcanti): Via Calzaiuoli, location of the home of the Cavalcanti;

Inferno X, 91–93 (Farinata): Palazzo Vecchio, first courtyard;

Inferno XII, 146 (Arno): small loggia of Ponte Vecchio;

Inferno XV, 82–87 (Brunetto Latini): Via Cerretani, Church of Santa Maria Maggiore, location of the tomb of Brunetto Latini;

Inferno XVII, 58–60 (Gianfigliazzi): Via Tornabuoni, location of the home of the Gianfigliazzi;

Inferno XIX, 17 (Baptistery): Baptistery, looking towards Via Martelli;

Inferno XXIII, 94–95 (birth of the poet on the banks of the Arno): Via Dante Alighieri, Dante's house;

Inferno XXXII, 79–81, 106–108 (Bocca degli Abati): Via dei Tavolini, where the house of the Abati once stood;

Purgatorio XII, 100–105 (church of San Miniato al Monte and Ponte alle Grazie, formerly Ponte Rubaconte): at the beginning of Via San Salvatore al Monte;

Purgatorio XIV, 16–18 (Arno): Piazza Piave, tower of the Zecca Vecchia;

Purgatorio XXIV, 79–84 (Forese Donati): Via del Corso, near the ruins of Donati Tower;

Purgatorio XXIV, 82–87 (Corso Donati): Piazza San Salvi, where the troops of Henry VII camped near the monastery during the siege of Florence;

Purgatorio XXX, 31–33 (Beatrice Portinari): Via del Corso, location of the home of the Portinari;

Paradiso XV, 97–99 (Florence): Via Dante Alighieri, near the Badia;

Paradiso XV, 112–114 (Belliccion Berti Ravignani): Via del Corso, location of the home of the Ravignani;

Paradiso XVI, 40–42 (Dante's ancestors): Via degli Speziali, location of the home of the Alighieri;

Paradiso XVI, 85–87 (Florentine dignitaries): Via delle Oche, market where the main families of Florence gathered each year;

Paradiso XVI, 94–96 (Cerchi family): Via del Corso, location of the home of the Cerchi;

Paradiso XVI, 101–102 (Galigai family): Via dei Tavolini, location of the home of Galigai;

Paradiso XV, 109–110 (Uberti family): Palazzo Vecchio, first courtyard;

Paradiso XVI, 110–111 (Lamberti family): Via Lamberti;

Paradiso XVI, 112–114 (Visdomini family): Via delle Oche, alongside the ruins of Visdomini Tower;

Paradiso XVI, 115–117 (Adimari family): Via delle Oche, location of the home of Adimari;

Paradiso XVI, 125–126 (Peruzzi family, with symbol of six pears): Borgo dei Greci, location of a gateway on city ramparts;

Paradiso XVI, 127–128, 130–132 (Della Bella family): Via dei Cerchi, location of the home of the Della Bella;

Paradiso XVI, 127–130 (Ugo di Brandeburgo): Via del Proconsolo, location of the Badia, a church where a commemoration service for Ugo di Brandeburgo, called Ugo di Toscana, is still held every 21 December;

Paradiso XVI, 133–135 (Gualterotti family): Borgo Sant'Apostoli, location of the home of Gualterotti;

Paradiso XVI, 136–139 (Amidei family): Via Por Santa Maria, alongside the ruins of Amidei Tower;

Paradiso XVI, 140–144 (Buondelmonti): Borgo Sant'Apostoli, location of the home of Buondelmonti;

Paradiso XVI, 145–147 (remains of the statue of Mars): Ponte Vecchio at the corner with Piazza del Pesce, where the remains of the statue once stood;

Paradiso XVI, 149–154 (old Florence): Palazzo Vecchio;

Paradiso XXV, 1–9 (baptism): Baptistery, looking towards the Duomo;

Paradiso XXXIII, 1–9 (St Bernard's prayer to the Virgin): Piazza del Duomo, but this last plaque has disappeared.

SCUOLO DEL CUOIO (LEATHER SCHOOL)

Santa Croce monastery
Via San Giuseppe, 5 red
• www.scuoladelcuoio.com • Tel: 055 2480337
• Open Monday–Friday from 10.30am to 6pm (for sale of goods)

> *Craft workshops in the monastery of Santa Croce*

After the Second World War two families of Florentine craftsmen who had links with the Franciscan monks of Santa Croce attempted to provide training and work opportunities for some of the numerous young people orphaned by the fighting. They decided to open up a Leather School, fitting out part of the monastery as workshops and teaching rooms. The orphan apprentices, attracted by the chance of training that was as rigorous as it was prestigious, dedicated themselves to their craft with such determination that the products of the Leather School were already attracting clients in 1950. The quality goods were particularly appreciated by the American armed forces, with the school becoming official supplier to the Sixth Fleet and the US Army Air Forces. With a reception like that, the school was guaranteed long-running success in the United States.

Nothing like the usual tourist trap, the school is unique in Florence: not only can you see the craftsmen at work, but its setting is a long frescoed corridor lined with individual monastic cells converted into miniature workshops. The visit ends in a display showroom, where you can buy some of the goods made here: bags, cases, diary covers, luggage and numerous other articles – all *definitely not* "Made in China". You can also enrol for one of the various courses in leather-working that the school organises for the general public. It only takes half a day to learn how to make a leather diary cover (which you then get to keep), or six hours to make a shoulder bag or leather picture-frame.

From the leather workshops you can pass directly into Santa Croce via the Medici Chapel, which was where Galileo was first buried. The grand duke of Tuscany (Ferdinando II de' Medici) managed to have the scholar interred within the church even though he had been considered a heretic. The passage through to the church is itself worthy of note for the display of dramatic photographs depicting the disastrous flood of 1966.
On leaving the school, you pass through a rear courtyard which affords a rare view of the gigantic ensemble formed by the apse of Santa Croce.

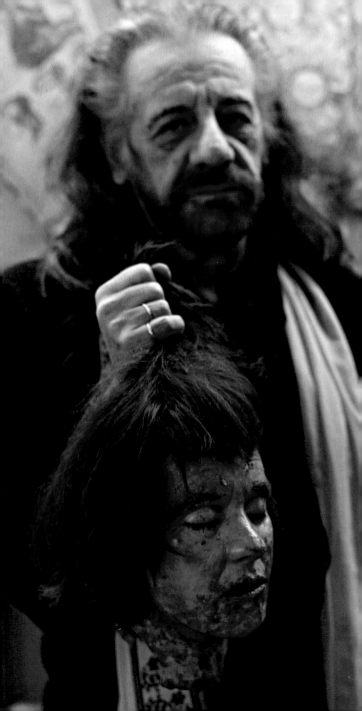

FILISTRUCCHI

Via Verdi
• Tel: 055 2344901
• www.filistrucchi.com
• Guided tours of the workshop on request only

Make-up studio

This shop opened in 1720, and a tour of the interior – and even more so, the back shop – is a real voyage of discovery through all the tricks of show business. The frontage already sets the tone, and when crossing the threshold you have the feeling of entering another era. A point of reference for Italy's actors, acrobats and experts in FX (special effects in both theatre and cinema), *Filistrucchi* makes and sells all sorts of accessories for disguise and make-up. It all began in the eighteenth century, with the fashion for perukes imported from France; then, when local hairdressers learned to make those wigs and perukes themselves, the shop changed its product range, first of all supplying products for stage make-up and disguise and later materials for photographers and advertising agencies. The business can boast collaboration with some of the world's great opera houses – from New York and Boston to all the major houses in Italy – as well as with eminent stage and film designers. Indeed, it is a real rarity nowadays to find a shop that still has its own workshop, where everything is

made to old "recipes" that have been updated to keep up with technical developments. The product range includes not only false moustaches, sideburns and beards, but also the shop's famous latex and papier-mâché face masks, its remarkable false noses and ears and any number of other prostheses (from a witch's pointed chin to a unicorn's horn). You'll also find a full range of make-up products, some intended for the theatre, some for more personal use: there are, for example, a number of wigs and toupees. For Filistrucchi, the entire surface of the human body is a place where three centuries of *savoir-faire* can be brought to bear for a make-over. And it's amazing to discover just how many "tricks of the trade" there are.

The miraculous response of St Minias to decapitation recalls that of
St Denis, Bishop of Paris (see *Secret Paris* in this series of guides). The
phenomenon even has a precise name: *cephalophoria*, from the Greek
kephale (head) and *phorein* (to carry).

STROLLING ROUND THE EDGE
OF FLORENCE'S FORMER AMPHITHEATRE

⑥

Via Torta
Piazza Peruzzi

*Imagine
you can hear
the crowds*

Near Piazza Santa Croce you can enjoy a stroll around an ancient monument that's no longer there. Perhaps disappointing for the tourist in search of spectacular ruins, this walk involves following an unusual curved line along these historic streets, where it takes an effort of the imagination to conjure up a vision of what once stood here.

The line follows the route of Via Torta (which, as a plaque notes, used to bear the significant name of Via Torcicoda (Tail Twister), Via del Parlascio (a *parlascio* or *parlagio* was a medieval term for a place of public assembly) and Via Bentaccordi round to Piazza Peruzzi. These streets form a loop unique in Florence, where roads are usually at right angles to each other. The curve reflects the semicircular outline of the old Roman amphitheatre; built in the second century AD, it could hold up to 20,000 people (Rome Coliseum held up to 80,000) and had an arena of 64 metres by 40. The location was marshy land, as revealed by a number of surviving street names – Via Isole delle Stinche, Via dell'Acqua, Via Anguillara (*anguilla* = eel) – or even the name of the church of San Jacopo tra i Fossi (St Jacopo between the Ditches) that stands in nearby Via dei Benci. As for the name Via Burella, between Via Torta and Via dell'Acqua, it comes from the *burii* of the old amphitheatre, the underground passageways leading to the arenas.

The arch of the doorway at No. 6 Piazza Peruzzi corresponds to the longitudinal axis of the coliseum, and some houses in this street have rooms arranged in a sort of open-fan layout, indicating that they were built using the stones – or perhaps even a stretch – of the old amphitheatre, of which they form the sole surviving trace. The stroll certainly gives an idea of the size of the ancient amphitheatre and of how it was incorporated within the fabric of the developing city.

The Roman amphitheatre of Florence was where St Minias (San Miniato) was martyred. Tradition has it that, in AD 250, the Christian was beheaded in front of a jubilant crowd. However, the decapitated saint then stood erect, picked up his head and, holding it under his arm, walked proudly out of the arena. He then walked quickly to the Arno, crossed the river and went up the hill nearest the city centre. Once at the summit, he fell to the ground – exhausted by his ordeal or overwhelmed by the view. The Basilica di San Miniato al Monte was later built here in his honour.

ORATORY OF THE COMPAGNIA DI SAN NICCOLÒ DEL CEPPO

Via de' Pandolfini, 2
• Monday–Friday, from 5pm to 7pm
• Donations welcome

Children's Oratory

A t the beginning of Via de' Pandolfini is a small door set in a roughcast wall with no decoration or identifying sign; this is the entrance to the now almost forgotten Compagnia di San Niccolò al Ceppo,* one of the oldest confraternities in Florence. Originally set up in the fourteenth century, its premises were located at various places in the city before being transferred here in 1561.

Initially established to provide catechism for the young people of Florence during the day and prayer meetings for adults (in particular, artisan workers) during the late afternoon, the confraternity is still active, although now restricted to offering Mass in this oratory.

Open to all, the oratory has a small vestibule which leads through into a warm and welcoming room with simple wood furnishings and a ceiling with frescoes by Giandomenico Ferretti depicting *Scenes from the Life of St Nicholas*. The *Crucifixion* over the high altar is by Francesco Curradi and replaces what was the oratory's artistic masterpiece: a *Crucifixion with St Nicholas and St Francis* formerly attributed to Fra Angelico but now thought to be the work of Paolo Uccello. (It is now in San Marco museum.) There are also two paintings by the sixteenth-century painter Giovanni Antonio Sogliani: *The Visitation* and *St Nicholas with Two Children of the Compagnia*; these were used during religious processions as the confraternity's banners.

If you'd like to become a member of the confraternity you can join by paying a small fee in the secretary's office. Quite apart from the "spiritual benefit" this affords, you'll then feel you really belong to this charming oratory. The space has recently been rediscovered as a venue for theatre productions, and even when it's still and quiet, the welcoming atmosphere gives some idea of what it must have been like when Florentine youngsters filled these rooms.

---

*Ceppo (trunk) refers to the tree trunk that was hollowed out to receive the offerings of the faithful.

PALAZZO BORGHESE

Via Ghibellina, 110
• Visits require a few days' prior booking and depend on staff availability
• info@palazzoborghese.it
• Tel: 055 2396293
• www.palazzoborghese.it

> *Nineteenth-century extravaganza*

Even though a little cramped in the narrow Via Ghibellina, Palazzo Borghese stands out for its ground floor of undressed stone surmounted by a *piano nobile* (first floor) of neoclassical columns. This exterior gives no idea of the neoclassical opulence within, which does however strike you the moment you step into the entrance hall, where large Egyptian-style statues seem to stand in attendance. A little further on and you come to more statues, more columns and a monumental staircase. These form the core of an architectural composition within which are set mirrors, paintings, marble artefacts and carved capitals. In total, the palazzo has dozens (some say more than forty) rooms, each of which is meticulously decorated in an individual style – and with a certain flamboyance.

The mirror-filled Ballroom contains finely decorated doors and overpoweringly elaborate stucco-work. Then come the Pink Room, the Red Room, the Yellow Room, the Green Room and the … run out of colours? … Middle Room (Salotto di Mezzo), each more sumptuously decorated than the next, and all with richly frescoed ceilings. Then there is the Council Chamber, with its gigantic fireplace, and the room that is the "apotheosis" of the entire palazzo: the Monumental Gallery, which is definitely more of a gallery than a salon, given that it's five times as long as it is wide. On entering you're overwhelmed by the unrestrained luxury of the place: there are huge mirrors with a myriad of ostentatious lamps, niches containing large statues, decorations in gold and white, the inevitable columns, and a large frescoed cupola – combining to make this one of the most luxurious interiors in Florence, indeed in Italy.

This was exactly the intention of Camillo Borghese, husband of Pauline Bonaparte. When he undertook the complete refurbishment of this palazzo in 1822, he didn't hesitate to spend a fortune on the project, employing the city's very best craftsmen and creating a centrepiece for Florentine high society. Later Prince Poniatowski of Poland opened the Casino Borghese here. After extensive restoration in the 1990s, the building is now only open for receptions and other social events.

ORPHEUS FOUNTAIN

⑨

Palazzo Vivarelli Colonna
Via delle Conce, 28
• Open April–October, Tuesday and Thursday from 10am to 6pm

*A
remarkable
pastiche*

The Orpheus fountain is undoubtedly the showpiece of the wonderful garden of Palazzo Vivarelli Colonna. This garden, now open to the public, was a private haven of peace and quiet in the eighteenth century, and this fountain was one of the features added to create a sense of theatrical monumentality. Preceded by a small and elegant nineteenth-century loggia, the fountain – which is so imposing it seems like a shallow grotto – is set against the end wall of the garden. It is a remarkable and very expressive pastiche combining bare rock with painting, mosaic and sculpture.

The melancholy pose and expression of Orpheus himself were probably intended to reflect the grief felt at the premature death of his wife by Francesco Niccolò Gabburri, owner of the palazzo and garden. However, the overall composition – with its two fine side statues, its composition of porous stone, and the large shield made to appear about to fall – seems much more light-hearted (not to say playful) in spirit. The three small satyrs shown holding onto the crooked family shield are in fact Gabburri's children, while the wide cracks in the stone arch are intended as a deliberate tribute to ancient ruins rather than the passing of time.

In the central avenue a small circular fountain with a sculpture of a swan is surrounded by fine examples of aromatic shrubs – orange trees, lemon trees and azaleas – and geometric lawns.

A small copse of magnolias, pine, laurel and oak adds another romantic touch to the garden. And the wrought-iron balustrades, the well-kept pathways, the large urns set atop the enclosing wall, and a third, smaller, fountain (within the loggia) – all make this garden typical of an era that found pleasure in its own image, delighting in what Talleyrand called "*la douceur de vivre*".

FLOOD MARKERS ⑩

Via Ghibellina, corner of Via delle Casine
Via de' Neri, corner of Via San Remigio

An "Arnometer"

At first glance there's nothing special about the corner of Via Ghibellina and Via delle Casine. But on moving a little closer to the building there, you'll find something that reflects an aspect of the city's history: markers of the levels reached by the Arno floodwaters on various occasions. About 1 metre above ground level is the inscription *1547 – ARNO FU QUI A 13 AGOSTO* (1547 – Arno reached here on 13 August), with a line indicating the high-water mark five centuries ago. That particular flood was all the more extraordinary because, unlike the others, it happened at the height of summer. Slightly higher up is a bronze plaque commemorating the disastrous flood of 1844, and then – much higher up (more than 4 metres above ground level) – is the third plaque which reads *IL 4 NOVEMBRE 1966 L'ACQUA D'ARNO ARRIVÒ A QUEST'ALTEZZA* (On 4 November 1966 the waters of the Arno reached this height). What we have here could perhaps be described as an "Arnometer", measuring the behaviour of the river in exceptional circumstances. On the corner of Via San Remigio and Via de' Neri are two other inscriptions, recalling exceptional floods more than six hundred years apart. Higher up – at 4.92m above ground level – is a plaque that indicates the level reached by the floodwaters of the Arno on 4 November 1966, while just below is another marker which refers to the year 1333 and bears the inscription "during the night of Friday 4 November

the waters reached here". Yes, quite incredibly, the two monstrous floods happened on the same date! Apart from those two floods, the worst were those of 1466, 1547 and 1844. None, however, match up to that of 1966, which killed thirty-four people, left 100,000 Florentines trapped on rooftops or in the upper storeys of buildings for a full day and night, swept away 15,000 cars and caused untold damage to the city's art treasures. A torrent of mud, for example, swept into the church of Ognissanti and damaged Botticelli's fresco of *St Augustine*; the magnificent tombs in the church of Santa Croce were buried under 4.5 metres of slime; in the Uffizi the floodwaters reached the third floor. However, miraculously, all the city's bridges withstood the flood.

WINDOW WHERE ELIDE BENEDETTI MET HER TRAGIC END

Via San Giuseppe, opposite the eponymous church

(11)

> *"The city's most moving tragedy"*

Opposite the parish church of San Giuseppe a recent plaque commemorates one of the most moving tragedies in Florentine history. Rather than the inscription, it is the window bars that attract attention, for it was here that Elide Benedetti, the most unfortunate of all the flood victims, died on 4 November 1966.

Elide was 66 years old and confined to a wheelchair. By the time rescuers reached her the water was too high to bring her out through the doorway. Some *carabinieri* therefore raised her in a sheet tied to the window, to keep her above ground level while they went for help – and for something to cut the bars from the outside. The parish priest, Father Giuseppe Baretti, stayed with the poor woman at the window, offering comfort as the situation became more and more dramatic. The flood waters, however, continued their inexorable rise, help did not arrive and Elide was drowned; Father Baretti found his courage failed him and he couldn't stay with her right to the end. A quote from the priest's diary is included on the plaque: "It was the most moving tragedy in the whole city. Assisting helpless while a woman who must die sees death approaching, and solely because we couldn't get through the window bars".

The plaque was raised by the parishes of San Giuseppe and Sant'Ambrogio in 2006, on the fortieth anniversary of the flood. And if you're amazed that it took so long for such a public act of commemoration, you'll be even more so to learn that it took years to obtain the official number of victims. It was only recently that the Associazione Firenze Promuove managed to publish a Police Headquarters document dated November 1966, which gives a total of thirty-four people – seventeen in Florence and seventeen in the surrounding towns – listing the names of each and the circumstances of their death.

PIAZZA DELLA MADONNA DELLA NEVE ⓬

Entrance from Via del'Agnolo or Via Ghibellina

> **Courtyard of the historic Le Murate jail**

This small pedestrian precinct with the poetic name (Madonna of the Snow) is one of the most interesting oases of calm and quiet within Florence as it occupies the courtyard of a former prison. And this was not just any prison, but the famous Le Murate, the main jail in Tuscany and one which was in use right up to the late twentieth century. The hulking presence of a prison within the historic city centre was due to the fact that the structure had originally been a convent for a cloistered Order of nuns (*murate* literally means "walled-up") founded in the fifteenth century.

Before they became cells in the more modern sense of the term, the cells here had housed the nuns who, prior to 1424, had lived in small houses flanking either side of the Ponte Rubaconte. Subsequently renamed Ponte alle Grazie, that bridge was destroyed in the Second World War and then rebuilt – but without the houses that had given it the air of a miniature Ponte Vecchio.

When it was decided in the 1990s to transfer the prison to the new facilities at Sollicciano, outside the city, this area became the object of one of the most ambitious and original redevelopment projects Florence has seen.

The result is that the prison courtyard has been converted into a pedestrian area complete with restaurants and public facilities. And you can finally see part of the exterior of the sixteenth-century Cappella di Santa Maria della Neve, the façade of which was subsequently incorporated within the high prison walls.

From the piazza, which in the summer is busy until late at night but is completely peaceful in winter, you can access some of the prison corridors and the cells leading off them. The whole restoration project was inspired by a desire to satisfy modern tastes while conserving certain features of the old prison; details such as doors, locks, bolts and spy holes are now all valid items of industrial archaeology. This careful attention to the historic past adds to our pleasure that the jail has been "set free".

OLTRARNO

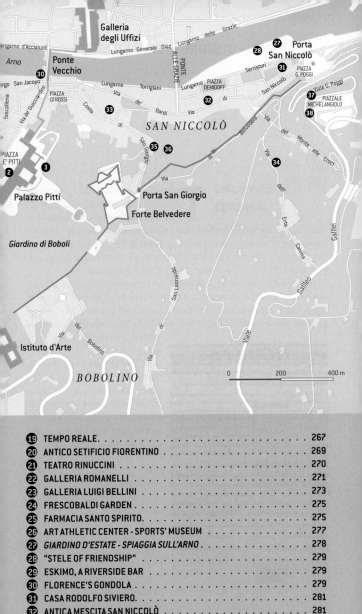

AN ENIGMA IN STONE AT PALAZZO PITTI ❶

Palazzo Pitti
Piazza Pitti

*Concealed
message*

The façade of Palazzo Pitti is powerfully seductive – in part because the frontage appears to extend beyond the field of vision of the naked eye. The very colour of the stones, whose ochre gives an impression of warmth, also adds to the charm of the building. And within the whole are set large, but slightly irregular, windows whose design and distribution reflects the aesthetic canons of the Renaissance.

However, the most striking feature is the arrangement of the protruding rectangular blocks of stone that make up the façade: of varying degrees of regularity, these decrease in size from ground level upwards. This change gives the impression that the stones towards the base were less completely

worked, with the blocks acquiring greater finish as the building rose from the ground. However, there is also an enigma in the organisation of the stones of the façade: in the lower section there are two incongruous blocks, one much longer than the others, one much shorter. It seems that when Luca Pitti had these two stones inserted here he intended that the larger should be identified as himself, and the shorter seen as a derogatory reference to his business rivals, jealous both of his financial success and this huge new palazzo. So this is a "mural jibe". And whether or not this story is true, it's surely no accident that a stone measuring 12 metres in length was set alongside one measuring just half a metre.

It's amusing to try and spot them yourself. But here's a tip: look to the left of the central doorway, between the projecting stone blocks about 2 metres from ground level.

NEARBY

PIAZZA PITTI, 1702

1702? Seeing is believing. Above the door of the building standing just opposite Palazzo Pitti are two numbers: 7 and 1702. Which is the right one? The 1702 is perhaps the last remaining trace of the old system for numbering Florence's houses, in which number 1 was Ponte Vecchio itself. This single system extended in a capillary fashion throughout the city, following an even more complex logic than that found in the street numbers of Venice, where at least the buildings are divided according to *sestieri* (the six districts that make up the city).

In Oltrarno, the first building was numbered 1289, with the numbers also continuing on the other side of the river, reaching beyond 8000 in the Santa Croce district. The whole system was reformed in 1865, introducing the present numbering by street or piazza. This was when the building once numbered 1702 became 7 Piazza Pitti. As for the old system, it's nothing but a memory, although traces can still pose the odd puzzler for the sharp-eyed visitor.

FLORENTINE STREET NUMBERS

There are two systems of street numbers in Florence: private residences have dark blue numbers, while public buildings and business premises have red numbers. As each system follows its own numerical order, it is possible for example to see a blue No. 25 alongside a red No. 3.

The addresses given in this guide respect this special numbering system – when the number is that of business premises, it is followed by the letter "r".

THE SYMBOLISM OF THE STATUE OF 'BACCHUS RIDING A TORTOISE'

③

Boboli Gardens

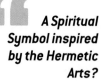

A Spiritual Symbol inspired by the Hermetic Arts?

I n the Boboli gardens – near the entrance to the left of Palazzo Pitti – one encounters a curious fountain showing an overweight male figure riding a tortoise. Setting aside the tone of playful burlesque which was such an integral part of Florentine Mannerist architecture, one might read this statue as combining traditional symbolism and a concealed meaning.

For the Greeks and Romans, Bacchus was the god of wine (here represented by the water of the fountain) and was popularly associated with the orgies that might result from drunkenness. But at a symbolic level, these libations might be associated with inebriating Wisdom, which plunges those who partake of it into an ecstatic state. This means that wisdom might be represented either by the vine or by the wine it produces. Indeed, since the earliest centuries of Christianity, wine had been seen as a symbol of *gnosis*, of divine Wisdom. Bacchus, in fact, was frequently associated with the Phoenician god Baal, "the Supreme Lord", whilst his Greek name, Dionysus, means "God with us".

Thus Bacchus represents the Supreme Godhead (the equivalent of Ganesh in Hinduism), what the Christian Gnostics of the third-fifth century AD called *Christus-Baal*. When Greek civilisation was at its height, the bacchantes were, in fact, chaste virgin priestesses dedicated to the veneration of the god of Wisdom. It was only later, when traditional symbols became distorted and traditional social values deformed, that Bacchus became the god of bacchanals, of excess, in a society that had itself become decadent.

Shown riding a tortoise, Bacchus becomes a symbol of the Supreme Godhead leading his creation: the Universe. In fact, for the Greeks and

Romans, the tortoise was the symbol of a universe made manifest by the power of the Spirit (what the Hindus call *Purusha*) and thus symbolises the Throne of God.

Similarly, the tortoise was a symbol of the Great Work of hermetism, which was based on the three main chemical elements of Sulphur, Mercury and Salt. Sulphur was associated with the head of the tortoise (symbolising Heaven or the Upper Level); the shell suggested the Earth (or Middle Level) and was associated with Mercury. Finally there was the tortoise's belly, an emblem of Hell and the Lower Level associated with Salt.

ALCHEMY AND THE HERMETIC ARTS IN THE BOBOLI GARDENS

Both Cosimo and Francesco de Medici are known to have been interested in alchemy and the hermetic arts, with the Boboli Gardens and the Pitti Palace being just two of the places within the city where one can find traces of this interest. Apart from the statue of Bacchus on a Tortoise (see opposite), another such trace is to be found on the raised walkway between Palazzo Vecchio and Palazzo Pitti, a walkway that Cosimo I commissioned Vasari to design. It is a depiction of a lion wearing a crown adorned at the front with a *fleur de lys*. A symbol of power and light, the lion was associated with the sun and, as the King of the Animals, was seen as embodying strength, wisdom and justice. A guarantee of temporal power and a representation of spiritual power, the lion adorned not only the throne of Solomon but also that of kings in France, Italy and numerous other countries; in the Middle Ages, it also figured upon the thrones of bishops. In medieval iconography, the head and upper body of the lion were taken to embody the divine nature of Christ, whilst the lower part of the body represented his human nature. These two natures were represented by a bridge that was seen as running from the human to the divine and *vice versa*. In alchemy, the "crowned Lion" represents gold, the solar metal. Furthermore, the sign of Leo is set right at the heart of the zodiac. Within the Boboli Gardens there are also columns bearing depictions of reptiles, which some say are lizards, and others dragons. Two of them are intertwined and seem to be fighting, forming the traditional circle "of eternity" which the hermetists called *ouroboros* (the serpent which bites its tail: *ob* means "serpent" in Hebrew whilst *ouro* means "king" in Coptic). This symbolises the resurrection of he who is reborn to a new spiritual life after sloughing off his mortal human condition. In the gardens immediately in front of Palazzo Pitti, an obelisk stands by the side of a water basin. The obelisk, in fact, has the stylised form of Celtic menhirs and ancient Egyptian pyramids. It was said to function as a catalyst of celestial energy and as a condenser of terrestrial energy – what in the East is known as *Fohat* and *Kundalini* and in the West as "sidereal tellurism" and "planetary tellurism". A central junction where these two types of energy are concentrated, the obelisk thus generates vitality in the surrounding area and in those who walk around it. This revitalisation is here represented by the circular water basin. This symbolises the Ocean of Life, the living waters of creation over which the Divine Spirit moved, indicated by the primordial energies captured by the obelisk. In alchemy, that obelisk represents the phases in the Great Work which link together Earth and Heaven, the solid and the subtle, Matter and Spirit. Finally, it indicates the gradual passage from an imperfect state to the raised state of Perfect Being, a veritable "Philosopher of Fire". This state of Perfection is represented inside the palace by the *Fontana della Coppa*, which is surmounted by an infant at whose feet is a bird that looks like the phoenix. This is an anthropomorphic rendition of the Divine Heir who, in the Great Work, corresponds to the Philosopher's Stone, the ultimate aim of alchemy and symbolised by the phoenix. Thus, for those who know how to look, Palazzo Pitti is rich in sacred significance, the silent language of symbols revealing itself to be rich and expressive once its mysteries are unveiled.

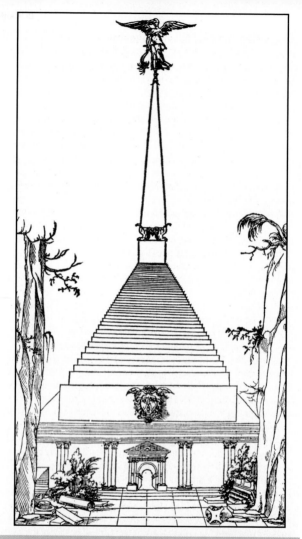

THE UNREQUITED LOVE OF LORENZO DE' MEDICI: AN INSPIRATION FOR POLIPHILO AND SHAKESPEARE?

The doomed love affair of Lorenzo de' Medici and Lucrezia Donati (who was married to Niccolo Ardinghelli against her will) seems to have directly inspired Poliphilo's quest: same name, same events, same timescale (1462-1464)…

The love life of Lorenzo the Magnificent is also thought to have provided the material for Francesco Cei, a poet close to Lorenzo, in his poem *Giulia e Romeo* which directly inspired Shakespeare to write the famous *Romeo and Juliet*.

***POLIPHILO'S DREAM OF THE STRIFE OF LOVE*, AN EXTRAORDINARY HUMANIST ROMANCE THAT DIRECTLY INSPIRED THE GARDENS OF VERSAILLES, BOBOLI (FLORENCE) AND BERNINI'S CELEBRATED ELEPHANT-OBELISK IN ROME**

Printed by Aldus Manutius at Venice in 1499, *Hypnerotomachia Poliphili* (Poliphilo's Dream of the Strife of Love) is perhaps the most complex *roman-à-clef* ever published. Illustrated with around 170 exquisite woodcuts, it is also considered one of the finest examples of early printing.

The book, written in a mixture of Italian, Latin, Greek, Hebrew, Arabic, Spanish, Venetian and a few other dialects, was long considered anonymous. Recent research, however, chiefly led by Emanuela Kretzulesco,* have pointed to Francesco Colonna, as the decorative first letters of each of the thirty-eight chapters spell out the following phrase: *Poliam Frater Franciscus Columna peramavit* ("Brother Francesco Colonna dearly loved Polia"). A nephew of Cardinal Prospero Colonna, Francesco Colonna was part of the circle of Enlightenment figures that included Cardinal Bessarion, the future Pope Pius II and Nicholas V, known as the Renaissance Pope, opposed to the succeeding popes and in particular to Alexander VI Borgia. At a time when the Borgias, against the advice of Pius II and Nicholas V, were seeking to grant the pontiff temporal as well as spiritual power, and the papacy was embarking on a dark period of its history, *Poliphilo's Dream* was consequently rendered deliberately obscure in order to escape papal censure. More than a story of Poliphilo's love for Lucrezia, the book is a spiritual quest of a philosopher passionately devoted to divine wisdom (Athena Polias).

Developing humanist themes, he transmitted in a cryptic way the spiritual testament of a circle of theologians united around Nicholas V, who had undertaken comparative studies of religious traditions going back to ancient Greece and Egypt with great openness of mind, thus reviving the heritage of Pope Sylvester II (Gerbert of Aurillac).

In concurrence with the Florentine Platonic Academy of the Medici and Marsilio Ficino, this group notably included the architect Leon Battista Alberti and Prospero Colonna, as well as being a great inspiration to Pico della Mirandola, Leonardo da Vinci, Nicolaus Copernicus, Giordano Bruno and Galileo.

Poliphilo's Dream reveals that the best way to know God is through Nature, divine creation. With the help of the codes held in the *Hyeroglyphica* of Horus Apollo (Horapollo), it also illuminates the spiritual road that leads there. In an absolutely extraordinary fashion for anyone interested in understanding the background against which *Poliphilo's Dream* evolved, it is clear that it also closely inspired the gardens of Versailles or Boboli in Florence, as well as Bernini's celebrated elephant-obelisk in Rome through the numerous symbols scattered along Poliphilo's route.

WHAT DOES *HYPNEROTOMACHIA* MEAN?

The etymology of the term *Hypnerotomachia* is based on the following Greek words: *hypnos* (sleep) *eros* (love), and *mache* (fight).

Les Jardins du songe. Poliphile et la mystique de la Renaissance. Paris, Magma (only in French and Spanish).

CASA GUIDI

Piazza San Felice, 8
• Tel: 055 354457
• Open 1 April–30 November on Monday, Wednesday and Friday from
3pm to 6pm
• Admission free but donations welcome
• To book the building for a night, consult the site
http://bookings/landmarktrust.org.uk

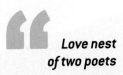

*Love nest
of two poets*

Casa Guidi, largely unknown to both tourists and locals, is a place of charming simplicity. While offering nothing extraordinary, it does give you some idea of the elegant retirement and intellectual peace enjoyed here by its two most illustrious residents. In fact, this apartment is reminiscent of the heyday of the English community in Florence. In a way it should be called Casa Browning, because in 1847 it was rented by one of the most extraordinary poetic couples in the history of literature: Robert Browning and his wife, Elizabeth Barrett Browning (she actually died here in 1861). Apart from a few fine mirrors, the contents of the house are of no particular value: the Brownings bought almost all their furniture from local second-hand dealers. However, the interiors that are still open to the public, more than 150 years later, reveal the sobriety and taste with which they decorated their living space. Indeed, the restoration carried out here by The Landmark Trust and Eton College was predicated on the desire to maintain the full character of the original, with the same woodwork, the same fireplace and the same colours in the painted and roughcast surfaces. Thus a perfectly intact period residence is waiting to be discovered here, complete with bedroom (containing the Brownings' piano), small study, small and convivial kitchen and charming library.

Two busts and two painted portraits give some idea of the affable appearance of Robert Browning and the more austere physiognomy of his wife Elizabeth, whose face is shown framed by thick brown hair. There are also various objects that conjure up some sense of their private life together. The plaque on the outside wall has an inscription by Nicolò Tommaseo, recalling the role this remarkable couple played in consolidating the bond between Britain and Italy at a time when the first wave of British artists was arriving to search for inspiration on the banks of the Arno.

NIGHT AT CASA GUIDI

One of the two bedrooms in the apartment can be rented (maximum six people). An unforgettable way to pass a night in Florence.

ASTRONOMICAL TOWER OF LA SPECOLA ⑤

Via Romana, 17
• www.msn.unifi.it
• Visits by appointment only, with paid guide; cost of guide in addition to admission fee
• To book, call 055 2346760 Monday–Friday from 10am to 2pm, or e-mail edumsn@unifi.it

> *Long-forgotten observatory*

Even though *specola* is an old Italian word for "observatory", few know that the present Museo della Specola was for a long time Florence's Astronomical Observatory. The observatory tower was once a key point of reference for the scientific community within the city. Curiously enough, however, the Specola observatory was built at the foot of a hill rather than on the summit, which would have been a much better place from which to observe the heavens, but the aim was to encourage links between scientific activities in the city centre. The observatory entered into service in 1807, furnished with the most up-to-date equipment and run by renowned scholars. However, it had been planned at the end of the eighteenth century, a period in which a large number of elementary scientific criteria were still unknown. Nevertheless, the Specola Observatory achieved a number of results that established its reputation within the European scientific community. For example, between 1855 and 1857, it identified three comets and carried out various metrological studies that confirmed the discoveries made by the Accademia del Cimento from the mid seventeenth century onwards. Ultimately, its poor location meant that the observatory proper had to relocate to Arcetri. As a result, the various rooms of this building – including the meridian room and the octagonal room allowing for 360° observation of the heavens – fell into disuse, and the place was virtually forgotten. After long and painstaking restoration, the old observatory was reopened in 2009, allowing the public to rediscover this exceptional room. However, if you want to observe the stars it is still better to go up to Arcetri.

NEARBY

FARMACIA PITTI ⑥
Piazza San Felice, 4 red • Tel: 055 224402
Over the centuries this building has served as the business premises of numerous apothecaries, whose ancient name in Italian was *speziali*. In 1427 Cenni di Niccolò owned various buildings in Piazza San Felice, and then in the eighteenth century the Pharmacy of the Grand Duchy was transferred here. The public at that point was only admitted to the first floor, with the apothecary's kilns being located on the ground floor. Later, at the beginning of the nineteenth century, the building was the property of yet another pharmacist, a certain Giuseppe Puliti. Nowadays, the refined interior of the building maintains the style of the Grand Duchy and is thoroughly imbued with a taste for the classical.

SKELETON ROOM

Museo della Specola
Via Romana, 17
• www.msn.unifi.it
• Open 9.30am to 4.30pm; closed Monday, 1 January, Easter Sunday,
1 May, 15 August and 25 December
• Admission to the museum: €6 (full price) and €3 (concessions)
Admission to the Skeleton Room, requiring telephone booking
(055 2346760), Monday–Saturday from 9am to 5pm, according
to availability
• Cost of the (obligatory) guided tour: €30 for groups up to a maximum
of thirty

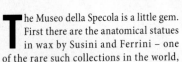

*Museum
of horrors*

T he Museo della Specola is a little gem. First there are the anatomical statues in wax by Susini and Ferrini – one of the rare such collections in the world, although there are two other little-known examples in Paris and Venice (see *Secret Paris* and *Secret Venice* in this series of guides). But this museum also has: a depiction of a decomposing head, which the Syracuse-born artist Zumbo based on a real skull; some rather disturbing *teatri della peste* (plague theatres); and a collection of stuffed animals. Furthermore, in what used to be the stables on the ground floor, you can now once more visit the astonishing Salone dei Scheletri, an even more staggering space that has been closed to the public for years.

With a name that sounds like the title of a horror film, this room has a spectacular collection of animal skeletons contained within 120 glass display cases, arranged like so many huge pieces of furniture. The largest are those of a whale (a sperm whale to be precise) and an elephant, the former suspended from the ceiling to form a sort of aerial exhibit, and the latter set in the centre of the room. There are also various human skeletons – those of a woman, several men and a number of children.

The 40 metre by 7 metre space itself gives the impression of extended perspective, which means that the skeletons have an even more dramatic impact. A period loggia provides further raised exhibition space, thus heightening the impression of being completely surrounded by skeletons.

The room is sometimes used for night-time performances.

SALA DELLE CICOGNE

Astronomical Tower of La Specola
Museo della Specola
Via Romana, 17
• www.msn.unifi.it
• Visits by appointment only, with paid guide; cost of guide in addition to admission fee
• To book, call 055 2346760 Monday–Friday from 10am to 2pm, or e-mail edumsn@unifi.it

*Storks
in full flight*

The "telegraphic-system" meridian in the Specola is almost unique in the world. The only other known meridians of this type are to be found in Bologna and Budapest. Located in the Sala delle Cicogne (Stork Room), this meridian was – together with the astronomical and meteorological observatories – part of the scientific apparatus of the Museo Imperiale e Reale di Fisica e di Storia Naturale that was set up in 1775 by Grand Duke Piero Leopoldo I.

Stretched between two clamps at 60 millimetres above ground level, a metal wire (once a thread of woven hair) traced a line parallel to the meridian. The technical precision here was ultimately nullified by the changes in ground level over the years. Looking at the wire, the meridian could be read on the band of marble and copper on the floor; at the centre of this band runs a thread of silver marked by the signs of the zodiac, which are not merely decorative but indicate the point that corresponds to the passage of the Sun through the various constellations.

This meridian also allowed an observer to identify solstices and solar eclipses, which are indicated by refined depictions of a shining Sun. High up on the wall can be seen the small hole where the ray of sunlight that served as the gnomon entered. Finally, there is the rail-mounted equipment which made it possible to slide a telescope along the axis of the meridian for nocturnal observations; these involved another astronomical instrument

called a *quarantale*.

Remarkable for its various scientific uses as well as its aesthetic qualities, the meridian is located in a room which itself demonstrates how the arts and sciences go together: the Sala delle Cicogne is decorated with a wealth of precious materials and admirable stucco-work depicting twenty storks in full flight.

MUNICIPAL BATHS ⑨

Via Sant' Agostino, 8
• Open daily from 9am to 1pm and 3pm to 7pm
• Closed Sunday

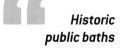

*Historic
public baths*

Whereas they clearly serve a useful purpose, public baths are generally not known for their beauty. But this is what makes the Via Sant' Agostino Baths so unique.

Opened in 1911, these superbly finished baths are a credit to the social policies of the day, which resulted in the creation of such facilities in the heart of one of the most heavily populated districts of Florence – an area where the densely packed housing was poorly ventilated, damp and totally bereft of running water, toilets and bathrooms.

The building as such is not as large as it looks, and is very different in style to those on either side of it: the "Late Secessionist" façade (early twentieth century) contains friezes which give it a rather imposing air.

What is particularly striking, however, is the clear effort that was made to establish an intermediate space between the interior and exterior of the baths. This protective, transitional, area forms a zone of passage, reassuring all those who entered that these public baths had a regenerative function;

they were clearly distinct from the world around them.

Unfortunately, almost nothing has survived of the original interiors. Regrettable restoration work carried out in 1982–83 stripped away the original decorations and finishings, bricked up the façade windows in the interior and completely altered the original layout (destroying the high-ceilinged rooms of the past in order to create an extra floor within the building). Indeed, the whole right wing of the public baths is now separated from the rest of the building and is occupied by the Public Assistance Offices of the Armed Services.

THEATRICAL CROSSROADS

There is certainly no other junction in Florence that has such a high concentration of theatres: within about 100 metres there are at least five, which makes this part of town a must for the theatre-lover.

Starting in Via Santa Maria there is the Teatro Granducale Goldoni, opened in 1817, which is part of the various theatrical arenas known collectively as the *Delices Goldoni*. The sombre façade, complete with small pergola, gives no idea of the magnificence of the interiors: a gallery, three levels of boxes and a central royal box, all within a space decorated with rich stucco-work. Following various vicissitudes, this theatre remained closed for almost fifty years before desperately slow restoration work was completed and it reopened in 1976 (with the boxes still out of use). It was not until the completion of the restoration work that the entire facility was available to the city's cultural life – among other functions it is now home to the *corps du ballet* that performs at the Maggio Musicale Fiorentino festival.

Just alongside is the Cantiere Goldonetta, also known as *Cango*. Long and narrow, this theatre is notable for having been home to Vittorio Gassman's Bottega Teatrale (Theatre Workshop) in the 1980s. It now hosts performances of various kinds as well as *avant-garde* plays.

A little further on is Via de' Serragli, with the now-closed Church of Sant'Elisabetta standing at the corner of Via del Campuccio. The church was once part of a convent of *convertite* – that is, women who had abandoned their former sinful ways and Jewish women who had converted to Roman Catholicism. Complete with a choir once occupied by nuns, the space has been used for the staging of "chamber" works by such dramatists as Beckett and Ionesco.

Opposite, on the corner of Via Santa Maria, stand the premises of the Istituto Artigianelli, onto whose central courtyard gives a theatre that was once the home of a resident theatre company known as *I Ragazzi*. In summer, the courtyard is still used for performances.

Not far from the Artigianelli, at number 105, is the Cinema Goldoni. Awaiting restructuring, this is the third theatre space in the city dedicated to the Venetian playwright. He is also honoured by a statue placed in an eponymous square at the end of Via de' Serragli (just over the Arno), which was raised in the nineteenth century by "Florentine theatre-lovers". The cinema actually stands on the site of yet another one of the *Delizie Goldoni*: the Arena Goldoni, which could hold up to 1,500 spectators and was surrounded by gardens laid out with lawns and shrubbery "for open-air entertainments, village fêtes and gymnastic displays". The site was then built over at the end of the nineteenth century, with Gordon Craig later leasing the premises to house an experimental drama school, now commemorated by a plaque on the façade. Craig's technique involved a revolutionary use of games, intended to transform the actor into a sort of "super puppet" whose mind had total and assured control over each movement of the body. Craig was also the backer of Florence's very first magazine dedicated entirely to theatre, *The Mask*. The "arena" was converted into a cinema in 1935, although it is still used periodically for variety theatre.

CORSI ANNALENA GARDEN

Via dei Serragli, 133
• Visits by kind permission of the owners
• Tel: 055 2280105 or e-mail scarsellistefania@yahoo.it

Modest in size, the Corsi Annalena garden is laid out in terraces overlooking Via dei Serragli, *Hanging garden of Oltrarno*

terracing undoubtedly being the best way of organising a garden when there is little surface area. The result affords a panoramic view of the countryside around Florence, extending from the urban fabric itself to the vast green area of Parco dei Torrigiani and the hills beyond. There is even an underground passageway linking this garden to the Boboli and to the Parco dei Torrigiani, making it possible to get from the Palazzo Pitti to the countryside beyond the city walls without being disturbed. However, this is only one of the secrets of this garden, which owes its name to Countess Anna Elena Malatesta. In the fifteenth century she had a monastery built here, which was subsequently destroyed by Cosimo I as a defensive measure during a war with the Sienese. Later the site was acquired by the Corsi family, who at the beginning of the nineteenth century commissioned Giuseppe Manetti to design the layout of what would be the first "Romantic" garden in the city, complete with all the associated amenities. You can anticipate what lies inside the garden from the external corner between Via Romana and Via de' Mori, where stands a Tempio del Canto (Temple of Song). A good 3 metres above pavement level – thus revealing the raised level of the garden itself – this "kiosk" is complete with a niche for a statue of Mercury, the god of travellers, who stood there to welcome the visitors who entered Florence by the Siena road.

The entire garden is, in fact, full of statues – from a complete series of *The Muses* in terracotta to a copy of Verrocchio's *Putto with Dolphin*. There is also a greenhouse, a fountain and, alongside the terrace, decorative stucco-work and a semicircular bench in wrought iron. This admirable garden forms a wonderful aesthetic ensemble – and it is well worth applying to the owners for permission to visit.

MULTIPLE REINCARNATIONS OF A FLORENTINE PALAZZO

Pensione Annalena - Via Romana, 34 • Tel: 055 222402

In his *Istorie fiorentine (Florentine History)*, Machiavelli tells the tragic story of the beautiful Annalena Orsini, an orphan who was adopted by Cosimo the Elder after her father had been killed in battle. Annalena later saw her husband killed as well – murdered by a man whose advances she had rejected – and she then took religious orders, turning her palazzo into a convent. This was just one of a long series of changes in the use of the building: later occupied by military headquarters (linked to Boboli Gardens by underground passageways), it subsequently became the residence of Bonaparte's sister, a religious school for young noblewomen, a casino, a luxury brothel and then a hospice at the beginning of the twentieth century. Since 1919 it has been a boarding-house popular with actors and artists.

GIARDINO TORRIGIANI

Via dei Serragli
• Visits, lasting 1½ hours, are organised on request;
contact susanna@giardinotorrigiani.it or call 349 2868449
• www.giardinotorrigiani.it

*Oltrarno's
private park*

Torrigiani is more than just a private garden, it is a proper park: the wonderful open space extends over 6 hectares of land between the old city walls in Viale Petrarca and Via dei Serragli. Indeed, at one time it actually covered a total of 10 hectares, thanks to various land purchases made by the Torrigianis in the years 1802–17.

It was Luigi Cambray Digny – later followed by Gaetano Baccani – who designed this park, which has a rich variety of plants and numerous decorative features – from trimmed hedges to geometrical layouts and stage-set style avenues. Note Pio Fede's neoclassical monument dedicated to Piero Torrigiani, and the large neo-Gothic tower. The tower was the work of Baccani himself and is complete with an external spiral staircase and a small observation platform at the top. It has actually become one of the symbols of Oltrarno – even if the Florentines themselves only catch a glimpse of it on the other side of the park walls.

NEARBY

RICCARDO BARTHEL

Via dei Serragli, 234 red • Tel: 055 2280721

For years now Barthel has been recycling old bathroom and kitchen fittings, turning them into choice items of furnishing that are appreciated by a clientele throughout Italy and beyond. A visit here is essential if you're looking for an old type of sink or stove that can't be found elsewhere; however, it is also a voyage of discovery in the history of domestic interiors, be they bathrooms, kitchens or dining rooms. Whatever your tastes in interior design, you won't regret stopping off here, where you'll get the impression of sampling the silent atmosphere of days gone by.

FARMACIA DE' SERRAGLI

Via dei Serragli, 94 red • Tel: 055 289880

This elegant little pharmacy is remarkably *bijou* in both appearance and atmosphere. In service since the nineteenth century, its fittings are entirely in white wood with a gilded trim, characteristic of the period. The space itself is contained under a vaulted ceiling. All in all, a real gem.

FRANCIABIGIO'S *LAST SUPPER*

Monastero della Calza
Piazza della Calza, 6
• Open daily 2pm to 3.30pm
• Book at least a day in advance; by phone at 05 522 2287 or write to calza@calza.it
• Guided tours can be organised
• Closed during the week of 15 August
• Admission free

> **The last *Last Supper* still in a working refectory**

The most unusual *Last Supper* in Florence is by the Italian Renaissance painter Franciabigio, who may be less famous than others who have tackled this classic theme but whose highly original work does have the distinction of being the only one still hanging in a working refectory (the dining room of the youth hostel run by the Monastero della Calza).

However, you don't have to be a guest here to view the work, which is remarkably dynamic in composition. Judas, undoubtedly touched by Christ's words, is so troubled that he appears about to upset the salt cellar and knock over the stool on which he is sitting; the other apostles are shown caught up in discussion, with one about to rise from the table; and the wind seems to have caught one of the window shutters. In contrast to all this, St John rests his head on Christ's right shoulder – a gesture of calm intimacy.

FLORENCE'S EIGHT *LAST SUPPERS*

Dating from 1514, Franciabigio's dynamic composition should be compared with the eight other frescoes of *The Last Supper* in Florence (more than any city in the world). These works are dotted across the city map like the stars of a constellation, featuring in the old city centre, in the Oltrarno district and even in suburban areas. You could visit them all, one after the other, to appreciate their variations on the theme – beginning for example with Andrea del Sarto's work at San Salvi, followed by Ghirlandaio's two *Last Suppers* at Ognissanti and the Monastery of San Marco, Andrea del Castagno's at Sant'Apollonia and Taddeo Gaddi's at Santa Croce. The lesser-known works are Andrea Orcagna's at Santo Spirito, Fuligno's at Sant'Onofrio and this Franciabigio at the Monastero della Calza.

The variety is explained by the rivalry between the Florentine monasteries and convents, and its art patrons – whose tastes may even be reflected in the trees or dishes depicted in these frescoes.

ACCADEMIA BARTOLOMMEO CRISTOFORI

Via Camaldoli, 7 red
• Tel: 055 221646
• www.accademiacristofori.it • info@accademiacristofori.it
• The museum can be visited during concerts
• Other visits, on payment and with a guided tour by a qualified musician, can be booked by contacting 349 2653334, with at least two weeks' notice • Groups must comprise at least ten people

> *Friends of the precursor of the piano*

A t the heart of the San Frediano district, the green doorway at number 7 (red) Via Camaldoli gives access to an old factory that has been refurbished by the architect Temistocle Antoniadis. The place now houses a veritable gem of Florentine cultural life, which is still largely unknown outside the district itself.

This exemplary private institution is named after Bartolomeo Cristofori, the inventor of the pianoforte, and it would be difficult to find a place that offered a fuller range of services and events within a warmer or more welcoming atmosphere.

The first part of the institute comprises a veritable museum of the pianoforte, with various organs and numerous rare examples of this precursor of the modern-day instrument. Now long forgotten, the pianoforte had its own very particular sound and was made entirely from wood, without any metal reinforcements. Within the instrument, the hammers that strike the cords are padded with leather rather than felt (as in a modern piano), although it was possible, by means of a special pedal, to insert a piece of felt between the hammer and cord to obtain a more diaphanous sound, perfectly suited to the repertoire that runs from Mozart through Beethoven to Schubert. Another pedal, known as the Janissary or Turkish pedal, created a very resonant effect, while a third produced the sort of sonorities associated with the bassoon.

Along with this remarkable collection of instruments, the academy has a specialist library and a workshop renowned for its restoration of musical instruments. Most importantly there is also a hundred-seat auditorium used for the two main activities of this charming institution: a season of chamber music concerts (on average, two per month) and master classes given by highly skilled musicians.

The "ABC", as the members of the academy like to refer to it, is open to the public during concerts and restoration projects, or on request for a private visit. It provides the perfect opportunity to learn something about the now rare pianoforte. There is even a chance to try out what it sounds like when played.

HISTORIC JEWISH CEMETERY

Viale Arisoto, 16
• Open the first Sunday of each month, from 10am to 12pm, with guided tours from 10am to 11am • Admission: €3 (full price) and € 2 (concessions) • At extra cost, guided tours for groups can be organised outside usual opening hours • Tel: 055 2346654
• Restoration work began in 2009 and is expected to continue for a few years, making more extensive visits possible

> *Old Jewish tombs in San Frediano*

Like Venice, Florence has a historic Jewish cemetery, even if this one dates from rather later: 1777. At the foot of the city walls and just a short walk from the San Frediano Gateway, this sacred place is curiously surrounded by buildings of several storeys – hardly a setting that creates a meditative atmosphere – and is located near a nursery school. In fact built on land that once belonged to the cemetery, this school was the fruit of building speculation that verged on profanation. One result, for example, was that certain eighteenth-century gravestones were moved haphazardly to near the entrance to the cemetery, with most being set upside down by workmen who clearly couldn't read Hebrew.

In line with Jewish tradition, there are neither images nor photographs of the deceased on the tombs. However, the tombs themselves are remarkably varied and it is this variety that makes the cemetery so eclectic and interesting. Along with simple gravestones and stelae, there are also tombs in the form of a sarcophagus or a small temple, or even an Egyptian pyramid (the Levi family tomb). Two other monumental tombs will certainly not pass unnoticed. One is a burial chapel designed by Treves, the architect of Florence's main synagogue, in the form of a sumptuously decorated colonnaded kiosk, while the other is a burial chapel in Egyptian style, which seems about to succumb to the weight of shrubbery covering it.

The cemetery is resisting real-estate speculation as best it can. It was closed in 1870, after having been in existence for almost a century, and only recently has the decision been taken to reopen it to the public one day a month. However, it still has a very neglected appearance. Nevertheless, the cypress-lined paths, the age of its strange tombs and the nonchalance that seems to be an integral part of Jewish culture, all retain the very particular charm of the place, in spite of its setting among the workaday buildings of this part of San Frediano.

NEARBY

MOLERIA LOCCHI

Via Burchiello, 10 • www.locchi.com • Tel: 055 2298371
If you are unlucky enough to smash the cut-glass decanter from your grandmother's dining service, do not despair. The craftworkers of the Moleria Locchi (set up at the beginning of the twentieth century), can help. The incomparable skill and technical know-how are, in themselves, a guarantee of the continuing traditions of Florentine craftsmanship.

SPAZIO ARTI E MESTIERI (SAM)

Florence Foundation for Artistic Crafts
Vecchio Conventino
Via Giano della Bella, 20–21
• Open to the public Monday–Friday from 8am to 6pm, on request
• Tel: 055 2322269
• www.spaziosam.it • info@fondazioneartigianato.it

> *In search of vanishing crafts*

Near Piazza Tasso, in the outlying area of the historic city centre, is an old convent that has been converted into a centre housing workshops and various other initiatives intended to keep the city's numerous traditional crafts alive. This cloistered structure, the last convent ever built in Florence (at the end of the nineteenth century), actually had a rather eventful history. Just a few years after its completion, it was requisitioned by the military authorities, serving first in the First World War as a military hospital and then as a sanatorium for those returning from the debacle of Caporetto. After the war, the building was in such a state that the nuns refused to set foot in it, thus the Conventino – "little convent", as it began to be known – passed into private ownership and then, during the twenty years of fascist rule, served first as the premises for numerous artists' studios and then housed the clandestine printshop of the Communist newspaper *L'Unità*. It was also a meeting place for various anti-fascists, including partisan fighters (one of whom was the future President of the Italian Republic, Sandro Pertini). Ultimately, the building became the secret headquarters of the Oltrarno National Liberation Committee. When, in the post-war period, the Conventino was threatened with demolition by property developers, it was saved through the intervention of the City Council, who ultimately bought back the buildings in this area in 1975. There followed, however, a long period of neglect, then apparently interminable restoration. Nevertheless, the "little convent" finally reopened its doors in 2002, with the aim of nurturing and promoting the quality crafts of Florence. Still, the facility has yet to attract the local attention that it deserves. What used to be the nuns' cells now house a total of thirty-five workshops, whose products are sold direct to the public. Those who create their wares here include bookbinders, engravers, ceramicists and marquetry-workers. The presence of these and other craftworkers means that a visit to the Conventino is rather like a promendade through a "craft skills reserve," where ancient trades are protected against the threat of extinction. The scope for cultural discovery here has now been further expanded by the addition of two spaces that will house workers from other countries, who come here to demonstrate different skills and techniques. Home to the Florence Foundation for Artistic Crafts and its own training school, the Conventino is thus a veritable museum of the "minor arts". And if you are tired out by walking around the place and inspecting the tempting goods on sale, you can always rest awhile in the old cloister, which together with the garden and well has been fully restored.

TEMPO REALE

Villa Strozzi
Via Pisani, 77
• www.temporeale.it
• Visits on request; info@temporerale.it; Tel: 055 717270; or during public events

> **Crystalline notes of electronic music**

Villa Strozzi stands on a hill overlooking Florence and its top floor is occupied by offices, artistic workshops and two "study spaces" that host events bearing witness to the long-standing relationship between the composer Luciano Berio and the city of Florence.

The Tempo Reale (Real Time) workshop that the famous composer founded remains a rare pearl in Italy. Reflecting a Florence very different to the usual "open-air museum", it demonstrates that the city can and must develop a future alongside its legendary past, participating fully in all the innovation made possible by modern technologies.

The researchers at this centre dedicated to electronic music have developed software for the "spatialisation" of sound, plus an instrument called a MEEG (Max Electronic Event Generator), which is used to programme works of electronic music, frequently for the centre's own productions. The entire scheme follows in the footsteps that Berio himself had taken within this new domain. In fact, his own compositions often figure in the events at Tempo Reale, which organises concerts; makes exceptional quality electronic instruments available to musicians and composers; and holds seminars and study workshops that are intended to "train" not only composers and orchestra musicians but also the general public.

A visit to the centre takes you through archives that are truly unique in Italy, offering the chance to see computers and other electronic instruments whose limitless musical potential is not immediately obvious. In short, this is a trip into the future, amid the most remarkable sounds – and silences. Those who are already familiar with contemporary music will discover more about the ever-shifting boundaries of what can be achieved through the creative use of electronics. And, for those who are being introduced to such music for the first time, Tempo Reale offers a glimpse into a future of things never seen, sounds never heard – a world as mysterious as the process of creation itself.

ANTICO SERTIFICIO FIORENTINO

Via Bartolini, 4
• www.anticosetificiofiorentino.it
• Open Monday–Friday from 9am to 1pm and 2pm to 5pm
• Tel: 055 213861

Perfect
silk

Access to the Antico Setifico Fiorentino is like something from a fairytale – through a gate and a silent garden. Inside is a craft workshop that stands comparison with any museum. Every corner of the place is rich in history, bearing witness to the skill – and power – of the glorious Arte della Seta (Silk Guild), one of those trade corporations that contributed to the wealth of Florence and to its reputation throughout Europe.

These premises in San Frediano became home to the guild in 1786, established thanks to the combined efforts of various Florentine families who obtained a licence to pursue the craft from the ruling powers of the day (first the grand duke, then the king).

Florence has been producing fine-quality silk since the fifteenth century, and despite competition from low-cost products on the international market, this ancient silkworks continues to manufacture fabrics using eighteenth-century looms and machines, old weave patterns and stencils, and hand-dyeing techniques. The range of patterns presently on offer has been updated on the basis of the fabrics to be seen in Renaissance and Mannerist paintings.

On display is a mule jenny, on which the thread was drawn from the skein and then wound around bobbins; a small cultural gem in itself, this seems to bridge the gap between craft tradition and industrialisation. And then, of course, there are the eighteenth-century looms.

Maintaining the tradition of Florentine silkmaking, this old silkworks has continued to innovate and add to its range of products, which now runs from original-style fabrics to high-quality modern-style upholstery. It also accepts individual commissions.

There's an amazing amount on offer at this workshop, where time seems to have stood still.

TEATRO RINUCCINI

㉑

Palazzo Rinuccini
Via Santo Spirito, 39

Well-hidden theatre

Standing in the heart of the Oltrarno area, Palazzo Rinuccini – after a period of glory – knew the fate of the numerous patrician residences within the city that became the premises of either a school or some official institution. However, this particular palazzo does hold a hidden treasure: to the side of the building at the corner of Via Maffia (on the left) nestles the Teatro Rinccini. This tiny space was built in 1753 to designs by Giulio Mannaioni, which envisaged the demolition of a few neighbouring houses in order to build an entirely new wing for the palazzo. Since 2004 the Provincia di Firenze (Provincial Government) has been undertaking restoration work. However, even before the theatre reopens, you can with a little luck and, above all, patience perhaps manage a glimpse inside by asking either the building porter or the site foreman. The Teatro Rinuccini is one of the few remaining examples of such private theatres. The ninety seats in stucco-work are contained within a space complete with a pretty balcony that runs around three sides, rather like a miniature gallery. The ceiling is frescoed and the large central chandelier gives the place something of the air of a private salon. Eduardo De Flippo was supposed to open his drama school here, and it was with this project in mind that the theatre was restored in 1975. But that scheme came to nothing, and now thirty years later Teatro Rinuccini is again undergoing work, without it being clear to what use the space will be put. Instead of theatrical performances, the place has recently served as a lecture hall for the Istituto Tornabuoni.

GALLERIA ROMANELLI

Bordgo San Frediano, 70
• Tel: 055 2396662

**Headquarters
of a dynasty
of sculptors**

S et in place in 1922, the plaque on the façade of 70 Borgo San Frediano commemorates the fact that this was the site of the studio of Pasquale Romanelli. A pupil of Lorenzo Bartolini, he was responsible for various Florentine monuments – for example, the statue of Francesco Ferrucci in the Uffizi arcade.

For six generations, the Romanelli dynasty has created works that are scattered throughout the city: Raffaello sculpted the statue of Donatello in the church of San Lorenzo, along with the famous bust of Benvenuto Cellini on Ponte Vecchio and the large monument to Cosimo Ridolfi in Piazza

Santo Spirito, whereas Romano created Hercules and the Lion in Piazza Ognissanti.

This centuries-old tradition is kept alive nowadays by the Sculpture School opened by another Raffaello Romanelli – and his brother, Vincenzo – in Borgo San Frediano, with the historic workshop of the famous family becoming a museum filled with works not only by the Romanelli but also by Bartolini and other Florentine sculptors. Together with original works in marble and bronze there are copies and plaster casts. Overall, the collection ranges from equestrian monuments to small reproductions, and portraits to mythological figures.

GALLERIA LUIGI BELLINI

Lungarno Soderini, 5
- www.bellinimuseum.org
- Open Monday, Tuesday and Friday from 10am to 1pm and 4pm to 7pm
- To visit the museum, call 055 214031 or e-mail info@bellinigallery.com
- Admission €10, but ticket can be used for three consecutive visits

Private museum of a dynasty of antiquarians

Among the grand palazzi that dominate the Arno waterfront is a small building consisting of just a ground floor and first floor, with a large window and central balcony. Classical in form, this light and airy structure dates from the beginning of the twentieth century and was designed by the local architect Adolfo Coppedè. On the façade you can't miss the imposing mosaic sign which reads Museo Bellini. However, most tourist guides fail to mention the existence of this museum, which is in fact the business premises of a dynasty of antiquarians who have been dealing in *objets d'art* since the eighteenth century.

Among the works on display there are some that undoubtedly make it worthwhile to make a special trip. The collection, fruit of the professional experience and expertise of the Bellinis, includes a portrait by Tintoretto, a *Holy Virgin* by Luca Della Robbia, a small bronze by Giambologna, and another bronze sculpture attributed to Donatello. Note also the antique furniture, particularly a marquetry-work cabinet by Sansovino.

In the museum library are manuscripts, rare books, specialist publications and art magazines.

While a visit to this patrician building is worthwhile solely for the spectacular view it affords of the Arno, its real charm is the exhibition of exceptional masterpieces within a private and rather intimate setting, making it possible to fully appreciate the history of the Bellini family and its centuries-old experience in the arts.

FRESCOBALDI GARDEN

Via Santo Spirito, 11
• Tel: 055 211330
• Visits on request to the caretaker on any day except Sunday, from 7.30am to 7.30pm, but preferably in the afternoon

In the heart of Santo Spirito

The palazzo of the Frescobaldi was once referred to simply as Casa del Cortile (House with the Courtyard) because of the vast garden that is tucked away within it. Although hardly noticeable from the outside, the enclosed garden does have a stunning backdrop: a remarkable view of the wonderful church of Santo Spirito. In the first half of the seventeenth century, Matteo Frescobaldi decided to redevelop a number of properties in Via Santo Spirit that belonged to his family in order to build the present palazzo. Part of that work involved the layout of the garden that can be seen today. The approach is through a large porch that acts as a sort of airlock between the dense urban fabric of the old city centre and this haven of greenery so richly suited to meditation. Passing through this "decompression chamber", you enter one of those small private gardens that are the pride of central Florence, where artifice and nature seem to work together to create an oasis of silence and beauty. Until a few years ago the place was also graced with two bronze sculptures that admirably exemplified the work of the great Arnaldo Pomodoro. However, even if they have gone, there is still plenty to discover in this impeccably maintained *hortus clausus*: the lawn surrounded with azaleas; the statue of the god of Arcadia himself, Pan; and a large fountain modelled from monumental sponges (an architectural reminder of the period in which Casa del Cortile was built).

NEARBY

FARMACIA SANTO SPIRTIO

Piazza Santo Spirit, 12 red • Tel: 055 214032

Anton Francesco Grazzini may have been a playwright, but he was above all one of the most famous apothecaries of Renaissance Florence, living in the building which stands alongside the present-day pharmacy. The Pharmacia Santo Spirito is in fact thought to be one of the oldest in the city, having been in business since the beginning of the sixteenth century; it was, however, reopened and revamped in 1908. Only the building itself dates back to the original period, with a chessboard-design floor and subtly modelled vaulted ceiling. The furnishings with white glass frontages, the rich collection of glass and porcelain apothecary vases, the chairs, woodwork and elegant counter – all give the place the atmosphere of a sitting room. However, this harmonious interior is the fruit of a recent restoration carried out to honour the memory of Anton Francesco Grazzini, who is also commemorated by a plaque in the nearby Via delle Caldaie.

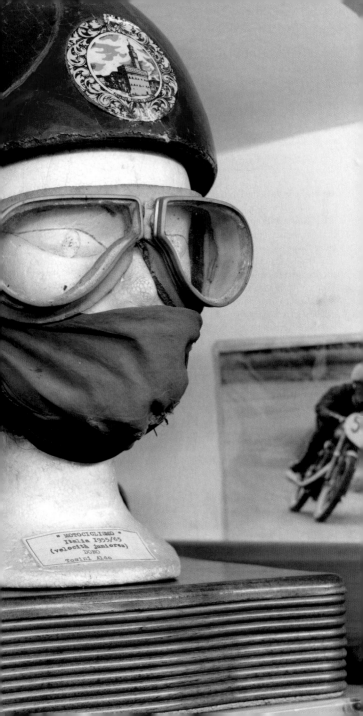

« MOTOCICLISMO »
Italia 1955/65
(velocità juniores)
UONO
Tosini Aldo

ART ATHLETIC CENTER - SPORTS' MUSEUM 26

Via Maggio, 39
• Free admission; visits by appointment
• Tel: 055 217294

> **The history of sport recounted within a Florentine Palazzo**

Amuseum of sports equipment is already a rarity in Italy. But this one is made all the more special by the fact that it does not stand alongside some sports hall but is contained within a *palazzo* in the patrician Via Maggio – with an interior of Florentine terracotta floors and coffered ceilings. The owner of the place is himself an "original": Florentine by birth, he has managed to combine his activity as a weightlifter (an Italian record-holder in 1969) and his taste for collecting sports artefacts. Since the 1960s, he has put together a collection that offers a very representative picture of sporting customs and practices.

The 200 m² of exhibition space are divided into two floors, and offers everything one might hope to find here: from the inevitable fencing masks to curious "insect traps for fishing", from balls to riding equipment. There is even a perfect half-scale version of an early-twentieth-century FIAT sports car in black and red, as well as golf clubs and bicycles made by the French company Michaux in 1865.

Each piece of equipment illustrates the history of a sport and the passionate interest of its practitioners. Look, for example, at the range of wooden cylinders which were worn over the hand and used to knock a ball back and forth in the game of *pallone col bracciale*; it was for this sport that the City Council built the Fascine Sphaeristerium in 1895, a structure which is now a listed building.

Though not part of the obvious tourist circuit, this unusual museum has continued to grow since 1964. In itself, it exemplifies the sort of persistence and resolution that are typically Florentine – qualities which have enabled the owner of the house to put together a collection which combines sport with art and history.

GIARDINO D'ESTATE – SPIAGGIA SULL'ARNO **㉗**

Piazza Poggi
June to September, 10.30am to 7.30pm

> **Sunbathing
> along the river**

Giardino d'estate – spiaggia sull'Arno (Summer garden – beach on the Arno) is the grand-sounding name (inspired by the famous "Paris-plage" on the banks of the Seine) given to designate a new way of enjoying not necessarily the Arno as much as its eroded banks. In the past few years, the city has begun to realise the potential of the riverbanks which, in any other European city, would be a favourite site for relaxation.

The beach project begins with an open-air bar on Piazza Poggi before heading to the river's edge where a large section of the banks have been pleasantly covered in green grass. This is followed by a wide strip of sand closer to the river; a row of bushes separates the sand from the water. This recreational area is dotted with a few wooden cabins (one equipped with refreshing jets of water), but also deckchairs, beach chairs, parasols and showers.

Despite their apparent curiosity, few Florentines, and even fewer tourists, venture onto this "beach", to the point that it's doubtful how many even know about it. Besides the sunbathing and the opportunity to relax in front of the superb palazzos and bell towers overlooking the Arno, this spot is a particularly advantageous place from which to observe sedentary and migratory species such as moorhen and grey heron.

NEARBY

"STELE OF FRIENDSHIP"

On Piazza Poggi, don't miss the "Stele of Friendship", a sculpture designed for the tenth anniversary of the Arno flood (4 November 1966), "in the good care of local organisations, in recognition of the city's gratitude to the angels of the river and all those who specifically demonstrated their solidarity to Florence in these tragic circumstances" – a commemorative initiative to thank the volunteers who helped Florence rise out of the waters.

ESKIMO, A RIVERSIDE BAR

Also in the Oltrarno district is the Eskimo, a riverside bar equipped with several beach chairs and parasols set up along the wall of the dam between Ponte alla Carraia and Ponte Vespucci. There may not be any green spaces here, but it's located right beside the Arno falls, which makes the experience all the more refreshing.

FLORENCE'S GONDOLA
Arches of Ponte Vecchio

On the Oltrarno side of the bridge, a Venetian gondola can be seen moored most of the time near one of the piers, out of the way but clearly visible at water level (less so from the embankment). In winter, the vessel is generally covered with a tarpaulin, although it is left uncovered in summer. This fine boat belongs to a Florentine boat-owner, who – with the permission of the nearby Florence Rowing Club – uses it along the stretch of water that runs from Ponte Vecchio to Ponte alla Carraia. However, it is only the lucky few who actually see the gondola gliding along the river Arno, whereas it is much easier to take advantage of the unusual "photo op" provided by the gondola when it is moored at night to Ponte Vecchio. Compared with Venice's network of narrow waterways or the broad sweep of its Grand Canal, this stretch of the Arno is nothing special, and the poor gondola may at times feel out of place. However, the Florentine palazzi overlooking the river are in no way inferior to their Venetian counterparts – nor are the city's muskrats in any way less "imposing" than Venice's famous *pantegane*. What is very different is the behaviour of the water itself, and the gondola must be very careful when negotiating the Arno's dangerous spates. It is said that a previous gondola was in fact carried away by the current and seriously damaged – to the great regret of the owner and of Florence itself (which lost this very special guest). It is also said, although you would be justified in doubting it, that Venetian gondoliers were so proud of this ambassador of their own city within Tuscany that they actually contributed to the cost of the new gondola.

CASA RODOLFO SIVIERO

Lungarno Serristori, 1
• Tel: 055 2345219
• Open throughout the year on Saturday from 10am to 6pm, Sunday from 10am to 1pm and Monday from 10am to 1pm
• Admission free
• To visit outside the above opening hours, consult the site www.museocasasiviero.it or apply directly to the museum curator, who himself takes round guided tours, by e-mail at casasiviero@regione.toscana.it

> **Collection of the guardian angel of looted collections**

A little gem in its own right, Casa Rodolfo Siviero is unlike any other Florence museum and yet has difficulty establishing a public reputation for itself, in spite of various attempts at promotion. The building stands alongside the Arno at the foot of the immense Porta San Niccolò, the only city gateway that has kept its original size. Being sheltered by hills it didn't suffer the fate of all the others, which were lowered to protect them from imperial artillery during sieges. Designed by Poggi, the structure is complemented by a pleasant garden and its contents recount the adventurous life of Rodolfo Siviero. During the Second World War, this hero would, with legendary success, undertake a long-running struggle against the Nazis who so avidly coveted the artworks in Italian collections. His work in fact continued after the end of the war, when Siviero revealed himself to have remarkable gifts as both diplomat and secret agent, using his personal charm and connections to recover innumerable works of art. Thanks to his tenacity and extraordinary knowledge of his field, he was responsible for the recovery of numerous masterpieces that had been taken from collections in Italy and, above all, France. The complexity of his personality is reflected in the eclecticism of the collection that is now on display in his house. Together with a small group of far from negligible twentieth-century works, which include pieces by such artists as Ardengo, Soffici, Manzù, De Chirico and Annigoni (all Siviero's friends), there are also paintings and sculptures from various periods, along with a few archaeological pieces.

Sometimes concerts and performances are held in Casa Siviero, the private rooms of which retain a sense of the owner and collector's presence – that mixture of good taste and sly wit which is so typically Florentine.

NEARBY

ANTICA MESCITA SAN NICCOLÒ

Via San Niccolò, 60 red • Tel: 055 2342836

This *antica mescita* (tap-room) is indeed ancient. When it served merely as a tavern, it sold wine that was exempt from customs duty, but then at the beginning of the nineteenth century it was converted to an inn. The room as such dates back to the tenth century, and in part comprises the crypt of the adjacent church of San Niccolò. The great boast of this hotel is that its interior is one of the few vestiges of Romanesque architecture in Florence, with columns and vaulted ceilings of bold simplicity.

VIA DEL CANNETO

Between Via de' Bardi and Costa delle Magnolie
• Not to be confused with the nearby Vicolo del Canneto

Urban country lane

The ancient Via del Canneto evokes centuries of history and embodies numerous aspects of the very identity of Florence. While there may be no hidden gem here, no artistic treasure or compelling local legend, the winding street is nevertheless unique in Florence for its continual shifts in gradient and the beauty of its stone paving.

Lined with buildings that are all different, the street is like a compendium of minor architectural details, whose very simplicity makes them a lesson in aesthetics. Everything in Via del Canneto seems miniscule: the narrow entrance, the little old houses with their miniature windows and doorways, and the bell-towers evoking a time long gone. The impression of being in some mountain village, or a reconstruction of a medieval town ... even a puppet-theatre stage set. The entrance is in part concealed, offering no idea of the gently sloping – then more steeply inclined – street beyond. Here and there, arches link the two sides of the street, as if to frame it; and towards the end Via del Canneto suddenly opens out onto the hillside. It is like emerging into the countryside, although in fact only 100 metres or so from Ponte Vecchio.

NEARBY

MARBLE PLAQUE OF AESOP'S TORTOISE AND EAGLE
Via dell' Erta Canina, 26

Just a few steps from the Arno and the city centre, this unusually named road (*erta canina* means "dog climb") is more like a country lane than a city street: at a very sharp gradient, it rises between drystone walls right up to the summit of the hill, revealing that to the south – as to the north and east – of Florence you pass almost imperceptibly from the city into the surrounding hills; to the west, on the other hand, the urban fabric extends into a plain.

At the lower end of the street, at a point where the road once forked into an area now occupied by a few restaurants, stands number 26, its door jamb bearing a marble plaque depicting a tortoise and eagle. This is a reference to Aesop's fable of the tortoise that begged an eagle to teach him how to fly. The more the eagle stressed that it was not in the nature of tortoises to fly, the more the tortoise insisted – until finally the bird of prey took him in his claws, lifted him up high into the sky and then dropped him.

If you're short of breath don't even try to hurry along this street; it really deserves its name of "dog climb".

MUSEO PIETRO ANNIGONI

35

Villa Bardini
Costa San Giorgio 2
• Open October–March, Wednesday–Friday from 10am to 4pm; Saturday and Sunday from 10am to 6pm; April–September, on the same days from 10am to 6pm

> *Discovering a twentieth-century classic*

In 2007 the Cassa di Risparmio di Firenze purchased the private collection that had belonged to Pietro Annigoni's children. All in all, this comprised some 6,000 works of art: oils, watercolours, sketches, drawings, lithographs, models and the notebooks that the artist had compiled during his frequent travels throughout the world. Less than two years later, the Foundation sponsored by the bank opened this museum dedicated to the Milan-born artist, who had had very close ties with Florence and the surrounding area; the Museo Chini in Borgo San Lorenzo is, for example, noteworthy for a few remarkable Annigoni landscapes, primarily of Mugello. Although housed in the magnificent Villa Bardini, the museum is largely unknown. This is regrettable for the general public, but fortunate for the happy few who can thus enjoy the elegance of Villa Bardini and a picture gallery that contains twenty or so Annigoni portraits. There are at least four self-portraits, each one remarkable for the intensity of the artist's gaze. Annigoni was, in fact, one of the greatest portrait painters of

the twentieth century, his sitters including Queen Elizabeth II and other members of the British royal family, Kennedy and Pope John XXIII. The collection here also comprises numerous other works – including landscape – which the artist painted between 1920 and 1970. Another point that won't escape the attention of the curious visitor is the very quality of the artist's easels and paint boxes, as well as the famous wooden mannequin that figured in so many metaphysical paintings. Given the wealth of its collection, the Museo Pietro Annigoni often replaces the exhibited works for special shows that explore a specific aspect of the art of a man who was a dedicated and keen-eyed traveller, embodying a sensibility akin to that of a Renaissance artist. Indeed, Annigoni was the favourite artist of a certain international elite, who saw in him a worthy descendant of the classical tradition in painting.

MUSEO DELLA FONDAZIONE ROBERTO CAPUCCI

Villa Bardino - Costa San Giorgio, 2 or Via dei Bardi, 1 red
• Open Monday–Sunday from 10am to 4pm; closed the first and last
Monday of the month, Christmas Day and New Year's Day
• Tel: 055 2654321

> **Villa where** *haute couture* **rivals sculpture and painting**

Villa Bardino, located at the top of Costa San Giorgio, has recently reopened after years of restoration work financed by the Cassa di Risparmio di Firenze, a local bank. With their numerous pathways, statues, garden adornments and belvedere, the gardens that extend across the hillside are as sumptuous as the villa itself. This is one of the most peaceful and elegant green spaces in the city; and the highest point in the garden is perhaps the most pleasant of all places from which to enjoy the famous panorama of Florence.

Following meticulous restoration, the villa has become a refined exhibition centre and home to the Museum of the Fondazione Roberto Capucci, a space which is, in a way, pendant to the Museo Ferragamo in Piazza Santa Trinità; it was Capucci's specific desire that his museum should be set up in Florence, one of the capitals of Italian fashion design.

Whether visiting a temporary exhibition or the permanent collection, you're bound to enjoy a feast of colour, with the forms and textures of fabrics highlighted by chromatic nuances. In the very way that the garments are exhibited, Capucci can be imagined striving to design clothes that can be appreciated like a painting or sculpture.

Within the hushed silence of each room, the clothes themselves put on a performance, each taking on a specific role. So compelling is this impression it would be no surprise to hear them speak.

The Foundation's purpose is to gather together archive material and full collections of the couturier's work. The marvellous exhibitions that it organises of Capucci's remarkable creations will convince even the most sceptical of the high artistic value of *haute couture*.

ROSE GARDEN

37

Viale Giuseppe Poggi, 2
Admission free
• Tel: 055 2625342
• From mid-May to end of June, every day from 8am to 8pm
• Undergoing restructuring to make it suitable for year-round opening
Only partially accessible to those with restricted mobility

> *Japanese oasis set among the roses of Florence*

One jewel box can enclose another. Although less famous than the iris garden alongside, the rose garden has the advantage of being open all year round, and of containing roses whose remarkable quality adds to the charm of the superb view of Florence to enjoy from here.

The garden was designed by Giuseppe Poggi himself, on terraces laid out by Attilio Pucci for the cultivation of roses. Complete with the narrow winding paths that were such a feature of nineteenth-century romantic gardens – together with numerous belvederes from which to enjoy the view – this garden is on a sloping site that required the creation of a very special irrigation system, with water from a cistern in Piazzale Michelangelo being distributed throughout the garden by a number of different channels. This carefully designed system reveals the scientific precision that went into the design of the entire layout of a garden which now contains a thousand different species of plant – and more than three hundred varieties of rose.

At the heart of this jewel box is another largely unknown gem: a Japanese garden. This was the creation of the architect Yasuo Kitayama, working in collaboration with seven gardeners. Inspired by the Zen principles of an oasis of *shorai-teien* (the future), the garden was laid out using materials imported directly from Japan in an act of homage to the Japanese city of Kyoto, which is twinned with Florence. Japanese monks from Kyoto's Kodai-ji Zen temple carried out a full ceremony of purification here in 2004, to mark the fortieth anniversary of the twinning of the two cities.

THE *PREMIO FIRENZE* EXHIBITION

Piazzale Michelangelo
• Admission free
• Open 24 April to 20 May (possible changes depending on which day national holiday of 25 April falls)
• Opening hours: 10am to 12.30pm and 3pm to 7pm; the competition is judged in mid-May and the prizes presented at Palazzo Vecchio
• Tel: 055 483112 • www.irisfirenze.it
• Only partially accessible to those with restricted mobility

Recreating in nature a flower invented for political reasons

For centuries, Florence has been identified by a flag now seen all over the city and at all sorts of urban events. Now used as everything from a logo for local crafts to a crest for sports teams, that symbol is as famous as Venice's Lion of St Mark or Rome's She-Wolf, even if it is less "imaginary" in nature or narrative in content. The lily associated with Florence does not really recall a specific episode or historical event, but could be said to symbolise the sobriety and elegance that are so much a part of the local temperament.

This is why in 1954 the City Council gave the *podere bastioni* (bastion lands) to the left of Piazzale Michelangelo over to the Italian Society of the Iris, which (in 1957) opened here a sort of temple to the lily (or rather, the iris), which can only be visited for the month of May, when the plants are in bloom, offering a spectacle of colours and scents.

What is less well-known is that the aim of the Premio Firenze which the Society of the Iris organises each year is to produce – through grafts and cross-breeding – a bloom that is close as possible to the famous Florence lily, whose particular red hue does not exist in nature. Indeed nobody has yet managed to obtain the desired colour, given that lilies (irises) tend to be either purple or white.

Originally, the Florence lily was white on a red background. The colour scheme was decided by the Ghibellines, who deliberately chose as their emblem a flower that grew wild in the Tuscan countryside. To mark their political opposition, the Guelphs therefore chose a red lily on a white background, and when they took power took this as the crest of the city. To keep both historical traditions satisfied, the Provincial Government of

Florence – as opposed to the City Council – has as its emblem a lily that is half red against a white background and half white against a red background.

The Iris Garden competition is, therefore, unique in that it strives to recreate a flower that was originally invented for political reasons.

THE SACRED SYMBOLISM OF THE *FLEUR-DE-LIS*

The *fleur-de-lis* is symbolically linked to the *Iris* and the *Lily* (*Lilium*). According to Miranda Bruce-Mitford, Louis VII the Younger (1147) was the first king of France to adopt the iris as his emblem and use it as a seal for his letters patent (decrees). As the name *Louis* was then spelled *Loys*, it supposedly evolved to "*fleur-de-louis*", then "*fleur-de-lis*", its three petals representing Faith, Wisdom and Courage.

In reality, even if there is a strong resemblance between the iris and the *fleur-de-lis*, the French monarch merely adopted an ancient symbol of French heraldry. In AD 496, an angel purportedly appeared before Clotilda (wife of Clovis, king of the Francs) and offered her a lily, an event that influenced her conversion to Christianity. This miracle is also reminiscent of the story of the Virgin Mary, when the Angel Gabriel appeared to her, holding a lily, to tell her she was predestined to be the mother of the Saviour. This flower is also present in the iconography of Joseph, Christ's father, to designate him as the patriarch of the new Holy dynasty of divine royalty.

In 1125, the French flag (and coat of arms) depicted a field of *fleurs-de-lis*. It remained unchanged until the reign of Charles V (1364), who officially adopted the symbol to honour the Holy Trinity, thus deciding to reduce the number of flowers to three. The flower's three petals also referred to the Trinity.

The lily stylised as a *fleur-de-lis* is also a biblical plant associated with the emblem of King David as well as Jesus Christ ("consider the lilies of the field ..." Matthew 6:28-29). It also appears in Egypt in association with the lotus flower, as well as in the Assyrian and Muslim cultures. It became an early symbol of power and sovereignty, and of the divine right of kings, also signifying the purity of body and soul. This is why the ancient kings of Europe were godly, consecrated by the Divinity through sacerdotal authority. Thus, theoretically, they were to be fair, perfect and pure beings as the Virgin Mary had been, she who is the "Lily of the Annunciation and Submission" (*Ecce Ancila Domine*, "Here is the Servant of the Lord," as Luke the Apostle reveals), and patron saint of all royal power.

The lily thus replaced the iris, which explains why, in Spanish, "*fleur-de-lis*" becomes "*flor del lírio*", and why the two flowers are symbolically associated with the same lily.

Botanically, the *fleur-de-lis* is neither

an iris nor a lily. The iris (*Iris germanica*) is a plant of the Iridaceae family that originates in northern Europe. The more commonly known lily species (*Lilium pumilum*, *Lilium speciosum*, *Lilium candidum*) are members of the Liliaceae family that originates in Central Asia and Asia Minor.

The true *fleur-de-lis* belongs to neither the Iridaceae nor the Liliaceae family. It is the *Sprekelia formosissima*, a member of the Amaryllidaceae family that originates in Mexico and Guatemala. Known in other languages as the Aztec lily, the São Tiago lily, and the St. James lily, *Sprekelia formosissima* is the only species of the genus. It was named in the 18th century by botanist Carl von Linné when he received a few bulbs from J. H. Van Sprekelsen, a German lawyer. The Spanish introduced the plant to Europe when they brought bulbs back from Mexico at the end of the 16th century.

OUTSKIRTS OF FLORENCE

BIKE RIDE IN RENAI DI SIGNA PARK

• Details at 349 885 2179 or e-mail: progettorenai.segreteria@tin.it, www.parcorenai.it
• Open from beginning of April to end of October (sometimes open later in the year, weather permitting)
• Open in spring 12pm to 8pm; Saturday and Sunday 9am to 8pm; in summer 9am to 2 in the morning • Admission free
• Cycle access through Cascine Park

Peaceful provincial pleasures

From Florence, following the new Cascine cycle track, you can ride as far as the green oasis of Renai di Signa Park. The route itself, along the banks of the Arno, follows a little-known part of the river, downstream from Cascine Park.

It takes about half an hour to reach the outskirts of this discreet haven overseen by the World Wide Fund for Nature (WWF). There you can observe birds and other wildlife, both permanent and transient residents in a completely original setting. This country park with its cooling lake waters brings together a range of amenities in an exceptional natural environment, allowing visitors to spend a relaxing day in the fresh air just a stone's throw from the historic centre. The idea is inspired by the principles of relaxing at the beach: sporting activities and refreshments within a strictly protected environment with facilities for closely observing the flora and fauna.

You'll find a variety of attractions, beginning with the genuine fine sand beach of the *Big Sur* enterprise, together with its associated infrastructure: "ecological" parasols made from straw and wood, deckchairs, pizzas, ice-creams, volley-ball court, table football, etc. Besides being able to swim there you can also take surfing or sailing lessons. Nearby you'll find a rock-climbing wall, a children's miniature golf, a climbing course, a playground and even a skatepark. From time to time, special days are organised around sporting events or local excursions.

Right at the edge of town, unsuspected amid the industrial suburbs, Renai Park has a peaceful provincial atmosphere, away from the hurly-burly of the city – there's even something exotic about it: a fine example of valuing nature within the urban fabric.

PARCO DELLA PIANA

Municipalities of Florence, Sesto Fiorentino, Campi Bisenzio, Prato
• www.parcodellapiana.it
• Guided visits organised by WWF at the Oasis de Focognano,
15 May–15 September, every Saturday and Sunday at the following
times: 10am, 11am, 12.00pm, 3pm, 4pm and 5pm; no need to book
• Details at 338 399 41 77 • Parking at the entrance to Campi Bisenzio
• Accessible by coach (No. 30) from Florence station: Campi Bisenzio stop
on Via Buozzi

> *Nature park between airport and factories*

Near the airport, the city waste recycling centre, the repair shops of the Italian railway company (Ferrovie dello Stato) and a motorway that is nothing if not invasive, Piana Park glows spontaneously like an implausible flower: this protected area, carved out from land that used to be out in the country, has become an industrial zone, with the exception of this extraordinary enclave that has been carefully safeguarded.

In a context of massive industrialisation, such perseverance in support of the environment is exemplary: hides and prepared tracks lead you around natural habitats (unsuspected considering the surroundings), diversions into open forest, recreational areas with specific itineraries (one of which is devoted to native trees) and lakeside oases, across the Gaine lakes zone (access by Osmannoro plain), the airport/university (follow the sideroads of Via Pasolini: Via dei Giunchi, Via Frilli, Via Lazzerini), of the "*Capitano*" (take Via del Lungo Gavine from the artisanal neighbourhood of Querciola), of Padule (from Via di Case Nuove, then follow Via di Focognano) and the oasis of the Italian Bird Protection League (Lega Italiana Protezione Uccelli) to the "knights' lake" (on Via del Pantano, turn into the little street just before the A11 motorway flyover). Depending on the time, day and season,

in this place that takes you in turn from lake, park, garden and canal, to country house and sugar cane plantation, you can spot birds such as the willow warbler, pine warbler, wheatear, water rail, crane, kingfisher, coot, wild duck, heron, egret and a variety of other wading birds that come to feed and nest, as the vegetation of this green oasis is just as varied: duckweed, reeds, red oak, bramble, hawthorn, laurel or even trees such as black alder, white poplar and the pedunculate (English) oak. So it is that the outer suburbs of Florence offer quite unexpected and exotic expeditions.

EQUOLAND SHOPS
Equoland showcases its products in three shops in Florence: via Ghibellina 115, via dei Pilastri 45 r and via de' Serragli 88 r.

EQUOLAND HANDMADE CHOCOLATES

Via delle Bartoline 41, Calenzano (FI)
• www.equoland.it/
• Monday—Friday from 10am to 1pm and 2pm to 7pm, Saturday from
10am to 1pm and 2pm to 7pm, and second Sunday of the month from
11am to 1pm and 2pm to 7pm

> **Ethical and
> multicultural
> chocolate**

Not far out of Florence, the handmade chocolate manufacturer Equoland is the only complete fair trade network in Europe: raw materials are sourced in the form of semi-finished products in cooperatives in developing countries, at a higher price than on the open market – to help local communities invest in social projects – then processed in this factory by multi-ethnic staff from three continents.

Inside the factory, an overhead walkway has been laid out so that visitors can see the different stages of the production line: from the mixing stage to the conservation of the product. This in itself constitutes a veritable museum of industrial culture, to the point of being a favourite site for school trips.

Once the factory visit is over, you can relax, for example in the factory's Florentine outlet (see box), in a large tasting hall where the chocolate is presented in all shapes and sizes: chocolate spread with selected ingredients (sunflower oil, cane sugar, Piedmontese hazelnuts, mint, chilli, etc.), chocolate bars for all tastes, praline, nuts or coffee beans covered with melted chocolate and an entire range to make children's mouths water.

The Equoland exhibition space also contains a collection of huge African statues (not for sale) and a fine assortment of Indonesian furniture and craft products from around the world: from Palestinian glassware to Senegalese toys made from recycled materials, pretty Malagasy photo albums to Indian scented soaps, even African musical instruments and Latin American textiles, hammocks, lamps, etc.

The food section itself goes way beyond the realm of chocolate because there are several types of honey and jam on offer, a variety of teas and infusions, as well as every kind of cake and snack. There's nothing but fair trade goods, as Equoland has become one of the world's largest import centres for community projects in addition to manufacturing its own chocolate. It's a unique pleasure for the curious or for a family looking for an unusual experience, far from Europe, through the senses of taste and smell.

MONUMENTO ALLA MEMORIA DEL PRINCIPE
INDIANO RAJARAM CHUTTRAPUTTI
MAHARAJAH DI KOLHAPUR, MORTO A
VENTUN'ANNO IN FIRENZE IL XXX GIORNO
DI NOVEMBRE MDCCCLXX QUANDO
DALL'INGHILTERRA TORNAVA ALLA PATRIA

MAUSOLEUM OF THE MAHARAJA OF KOLHAPUR

Piazzaletto dell'Indiano

❹

> *A maharaja in Florence*

A lthough the whole city is familiar with this mausoleum, if only because the famous "Indian viaduct" (Viadotto dell'Indiano) is named after it, hardly any local people go there, and understandably very few tourists visit it either. To add to its interest, the place is off the beaten track, in the depths of the vast Cascine Park. You can reach it by two different routes, the easiest being to drive the length of the park as far as Piazzaletto dell'Indiano, at the western limits; the other is to follow Via Pistoiese, going under Ponte dell'Indiano, then on the left, take Via Piemonte and then the little tunnel under the railway lines and pass under the bridge again to finally reach Cascine, where you can park. A footbridge across the Mugnone waters takes you back to the Piazzaletto.

There you'll find an extraordinary funerary monument, erected by Charles Francesco Fuller in 1874: the statue of an elephant protected by a baldaquin which features a commemorative epigraph in Italian, reproduced in English, Hindi and Punjabi on the other three sides, the only public inscription in these Indian languages in Florence, at least to our knowledge.

A little contemporary house and some decorative features add to the picturesque air. It was here that Rajaram Chuttraputti, Maharaja of Kolhapur, was cremated in 1870 at only twenty years of age, having succumbed to a mysterious ailment on his return from England, in a hotel room at Piazza Ognissanti.

The painful demise of this charming Indian moved the whole city at the time, and cosmopolitan nineteenth-century Florence proved itself diplomatic enough to find a site to honour the remains of the young maharaja according to an age-old exotic ritual, to ease the departure of his soul thousands of kilometres from his native land. The convergence of two rivers, the Arno and the Mugnone, an auspicious site for a cremation in Brahmanic ritual, thus allowed tradition to be respected: the funeral cortege crossed Cascine Park and the ashes were scattered on the water.

Ever since, the "Indian" has been a popular character in Florence, even though many residents have now forgotten the story behind his name.

MUSEO DELL'ISTITUTO AGRARIO (AGRICULTURAL SCHOOL MUSEUM) ❺

Viale delle Cascine, 11
• Access on request if places are available, when the faculty is open, by calling 055 362 161 between 8am and 1pm, or faxing 055 360 003

> *Natural science treasures at Cascine*

ittle known to Florentines and a real gem to specialists, the Istituto Tecnico Agrario Statale (State Agricultural Technical School), is the successor to the grandly named Regia Scuola Agraria di Pomologia e Orticoltura (Royal Agricultural School of Pomology and Horticulture), founded in 1882 in Cascine Park, near Le Pavoniere swimming pool.

Seriously damaged during the Second World War, then by the 1966 floods, but always rising from the ashes, this school was planned in an innovative way, with a stress on experiment and research. Thus major collections were put together here: botany (herbarium, superb reproductions of flowers and fungi), zoology (reptiles, invertebrates, mammals, amphibians); anatomy (reproductions of skeletons and bones); geology, mineralogy and even palaeontology (fossils from Tuscany), to which have been added several sets of plaster, resin or wax reproductions, real works of art.

The exhibition space also includes hundreds of devices used in physics, chemistry, agriculture, topography and meteorology, as well as a special

attraction: a model showing the development of Italian overseas colonies.

Finally, the museum has greenhouses filled with rare plants, an interesting seed collection – notably olives – and a remarkable scientific library in which some volumes date back to the 16th century. In addition, the institution itself is continually enriched with important private collections of minerals, books, photographs, botanical specimens, and so on. It's a pity that this heritage is not displayed to its best advantage, but the reason why this collection has been relegated to the idiosyncratic category is probably the important legacy of the Renaissance and a culture not predisposed to science. We find this regrettable as a museum so varied and fascinating deserves far more than a quick visit.

LORENZO IL MAGNIFICO: AT THE HEART OF NEOPLATONISM

Lorenzo de' Medici (Florence, 1 January 1449 – Careggi, 9 April 1492), as well as being a politician and statesman, was also a great patron and protector of scholars, writers, poets, artists and hermetists. A man who encouraged the development of Italy's first printing shops, he also nurtured the Renaissance humanism that rejected scholasticism in favour of an exploration of life that focused more upon humankind as the centre of the universe. Lorenzo the Magnificent was a particular supporter of the Neoplatonism whose relations with the hermetism of the day have long been accepted. It was under his protection, for example, that Marsilio Ficino translated the *Corpus Hermeticum* from Greek into Latin (published in Florence in 1471), as well as such works at the *Chaldean Oracles* and *Orphic Hymns*. Another eminent figure, Pico della Mirandola, dedicated himself entirely to the Christianisation of the Jewish Kabbalah, with the result that he was initially condemned by the Church and was only saved from these accusations of heresy by Lorenzo's intervention. His argument was that numerous monastic orders within Europe had engaged in the study of magic and astrology and that Pico della Mirandola's motivations had been purely scholarly. Fearing the power of the Florentine duke, the Church accepted this defence and there the matter came to an end. Others interested in Neoplatonism were the poets Pulci and Politien and such great artists as Botticelli and Ghirlandaio, while Michelangelo himself began his studies in a workshop under the patronage of Lorenzo il Magnifico.

VILLA MEDICI CAREGGI

Viale Pieraccini, 17
- Tel: 055 427 9755 or 055 427 9080
- Monday–Friday from 9am to 6pm, but we recommend afternoon visits
- Admission free; booking required for groups

House of Lorenzo the Magnificent and the Neoplatonists

Although the Careggi villa and its grounds are located in a suburb on the outskirts of town, just after the Careggi hospital complex, this was the favourite residence of Lorenzo de' Medici (Lorenzo the Magnificent), the site of his death and of his Neoplatonic Academy, a philosophical and theological research and study centre unequalled in Europe. Far from the Florentine hurly-burly, outwith the tourist circuit, it is also a place of beauty and calm not to be missed. Inside these walls the Hebrew Kabbalah and the texts of Averroes, the Apocryphal Evangelists and the works of the philosophers of antiquity, like Plato and Plotinus, were studied, in search of a common source of human thought and spirituality. It was a fundamental attempt at synthesis and wisdom which, if it had been continued after Lorenzo's death, may have made it possible to avoid the schisms, wars, repression and persecution of religious minorities, and to spare Europe's destiny a great many trials. It is an extraordinary experience to visit what used to be the Laurentian headquarters, passing through the offices of the Azienda Sanitaria Locale (ASL, equivalent of Social Security) which are based here. To its credit, the ASL has opened to the public a group of buildings, certain parts of which are not lacking in charm, despite the many renovations over the centuries. The first include a small lodge painted with frescoes which lends itself particularly well to the astronomical flights of fancy of Italian scholar Pico della Mirandola, a salon with a monumental fireplace where you can imagine his protégé Ange Politien composing his verses, and a large citrus glasshouse where Platina (the Italian Renaissance writer Bartolomeo Sacchi) no doubt studied the herbs needed for his medical gastronomy recipe books, not to mention the beautiful park, an ideal place for philosophical debates in the shade of the lush foliage.

NEOPLATONIC ACADEMY

The importance and ambition of the Neoplatonic Academy are still not fully understood. Founded in Villa Careggi by the philosopher and theologician Marsilio Ficino in 1459, on the initiative of Cosimo de' Medici, its purpose was to study the great traditions of thinking and spirituality – Judaism and the Kabbalah, Christianity, Platonic and Plotinic philosophy, Pythagoras, Orphism, Hermes Trismegistos (see p. 214) and other sources of antiquity – in order to attain "theological peace". This field of esoteric study and research exalted the subject of personal freedom in the image of God, as marvellously expressed by Pico della Mirandola in *Oration on the Dignity of Man*: "We have given you, O Adam, no visage proper to yourself, nor endowment properly your own, in order that whatever place, whatever form, whatever gifts you may, with premeditation, select, these same you may have and possess through your own judgement and decision. The nature of all other creatures is defined and restricted within laws which We have laid down; you, by contrast, impeded by no such restrictions, may, by your own free will, to whose custody We have assigned you, trace for yourself the lineaments of your own nature. I have placed you at the very centre of the world, so that from that vantage point you may with greater ease glance round about you on all that the world contains. We have made you a creature neither of heaven nor of earth, neither mortal nor immortal, in order that you may, as the free and proud shaper of your own being, fashion yourself in the form you may prefer. It will be in your power to descend to the lower, brutish forms of life; you will be able, through your own decision, to rise again to the superior orders whose life is divine." Another extraordinary aspect of the Academy was its rapport with political power, first with Cosimo, then with Lorenzo the Magnificent. After the latter's death in 1492 and the Academy's move to the Oricellai gardens, their political relations continued with the republicans and anti-Medicians, not to mention Niccolò Machiavelli, among others. It went so far that the implication of some academicians in the conspiracy against Cardinal Giulio de' Medici in 1523 forced the institution to close. It was exactly this rapport with the powerful that made the ambitions of Florentine Neoplatonism pragmatic, to such an extent that Pico della Mirandola turned up in Rome to try to convince the papacy of an ecumenical theological vision in which Christianity should appear as the apogee of other traditions – Greek, Jewish and even Islamic – which had always been in communication thanks to common truths to which only initiates held the secrets. Inevitably, the Academy's ideas on beauty influenced the arts (da Vinci, Botticelli, Signorelli, Perugino and the Pollaiolo brothers, to name a few) because, for Marsilio Ficino, it was through the creative power of the imagination that the condition of humanity is revealed. Even the poetry of Lorenzo the Magnificent was motivated, like the works of Ange Politien, by the principles of affirmation of the will and the need to "seize the day", while studies on perspective by Leon Battista Alberti were also driven by the quest for the "third dimension", an "in-depth approach" typical of Neoplatonic man. The proportion of forms and the value of numbers, not only symbolic but revealing hidden truths – research similar to the Kabbalistic quest – constituted one of the esoteric itineraries of Florentine Neoplatonism, as an individual discipline to access a body of knowledge which, in a state of permanent tension between good and evil, vice and virtue, reason and obscurity, followed the absolute of True Ideas or Eternal Truths. Among the vast fields that the academicians researched can even be found one of the earliest gastronomic treatises, a work by Bartolomeo Sacchi (a.k.a Platina): *On Honourable Pleasure and Health.* Published in 1474, the work not only included recipes, but also prescribed physical exercise and a suitable diet, while praising regional food. It is no surprise that this recipe book has now been republished (Éditions Einaudi), as a pioneer of *slow food* and the recommendation to eat local produce.

GUIDED TOUR OF THE NEW LAW COURTS ❼

Viale Guidoni
• Guided tours on particular days (apply to Tourist Information Offices or City Hall, Tel: 055 212245)

Florence's new sentinel

For some years now, anyone looking out over Florence from the belvederes that afford panoramic views of the city has been struck by an enormous structure that protrudes – that is the only word for it – from the recent buildings in the Novoli district. As all Florentines know by now, these are their new Law Courts. It is the sheer scale of the building that is so remarkable. A labyrinthine complex of five separate structures, it rises like a modern and secular cathedral. The various geometric volumes are arranged in staccato rhythm but with unmistakable vertical thrust, expanding over a total area of 126,000 square metres – a virtual fortress. These are the second largest Law Courts in Italy, after those in Turin. The architects were a husband-and-wife team – Leonardo Ricci and Maria Grazia Dall'Erba – and their designs make ample use of huge windows: in part to take advantage of natural light, in part to highlight volume through the use of vast high ceilings. Occasionally tours of the building are organised, when groups of visitors – each with their guide – can be seen exploring spaces on a scale unmatched anywhere else in the city. This tour is like a voyage of architectural

discovery, down interminable corridors to the vast underground archives, the oval halls of the mezzanine and ground floor, the large courtrooms themselves and numerous offices. The building also contains restaurants. Standing some 76 metres high, the new Law Courts have altered the traditional Florentine skyline, being the third tallest building in the city after the cathedral (Brunelleschi's cupola is 114 metres) and the Palazzo Vecchio's Arnolfo tower (95 metres). For those arriving from the airport or along the motorway from the north, the structure marks the approach to the city, seeming to stand guard over Florence like a latter-day sentinel.

HEADQUARTERS OF THE CASSA DI RISPARMIO DI FIRENZE

❽

Via Carlo Magno, 7
• Admission free from 8.30am to 5.30pm, Monday–Friday

L ike an unexpected stage in an itinerary devoted to contemporary Florentine architecture, the headquarters of the Savings Bank of Florence at Novoli, this new district to the north-west of the city, is particularly interesting in that a part of the premises is open to the public. With the presence of the courthouse, the university social science faculty and the dilapidated headquarters of the Regione Toscana, the whole district is becoming one of the new nerve centres of Florence.

New suburban centre

The Savings Bank is an exceptional building, the form and especially the dimensions of which are remarkable: over 25,000 square metres divided into three large wings of four to five storeys. Like the courthouse, it is immediately noticeable on the outskirts of the city coming in from the airport or the motorway to the north. Nevertheless, unlike the extravagant silhouette of the new law courts, the bank headquarters rather bring to mind the tranquil architecture of twentieth-century metaphysical painting: uniform ochre colouring, no clashing decoration or variations on the theme, the identical large classical windows, and the traditional materials of stone and brick. The work is by Giorgio Grassi of Milan, the winner of an international competition in which the British architect Norman Foster notably took part.

Between the buildings extends the large garden on circular themes that counterbalances the vertical rationale of the buildings, off which opens

out an auditorium made entirely from wood and thereby very welcoming. Other interiors, beginning with the dazzling entrance hall, also evoke a luminous and modernist architecture, comprising austere columns, openings, balconies and piercings for natural light. Of course, not all of this is open to the public: the Savings Bank is first and foremost a place of work, although it is open to cultural initiatives as evidenced by its auditorium, public exhibitions and garden. In this way the Florentine suburbs are little by little beginning to offer places of amazing freshness and freedom from ordinary venues.

CENTRALE TERMICA E CABINA APPARATI CENTRALI   ❾

Lines into Santa Maria Novella station
Via delle Ghiacciaie and Via Cittadella

*Futurism
in Florence*

Even if trains where you can stick your head out of the window have become rare (French writer and film-maker Georges Perec wrote that *vietato sporgersi* [do not lean out] is the best-known Italian phrase in France), if you arrive by train at Santa Maria Novella station look out on the right for a building striking for its size, its curious shade of red and especially its shape worthy of a science-fiction set.

This bizarre construction, which dates back to the 1930s and of which only the façade can be seen from the train, has an enigmatic name to say the least, Centrale Termica e Cabina Apparati Centrali (Thermal Power Plant and Central Equipment Room). There is nothing like it in Italy, perhaps not in Europe.

A favourite with architecture enthusiasts, and just as much ignored by the general public who never go near it, this feat is the work of Bolognese architect Angiolo Mazzoni. It is rather like an immense "machine" in the heart of the city, a machine that Filippo Tommaso Marinetti, the leader of futurism, had exultantly raised to the heights of futurist construction *par excellence*.

Its most astounding feature is that it is actually a dual machine: the thermal power plant, designed to heat the whole station by burning coal, equipped with four colossal boilers with standpipes, supply and distribution pumps, and an airlock for breaking down the coal; and the electrical control room with some 280 levers for railway signals and points, and an observatory fitted with a vast semi-circular bay window overlooking the railway lines. This aesthetic is unmissable, even seen from a passing train.

The thermal plant offers an impressive range of shapes: rectangular façade, glazed partitions with vertical bands and windows stretched out like cornices, a semi-circular section to rejoin the equipment room, blunt-tailed, flat-roofed and bulging into an apparent oval. Moreover, if you're looking at the building from the two quiet streets – Via delle Ghiacciaie and Via della Cittadella – you'll find the same collection of bay windows, circular surfaces and plane parallel shapes, as well as four chimneys interlinked by an aerial walkway reached by climbing up a perilous spiral staircase.

We are far from the Renaissance here.

CURIOSITIES OF A UNIQUE STADIUM

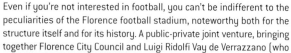

Stadio Artemio Franchi, Viale Manfredo Fanti, Campo di Marte

Even if you're not interested in football, you can't be indifferent to the peculiarities of the Florence football stadium, noteworthy both for the structure itself and for its history. A public-private joint venture, bringing together Florence City Council and Luigi Ridolfi Vay de Verrazzano (who

financed one-third of the project by selling two of his properties in Chianti to the owner of the Florence newspaper *La Nazione*), the stadium was built very quickly, from 1929 to 1932. The head of the design team for the city stadium, Pier Luigi Nervi, created a structure that was very *avant-garde* for the Europe of the day, with extensive use of reinforced concrete and a very "aerodynamic" structure for the stands. The roofing over the stands projects for 22 metres without columns or supports, a masterpiece of roof engineering again

due to Nervi. Another miracle of statics is to be seen in the elegant access ramps. Such helicoidal forms had never been built on this scale before, and original systems had to be developed to assess their stability. Even today, these ramps look perilously daring. The massive structure of the stadium is relieved by the colonnade which the engineer Giuntoli designed to give access to the VIP stand. Indeed, the whole scheme is noteworthy for being almost entirely the work of engineers and involving practically no architects. The Marathon Tower, which has become the symbol of the stadium and was again designed by Nervi, stands some 60 metres high. The vertical thrust of its outline counterbalances the horizontal expanse of the staircase.

When it was redeveloped for the 1990 World Cup, the stadium lost its excellent athletics track. The work on that occasion, under Italo Gamberini, modified various details of Nervi's creation, to the point that some spoke of it as "a cynical act of destruction that showed no regard for the cultural heritage; that was perpetrated amidst general indifference in Florence and in Italy as a whole, with the obliging consent of the bodies responsible for protecting the fine arts".

The sector reserved for VIPs was nicknamed the *formaggino* (small cheese) because the curved enclosed iron walkway makes it look like a section of cheese.

The name given to the stadium offended sensibilities in Siena, which saw Florence as "appropriating" the memory of Artemio Franchi. In fact, Franchi – long-time UEFA president and a recognised "wise man" of Italian football – was Siena-born but Florentine by adoption. Thus, this is a unique case of two cities naming their football stadium after the same man – not that the shared name brings the supporters of the two teams any closer.

FIRENZE STATUTO RAILWAY STATION

Via dello Statuto

Phantom station with an enigmatic window

I n Via dello Statuto, heading towards the ring road, you'll come across the stunning Firenze Statuto railway station built by the Florentine architect Cristiano Toraldo di Francia: a kind of long and narrow bridge made from cylindrical tubes, glazed bays, large portholes and brick cylinders, typified by a curious central window in stonework, surmounted by a half-arch -- an elegant reference to Renaissance architecture in a modern building which welcomes all those who enter the historic centre by passing under the elevated station.

Even if this building had been harmoniously inserted into the pre-existing context, which thereby saw its character changed, it is nonetheless a foreign body. Despite the large noticeboards on display, travellers rarely use the station, to the point that many Florentines don't even know it exists.

The history of this station turns on a series of conflicting decisions. Originally planned as a stop for regional trains, it appeared in the initial project with its numerous turrets and its clock, as a reference to Ponte Santa Trinita, one of the bridges over the Arno in the historic centre. The next plan was to build a station for high-speed (TGV) trains, to avoid arrivals at Santa Maria Novella, hence a large waiting room and long glass roofs were designed, at a stroke abandoning the bridge design by Bartolomeo Ammannati, who had inspired the project.

Once work was complete the plans were again changed, and the TGV station was transferred first to Rifredi then to Santa Maria Novella. So Firenze Statuto station was reconverted, with various sections given over to post offices and shops, while others sadly remained unoccupied. But the long walkways, 250 metres, were retained along with the elevated facing, almost 150 metres long, which explains why this building, which is oddly imposing for a suburban station, has such a bizarre look about it. Its central

window remains an enigma and a dual symbol: a gateway to the city, but also a blank window on a phantom palace, for you won't find a ticket office or any other services inside, where only a handful of regional trains stop daily, and none at all at the weekend. This is, as it happens, the best time to discover this architectural curiosity of Florence.

Giant "alien" mollusc from Asia

Banks of the Arno, especially near Ponte della Vittoria, the Rovezzano water barrier, Ponte Marco Polo and the stretch known as I Renai

Nobody in their right mind would dream of making a plate of seafood spaghetti with molluscs fished from the Arno: your stomach would probably appreciate it as much as a dose of cyanide.

However, you can find shellfish along the banks of the river – some of quite extraordinary size. You're most likely to see them around Rovezzano, near the Teatro Saschall (on the short stretches of sandy bank) and – even more likely – on the stretch beyond the Ponte della Vittoria. In these places a variety of shellfish can be found up to 30 cm long, 12 cm high and 7 cm thick. These gigantic bivalves are scary in themselves, but the name by which they are known is even scarier: *alieni*. In effect, these "aliens" originated far from the ecosystem of the Arno, in Indochina. They arrived in the Arno – as they did in many other places in Europe – at the end of the nineteenth century, and though the actual timing of their introduction is unknown, they firmly established themselves throughout Europe during the twentieth century. Going by the curious scientific name of *Sinanodonta woodiana*, these plump-looking shellfish are deceptive in appearance, for they are totally inedible – something you should *never* forget.

They also have a rather ambiguous effect. True, they overrun the environment and drive out local water fauna, but they also filter – and thus purify – up to 50 litres of water per day, each *Sinanodonta* drawing from the water not only the organic material on which it feeds but also such heavy metals as bronze and zinc (which are stored in its flesh). And they do all this without leaving the mudbanks, sometimes emerging to flaunt their corpulent mass on the sand. Perhaps they are trying to attract the attention of Florentines, who seem to take little notice of the fact that they are now surrounded by these monstrous prehistoric-looking creatures – yet further proof that globalisation began long ago.

MANHOLE COVERS: A MEMENTO OF FASCISM

"Giovanni Berta" fascist manhole covers

At various places in Florence you can see manhole covers with fascist insignia – for example, in Piazza della Repubblica, in Piazza del Duomo or in Via de' Pescioni, to name but three. Produced under fascist rule (1924–1945), they bear the symbols of the city – the Florentine lily and the inscription *Comune di Firenze* – plus the symbol of the lictor's *fasces* and the date in Roman numerals.

There are also the words *Fonderia Giovanni Berta*. Giovanni Berta, the son of Florentine industrialists and a young fascist, died at the age of 19 when workers dragged him from his car to throw him into the Arno. As he gripped the edge of Ponte Sospeso (now Ponte alla Vittoria), they cut off his hands. Throughout Italy, squares were named after this young victim and monuments raised in his honour. As the birthplace of the "martyr", Florence saw its city stadium renamed after Giovanni Berta (later named Stadio Municipale, then Stadio Artemio Franchi).

Even the metal foundry located in the Cure district – the very place that produced these manhole covers – was named after the young man.

DRAGON FOUNTAIN IN ORTI DEL PARNASO ⑫

Giardino dell'Orticoltura - Via Trento
• Open from 8.30am to 6pm (January–March), 8.30am to 7pm (April,
May, September–December), 8.30am to 8pm (June–August)

> **One of the most stunning panoramas in Florence**

With its historic entrance in Via Puccinotti and paths leading to the district library, the Logetta Bondi and the Tepidarium (one of the largest glasshouses in Italy, inaugurated in 1880 to the design of engineer Giacomo Roster), the Horticultural Garden is almost as popular as the upper part of the park, recently opened to the public. Access is equally easy from the rear of the Tepidarium or from the overhanging Via Trento; here, the entrance gate opens directly onto a panoramic terrace from which you can enjoy a stunning view of Florence, seen from a lower vantage point than Piazzale Michelangelo or Forte di Belvedere, but away from the constant urban hurly-burly: an ideal spot for admiring the sunset in perfect peace. This solitary part of the garden is known as the Parnassus Garden (Orti del Parnaso) in tribute to the extraordinary fountain curiously sculpted in a dragon shape and recently installed for the reopening. Although this fountain is little known, it is one of the most imposing in Florence, extending over forty-eight steps and three terraces along the length of a canal encased within the long tail of the dragon, ornamented with stone, coloured glass and mosaic, ending with the final cascade which gushes from the mouth of this likeable monster. The link between the dragon and Parnassus is of course from Greek mythology and the story of Python, son of Gaea (Mother Earth), the fabulous serpent covered with the mud of the Deluge. It was on Mount Parnassus, near the Delphic oracle, that Python was slain by the young Apollo who was avenging his mother, Leto, leading to the "Pythian" or Delphic Games, a sporting and sacred festival established in honour of Apollo. For lack of a Greek mountain in Via Trento, however, strollers will just have to content themselves with an unparalleled panoramic view over the city, away from the crowds of tourists.

NEARBY

CANTINA GUIDI ⑬
Via Pagnini, 22r • Tel: 055 480205
Opened in 1946, this wine merchant's (*cantina*) was one of the first specialist food shops in Florence. Although now closed, the original façade covered with Art Nouveau panels, the work of a great Italian ceramist, Antonio Chini, has become an object of curiosity. The Chini were a family dynasty of Art Nouveau architects and decorators, whose work features in houses and chapels along the main roads of their native village of Borgo San Lorenzo, in the Mugello district. Their work can of course also be seen at Villa Pecori Giraldi, where a large museum is dedicated to the Chini.

GIARDINO DEI GIUSTI

Giardino dell'Orticultura
Via Trento
• Opening hours: 8.30am to 6pm (January–March), 8.30am to 7pm (April, May, September–December), 8.30am to 8pm (June–August)
Sound and light installation: 5pm (October to March), 7.30pm (April–September)
• For a guided tour, call 055 262 5331

Mark of nobility on a silent place

O pen since 2007, the little Giardino dei Giusti (Garden of the Righteous) is set lower down than the Parnassus Garden but shares the same romantic setting and splendid view of the city. This quiet place is animated each evening at dusk by a sound and light show that transforms it into a "listening garden". Sound and light-emitting earthenware objects,

symbols of the memory of the Holocaust, blend in with the trees along an itinerary bordered with hedges and climbing plants (guided tours available).

In this park with its great variety of plantations – from bay trees to Chinese mulberry, as well as irises and cypresses – also look out for an oak tree (where a visitor has corrected the label by hand, adding that it is a green or holm oak – *leccio* in Italian) from a Polish cemetery and which is dedicated to the 40,000 Italians, both Jews and non-Jews, who died in the Nazi concentration camps.

WHEN GINO BARTALI CARRIED FAKE DOCUMENTS TO SAVE JEWS
The Garden of the Righteous also features *Lagerstroemia*, originating from the floral horticulture centre of the Municipality of Florence. It is said to commemorate the Italian cycling champion Gino Bartali who saved a number of Jews during the Second World War by smuggling fake documents to them in his saddle and handlebars.

FROM JERUSALEM TO FLORENCE
The Garden of the Righteous theme is inspired by the Yad Vashem Memorial in Jerusalem, where each tree is dedicated to a non-Jew who saved human lives during the Nazi persecution by laying themselves open to all kinds of risk, sometimes at the cost of their own lives. All who have visited Yad Vashem have been touched by the symbolic force of these trees, such that the project launched by Gabriele Nissim to open "Gardens of the Righteous" around the world has spread in recent years.

PUTTI FOUNTAIN

Piazza Vasari

> ## *Children piled on a tortoise's back*

The Ponte del Pino is a bridge over rail tracks that links the Via Massacio area with Viale del Mille. A garden here, raised above the level of the tracks, is remarkable for one single feature: a fountain in which the *putti* are not the chubby-cheeked and curly-haired cherubs usually found in Florentine paintings. This bronze sculpture depicts four toddlers shown on their hands and knees, one on top of the other, forming a sort of human pyramid on top of the unperturbed tortoise that forms the pedestal for this very unusual column. The back of the topmost child supports a large basin from which water trickles. The 2008 work financed by the City Council and carried out by the Opificio della Pietre Dure (Workshop of Semiprecious Stones) restored the fountain's water jet.

Is there perhaps some esoteric significance behind this very unusual composition?

The fountain is the work of sculptor Mario Moschi (1896–1971), who belonged to the Gruppo Donatello and in his youth (1925) produced the *Monument to the Dead of Rifredi* which now stands in Piazza Dalmazia. This *putti* composition dates from 1952 and seems to reveal a real sea change in the artist's temperament over the intervening decades. These figures of children had actually been modelled ten years before the erection of the

fountain, but their affectionate and ironic view of childhood makes it clear that the artist had drawn direct inspiration from his own private life.

There is, however, no mysterious symbolism here, just a celebration of Mario Moschi's granddaughter, a girl "as lively as four little children together", who used to crawl around the house on all fours – that is, when she wasn't happily playing with the family tortoise. Thus the inspiration for this original public work came from personal feelings stirred by a very domestic subject.

GALERIA RINALDO CARNIELO

16

Piazza Savonarola 3
• Open Saturday morning from 9am to 1pm
• www.museicivicifiorentini.it/carnielo
• Further information: l.lucchesi@comune.firenze.it

Workshop from the Florentine *belle époque*

Because of a notorious remark by Don Abbondio, a character in Alessandro Manzoni's novel *I promessi sposi* (*The Betrothed*), Carnielo, has become synonymous with the "perfect nobody" in Italy. By analogy, Florentines can be heard exclaiming: "Carnielo? Who was that guy?" Such being the case, it should be no surprise that the gallery dedicated to him is little known in Florence. Yet it is the only institution that gives an insight into Florentine artistic life of the *belle époque*, a period when painters' and sculptors' studios were ubiquitous in the neighbourhood (as the name Via degli Artisti illustrates).

This gallery occupies the ground floor of a small building that was the home and workshop of the sculptor Rinaldo Carnielo, set in the middle of Piazza Savonarola in a neighbourhood rich in Florentine *belle époque* villas built in a sober and elegant style. This house is one of the most significant examples of the influence of Art Nouveau in Florence, with its central façade flanked by two wings, characterised by this striking warning: Onora l'arte che è vita della vita ("Celebrate art, which is the life of life"). Another inscription can be read on the Via Benivieni side: Per aspera ad astra ("Through hardships to the stars"). The ensemble is imbued with a strange atmosphere at once serious and bizarre, while the peaceful Piazza Savonarola opens up before you, dominated by a monument to the Dominican preacher that used to stand in Palazzo Vecchio and graced with other *belle époque* buildings, such as the remarkable angled houses and the characteristic red of the headquarters of Syracuse University.

Once inside the gallery, you'll find an exhibition space rare in Florence: three rooms filled with a large number of plaster moulds, bas-reliefs, models and marble or bronze sculptures by Carnielo, bequeathed by his heirs in 1958 to the Municipality of Florence along with the workshop. Despite a few allusions to Renaissance motifs, Carnielo favoured a portentous style particularly evident in his funerary monuments and commemorative pieces, such as the *Dying Mozart*, *Angel of Death* and *Lion's Head*.

Carnielo's academic technique is rather removed from the *avant-garde* overturning of artistic expression a few years later, being closer to the taste for *verismo* (realism) and stressing the dramatic intensity of imagery.

VILLA GAMBERAIA

Via del Rossellino, 72
• www.villagamberaia.it
Visit the gardens daily from 9am to 5pm in winter and from 9am to 6pm
in summer
Booking recommended, particularly at the weekend
Admission: €10 (full price); €8 (concessions); public holidays and
preceding day: €12
The interior of the villa can be viewed by groups of at least ten for a
supplement of €5 per person
Tel: 055 697 205, or e-mail villagam@tin.it

*Florentine
villa par excellence*

The sumptuous villa Gamberaia de Settignano, by which there once flowed a stream famed for its crayfish (hence its name, from *gambero di fiume*, crayfish), has a history which is unforgettable to say the least. It was built by an ancestor of the sculptor Rossellino and belonged, among others, to the illustrious Capponi family, then at the end of the nineteenth century to Princess Giovanna Ghykha, sister of Queen Natalie of Serbia, before being bought by Baron von Ketteler. After the Second World War, it was taken over by the Vatican, and finally in 1952 by Marcello and Nerina Marchi. Over the centuries, each owner left their mark, leading to the current development which sets off the park. The villa complex has been transformed into tourist accomodation and facilities for ceremonies and seminars. The view of Florence is worth a detour : a stretch of pink roofs along the banks of the Arno, from which the Brunelleschi cupola emerges with the Amennines in the background. The park itself includes two elegant monumental gardens graced with ornamental ponds and geometrical alleys, rows of cypress trees, a grove of hom oaks and a bowling green. Enough delights to wander among open-mouthed in a labyrinth enriched with flights of steps, passages, fountains – an ideal place for touring Shakespeare plays or for playing hide and seek or blind man's buff.

With its two magnificent salons and interior courtyard surrounded by arcades, the villa equals the gardens. But its most beautiful aspect is incontestably the apartments in the 17th-century former chapel and a 14th-century country house converted into a lemon press. They do credit to the canon of Tuscan interiors: large fireplaces, exposed beams and box ceilings, brick floors, period furniture – and the unmissable view over Florence. You'll be loath to leave.

NINFEO DEL GIOVANNOZZI

Via del Paradiso, 5
• To arrange a free visit, call Mr Vangelisti (owner) at 347 796 2509

> **Surprising grotto at Gavinana**

I n the Florentine suburbs near Gavinana there is a private garden with a hidden grotto built in an eccentric style that forms part of Villa del Bandino, later inherited by the Niccolini family. It was the Niccolinis who in 1746 commissioned the painter and sculptor Giuseppe Giovannozzi da Settignano to build a "nymphaeum", a sanctuary consecrated to water nymphs, a rustic construction with three arches topped with ornamental vases and decorated with rich Baroque mosaics encrusted with shells.

All this shows that Giovannozzi took pleasure in creating this architectural diversion, which he built himself with the help of his son and a workman. In the grotto you'll find a number of benches and notably the pool, which used to be fitted with intermittent jets of water linked to the Bigallo wells.

In the centre rose the statue of Venus, which was stolen during the First World War and never heard of again. Its presence was more than justified among the coloured pebbles of the grotto because the goddess of Love presided over this sanctuary, which not only served as an imaginative refuge from the heat, or an unusual setting for fêtes or al fresco refreshments, but could also be used as a natural boudoir for courting couples.

The nymphaeum has its roots far from Boboli or Villa Demidoff, but

it has the same "rocky" spirit that dares and defies the commonplace, not afraid of ridicule but on the contrary giving free rein to the imagination, a witness to a carefree Florence. Recently restored by scrupulous owners and developed a few years ago as a unique setting for theatrical performance, the nymphaeum is now set in a simple green space overlooked by some modern buildings, as if playing hide and seek in the beautiful panorama surrounding it.

COMPLEX OF GUALCHIERE DI REMOLE ⑲

Left bank of the Arno, along the SP34 secondary road linking Florence and
Rosano, around 9 km from Viale Europa

*Treasure
of industrial
archaeology*

Shortly after leaving the city, on the road leading to Rosano, you can still see a textile factory on the banks of the Arno, whose waters it formerly used. The original woollen mill that was set up after the 1333 floods stayed in production for centuries. It belonged to the Albizi family until 1541, then to Arte della Lana, one of the seven Florentine arts and crafts guilds, and later to the Florence Chamber of Commerce. This factory, an authentic monument to the culture of technology, thus shaped over the centuries the urban identity of the cradle of the Renaissance in the arts. Moreover, it bears witness to the organic and economic rapport that the city has always had with its river, which alone might make you curious to visit the Gualchiere complex, a still impressive industrial site where you can see the château-like structure with its mills and hydraulic wheels. The complex extends over 4,000 square metres, a large part of which is now in ruins, although there is a restoration project to use it as the headquarters of the International Centre for Traditional Knowledge (but there has also been talk in recent years of a hotel complex). On the initiative of UNESCO, the aim of this centre will be to promote and disseminate knowledge of traditional techniques, as well as the recovery and safeguarding of popular scientific culture. Today, left to its own devices, the former complex is a treasure of industrial archaeology at the very gates of Florence. This treasure is unique in Europe not only because of its equipment but also because of its medieval origins, even though it has been converted more than once, let alone its fundamental role in the organic rapport that human labour has always held with the river. In addition, for centuries Gualchiere was linked to the Sieci district, on the opposite bank of the Arno, by a ferry service.

This forgotten site, unsuspected from the road, is not without charm, and neither is the short walk that takes you back to the tranquil and well-maintained banks of the Arno.

GUALCHIERE: A GENUINE "EXCLAVE" IN FLORENCE
Gualchiere holds another secret, another reason why this site merits a place in a guide to Florence: although the complex lies within the territory of the municipality of Bagno at Ripoli, it belongs to the municipality of Florence, so it is a genuine (and unusual) "exclave".

CANTO DEGLI ARETINI

Via di Ripoli, 51, at the corner of Via Benedetto Accolti

> **Former communal grave, enclave of Arezzo**

The phrase *canto degli Aretini* ("the Aretini corner") can lead to confusion because *canto* also means "song" in Italian. But you won't find anything particularly musical at this corner of Via di Ripoli, which forms a strange sort of enclave: this tiny part of Florence, as announced on a column surrounded

by a guardrail, is actually administered by the city of Arezzo, as the inscription on the plaque recalls – QUESTO COSIDDETTO CANTONE DI AREZZO CHE È DEL COMUNE GHIBELLINO PROPRIETÀ – which goes on to evoke the "MEMORIA DEGLI INFAUSTI ODII DA CITTÀ A CITTÀ OGGI NELL'ITALIANA CONCORDE POTENZA ABOLITI PER SEMPRE".* This *"canto"* marks the burial place of several hundred Aretini who had died in Florentine prisons. They were the poorest among 1000 soldiers that the Florentines took prisoner in 1189, at the end of the battle of Campaldino. Most of them were freed shortly afterwards, following the payment of a ransom, but the others stayed in their dungeon where they soon perished. Their memory has been perpetuated in this little patch of ground under the care of the curiously extra-communal administration of the city of Arezzo, which on 11 June each year places a floral wreath there at the same time as the Municipality of Florence.

"This so-called canton of Arezzo which belongs to the Ghibellino municipality ... in memory of the fatal hostilities which [divided] the towns, but which modern Italy, a united power, has abolished for evermore."

CIMITERO ALLORI

Via Senese, 184
• Open 1 October—31 March from 8am to 12.30pm and 2.30pm to 5pm, and from 1 April—30 September from 8am to 12pm and 3pm to 6pm; closed Sunday

Non-Catholic cemetery

O n the southern outskirts of Florence, in the suburb of Galluzzo, the little cemetery of the Allori ("laurels") is a haven of eternal peace whose history is little known. Although it is not exactly a monumental burial ground, from an artistic point of view there are several interesting tombs that give a certain cohesion to an otherwise rather eclectic place. Besides, the surrounding countryside is fairly typical of the Florentine landscape, which has had to adapt to the vagaries of the road network, such as the petrol stations and the often heavy traffic.

The site nevertheless complies well with the new norms which, in the nineteenth century, led to the closure of the English cemetery at Piazza Donatello and the removal of most cemeteries outside the city. The Allori cemetery was opened to cater to Florentine residents who were non-Catholics: Protestant, Orthodox, atheist and even Jews and Muslims.

Thus you'll discover among the tombs unusual sectors of Florentine society: the evangelical and English communities, and even some Russian aristocrats. The variety illustrates the diverse characters who have been buried here, from the British historian and writer Harold Acton to the antiquarian Frederick Stibbert, the Swiss painter Arnold Böcklin, or that magnificent and controversial writer Oriana Fallaci, who was very proud of his Florentine identity.

This diversity came from the Protestant community, whose deceased were laid to rest in the Swiss or "English" cemetery of Piazza Donatello. When major works were undertaken in order to turn Florence into the capital of the Kingdom of Italy from 1865 to 1870, the ramparts were demolished and the English cemetery found itself not only in the urban area but encircled by roads. It was at that time that the Allori cemetery was established, in 1860, in the Galluzzo district: the last resting-place with its simple gateway for all those who could not or would not be buried in Catholic ground.

VIUZZO DEI CATINAI

> **The old Impruneta road**

Drive up into the Florentine hills of Oltrarno, on the Arcetri and Montici side, and you'll climb through a maze of narrow tracks with walls covered in yellow or ochre plaster, dotted with villas and pavilions perfectly integrated into the landscape. Here and there, a chapel or panoramic view confers an almost medieval charm to these excursions on the outskirts of the city, which you can also follow on foot to discover the countryside and the town-planning of yesteryear. Among the various routes, the Viuzzo dei Catinai, a track with a solitary and timeless air lying below Pian dei Giullari, is one of the most unusual.

Today you'd think that people no longer came this way, despite the fact that for centuries it was the only route from Impruneta to Florence. Merchants especially could be seen heading down into the town with their carts loaded with bricks or glazed earthenware jars and bowls.

This is why the track was known as *viuzzo dei catinai* ("bowl-sellers"), but it was also used by the solemn procession of the miraculous Virgin of Impruneta. It's difficult to imagine such traffic on the semi-wild slopes that exist today. A few details even more striking as they are now rare in Florence clearly show that this was not just any country road.

First of all, you'll notice the pond (*zanella*) to collect rainwater to avoid flooding, a painstaking work of hydraulic engineering at the time and still in perfect condition. In addition, if you examine the road surface you'll see that many of the paving stones are perfectly squared off, a testimony to the skill of the craftsmen who set them there, while at the sides of the road bushy foliage has overrun the walls, such that the track seems to be snaking through a wild landscape.

Finally, when you arrive at the bottom, you'll discover a small fourteenth-century chapel, unusually shaped and distinguished by a Gothic archway, yet another sign of the antiquity of this route. So this short excursion in space and time comes to a very pleasant end.

NEARBY

THE PLAQUE OF VILLA IL TASSO

At the entrance to Villa Il Tasso (Via Benedetto Fortini 30), just beside the gateway, you'll see a plaque dating from 1704 which indicates that Florence is one mile away. Further along the road on a boundary wall can be seen some graffiti including one dated 1830 in a cartouche. Moving traces of the "*admirable tremblement du temps*" (admirable trembling of time), in Chateaubriand's words.

GIARDINO DI ARCHIMEDE

Museum of Mathematics
Via san Bartolo a Cintoia, 19
• Tel: 055 787 9594, open Monday–Friday from 9am to 1pm and Sunday
from 3pm to 7pm (closed August and public holidays)

> **Incredible museum for playing with numbers**

I n the suburbs of Florence you might suddenly notice an unusual house equipped with strange aerial walkways and striking tilted features, architecture which is bizarre to say the least and out of place in the sober urban uniformity. This curious building is home to a museum known particularly to schools, as there is no equivalent in Italy and perhaps not in the whole of Europe. The museum is the result of an innovative and ambitious project: to familiarise the general public with mathematics by offering entertainment and interactive participation, in order to arouse their curiosity about numbers and shapes. As we are in Tuscany, the museum had to begin with a programme dedicated to the mathematician Leonardo Fibonacci, also known as Leonardo of Pisa, author of the "golden laws" on the numerical structure of nature, as well as the famous *Liber Abaci* (*Book of Calculation*, 1202), a cornerstone in the transmission of medieval mathematical sciences to the West. However, the historical approach is only part of this museum, which includes an

interactive section on Pythagoras' theorem, explored through a series of puzzles, while the section entitled "*Oltre il compasso, la geometria delle curve*" ("Beyond the compass, the geometry of curves") reprises and expands on a successful exhibition of the 1990s, devoted to geometry and organised entirely around games and interactive experiences. Besides these permanent features, the museum offers temporary exhibitions and a series of recreational workshops on the practical applications of mathematics: you can for example learn how to fold paper into special shapes, let yourself be seduced by fascinating musical exercises, or count like the Sumerians. If you're looking for an unusual museum, you'll find it here, all the more so as Florentine museums are often conservative places, and almost all are in the city centre, whereas here for once the suburbs come into their own.

IMPRESSIVE REMAINS OF THE CITY'S FORTIFICATIONS

In some ways, the ancient ramparts of Florence remain a mystery. There is, for example, continuing disagreement as to the number of times the ring of city walls was expanded as Florence grew, with estimates varying from four to six. What is certain is that the construction of these fortifications turned Florence into a sort of building site from the Roman period right up until 1333, when the ring of walls attributed to Arnolfo di Cambio was completed. These fortifications then remained unchanged except for some additions and modifications made after the sixteenth century. When, in 1870, Giuseppe Poggi began working on the ring-road boulevards that were to give Florence the appearance of a capital city, a large part of the old fortifications was demolished. However, today's curious visitors can still have fun searching out the last remaining traces.

First ring of walls: In Via del Proconsolo, near the Badia Fiorentina on the Piazza San Firenze side, a curious circle is marked in the paving. This is a trace of the excavations that brought to light the ruins of certain towers and fragments of the ramparts of the first ring of walls (the *castrum*), which was built by the Romans at the beginning of the first century AD and enclosed a perimeter of only 400–500 metres.

Another trace of this first ring is the street name of Via Por Santa Maria, which comes from the medieval name for one of its four gateways (*porta*).

Second ring of walls: The second ring is known as the "Byzantine" fortifications because it was built by the Greeks in AD 550. Its perimeter was smaller than the Roman wall, because *Florentia* had shrunk as the result of barbarian incursions. Some argue that this ring was just a reworking of the Roman walls. The only surviving trace is the Torre della Pagliuzza.

Third ring of walls: There is no visible trace of the third ring, which largely followed the outline of the first ring.

Fourth ring of walls: The fourth ring is the result of an extension dating back to the eleventh century. It enclosed the river port near Palazzo Castellani. In his *Canto dei Cacciaguida* (*Paradiso*, Canto XVI), Dante describes these as the "old walls" which protected a still-united Florence, a flourishing civic and commercial entity.

Fifth ring of walls: The San Pierino Arch was undoubtedly a gateway in the fifth ring. At the end of the twelfth century the fortified protection of the city was extended for the first time to include part of Oltrarno district, with the walls now embracing an area of 75 hectares, as opposed to the 20 hectares of Roman times. By this period the city population was close to 30,000.

Sixth ring of walls: In 1280 the city population totalled 80,000 and would soon be more than 100,000. Arnolfo di Cambio – together with Giotto and others – worked on the construction of the sixth ring, which extended the area of the fortified city to 430 hectares. The ramparts measured 8 kilometres in total, with the walls standing 6 metres high and containing a total of twelve city gateways, each 35 metres high. Some were equipped with a drawbridge (for example, Porta San Gallo), serving as customs barriers and also protecting the city against night incursions by wrongdoers. At the time, the scheme for the city's fortifications was the most ambitious in Europe, and work continued until 1333. When completed, the walls enclosed the old "city centre" as we know it; population growth levelled out to such an extent that the number of residents in the mid nineteenth century was the same as it had been five centuries earlier.

At San Miniato stands the sole bastion that the Republic of Florence managed to build to withstand the siege by imperial forces in 1529, designed by Michelangelo.

If you look carefully at Porta San Niccolò, you'll notice that it is the only city gateway to have kept its upper part. This is because it was protected by the hills: during a war with Siena in the sixteenth century, Cosimo I had all the other city gateways lowered so that they would not be vulnerable to artillery.

The Fortezza di San Giovanni, later renamed Fortezza da Basso, was designed by Ammannati, while the Forte Belvedere was designed by Buontalenti. These two completed the city's fortifications, with the exception of a few bastions, of which only the San Giorgio (or Ginevra) bastion survives.

At the beginning of the nineteenth century, the very last city gateway was opened: a double-arched structure at the end of Via della Scala. The only surviving trace of this is in the street name of Via delle Porte Nuove.

Although in Oltrarno, Giuseppe Poggi left the old gateways and ramparts standing alongside the new boulevards, on the right bank of the Arno he decided to demolish them all. Many have seen this as an act of vandalism, given that the boulevards could very well have run for their entire length around the perimeter of the old walls. Other city gateways demolished include the gateway at the top of Borgo Pinto; the Porticciola (which stood alongside

the Arno by what is now the American Consulate); the Porta Guelfa, through which passed those condemned to death (alongside the Torre della Zecca). The Porta a Faenza had already been incorporated within the Fortezza da Basso.

A complete tour of the surviving city gateways would take in the following: Porta a Prato, Porta San Gallo, Porta alla Croce, Porta San Niccolò, Porta San Miniato, Porta San Giorgio, Porta Romana and Porta San Frediano. Some of these have been vandalised by drilling holes to attach Christmas decorations – a barbaric practice which began in 2004 but was fortunately stopped by the city magistrates.

FLORENCE THE UNFINISHED

Via del Proconsolo, 12
Piazza San Lorenzo
Piazza del Cestello
Piazza San Paolino
Piazza del Carmine

The modelling of a city as rich in architectural treasures as Florence is never an easy matter. Debate can be heated and finance is always a problem, with funds perhaps not as much as expected and the resulting adjustments to projects leading to rather disappointing end results. The polemical inscription that figures on Baccio d'Agnolo's Palazzo Salimbeni in Piazza Trinità could well be taken as summing up the whole thing: *carpere promtius quam imitari* (it is easier to criticise than to imitate).

Perhaps in Florence more than anywhere, the construction process makes excessively high demands. Indeed, all the unfinished buildings within the city could form a proper tourist route, starting with the *palazzo non finito* at No. 12 Via del Porconsolo (now home to the Museo Nazionale di Antropologia e Etnologia). Seen from the outside, the façade is clearly asymmetrical, with cornices at different levels on either side of a main doorway surmounted by two columns for which there is no continuation on the upper storey. Designed by Buontalenti for Alessandro Strozzi, this unfinished palace was subsequently taken in hand by a number of architects – Scamozzi, Cigoli, Caccini, Nigetti – the final hybrid being the result of each wanting to impose his own ideas. A local legend has it that the infernal monsters seen arising from the ground-floor windows refer to another reason why the building was never finished: Strozzi had made a pact with the devil.

Numerous other unfinished buildings could be cited in Florence, above all façades that never got further than the drawing-board. Indeed, both the Duomo and Santa Croce church have "fake" façades – designed in the nineteenth century, their neo-Gothic frontages put an end to centuries of hesitation between the various solutions that had been put forward. Other churches are still unfinished, and will probably remain so forever, like San Paolino.

The **Basilica of San Lorenzo** is one of these, even though it was the family church of the Medici and contains their mausoleum. The original church here was founded in the fourth century AD, but over the centuries the façade was never finished. Michelangelo himself produced a wooden model of a possible design, but this was never built because of lack of funds.

San Frediano in Cestello is another unfinished church. In 1680 the Cistercians decided to renovate their church by changing the position of its façade (to face the Arno) and adding a cupola. While the cupola was built and frescoed, the façade never got beyond the bare brick phase – which contrasts sharply with the sober Baroque style of the church as a whole.

Yet another example is the **Basilica of Santa Maria del Carmine** in Oltrarno. Built in the thirteenth century, the church was gradually embellished with numerous artistic masterpieces, including the Brancacci Chapel frescoed by Masaccio. Then a disastrous fire badly damaged the building in 1771, and the church had to be almost entirely rebuilt. However, agreement could not be reached on the new façade and once again it was decided to concentrate on the nave – with the risk that funds would run out or suitable artists would no longer be available when it came to work on the exterior.

ALPHABETICAL INDEX

ALPHABETICAL INDEX

ALPHABETICAL INDEX

THEMATIC INDEX

ARCHITECTURE

CONTEMPORARY FLORENCE

CURIOSITIES

THEMATIC INDEX

ESOTERICISM

GARDENS - NATURE

HISTORY

HOTELS/RESTAURANTS - SHOPPING

LITERATURE - DANTE

MUSEUMS

THEMATIC INDEX

RELIGION

SCIENCES

NOTES